BLACK FOOD MATTERS

BLACK FOOD MATTERS

● ● ●

RACIAL JUSTICE IN THE WAKE OF FOOD JUSTICE

● ● ●

HANNA GARTH AND ASHANTÉ M. REESE, EDITORS

University of Minnesota Press
Minneapolis
London

Published by the University of Minnesota Press
111 Third Avenue South, Suite 290
Minneapolis, MN 55401-2520
http://www.upress.umn.edu

The University of Minnesota is an equal-opportunity educator and employer.

Library of Congress Cataloging-in-Publication Data
Names: Garth, Hanna, editor. | Reese, Ashanté M., editor.
Title: Black food matters : racial justice in the wake of food justice /
  [edited by] Hanna Garth and Ashanté M. Reese.
Description: Minneapolis : University of Minnesota Press, [2020] | Includes
  bibliographical references and index. | Summary: "An in-depth look at
  Black food and the challenges it faces today"—Provided by publisher.
Identifiers: LCCN 2020020391 (print) | ISBN 978-1-5179-0813-3 (hc) |
  ISBN 978-1-5179-0814-0 (pb)
Subjects: LCSH: African Americans—Food. | African Americans—Social
  conditions. | Food security—United States. | Equality—United States. |
  Racism—United States.
Classification: LCC E185.86 .B52555 2020 (print) | DDC 305.896/073–dc23
LC record available at https://lccn.loc.gov/2020020391

UMP LSI

CONTENTS

BLACK FOOD MATTERS

An Introduction

Ashanté M. Reese and Hanna Garth

• • •

The global food system is plagued with inequities. On the one hand, the U.S. food supply is so abundant it could feed everyone in the country nearly twice over—even after exports are considered (Nestle 2002, 1). Yet the United States Department of Agriculture (USDA) reported that in 2018, 14.3 million Americans were food insecure.[1] The burden of food insecurity is especially felt by communities of color. In an effort to understand how race and ethnicity influence food insecurity, Ana McCormick Myers and Matthew Painter (2017) find that Black and Latinx people—regardless of immigrant status—are significantly more food insecure than foreign- or U.S.-born whites, suggesting that the food system is part of a larger structure of inequity. In an effort to address both food insecurity and unequal food access, activists and scholars have turned their attention to creating an equitable food system, framing their work under the umbrella of food justice. Growing out of the environmental justice movement that is largely led by women of color, food justice has become a theoretical, methodological, and aspirational framework for reenvisioning a world in which access to healthy, affordable food is not a dream but a reality for all.

In recent years, nuanced examinations of this movement reveal that what was once characterized as a singular movement is more a collection of similar (though sometimes diverging), fragmented approaches to food inequity, resulting in varied definitions and applications of the term *food justice*. At minimum, food justice highlights the problems of a contemporary food system that relies heavily on undervalued labor and the quick and efficient circulation of food products and is concerned with the unequal distribution of and access to healthy, affordable food. Robert Gottlieb and Anupama Joshi (2010, 6) assert that "food justice" ensures that "the benefits and risks of where, what, and how food is grown and produced, transported and distributed, and accessed and eaten are shared fairly" and as part of the process, knowing how food injustices are distributed and experienced form the basis for which a movement can grow.

Many Black activists and scholars theorize and frame food inequities as a by-product of the contestation to Black life, specifically grounding their food justice work from the starting point that just as racism produces increasing surveillance, disproportionate rates of mass incarceration, and income inequities, it also produces food inequities. Leah Penniman argues,

> Racism is built into the DNA of the US food system. Beginning with the genocidal land theft from Indigenous people, continuing with the kidnapping of our ancestors from the shores of West Africa for forced agricultural labor, morphing into convict leasing, expanding to the migrant guest worker program, and maturing into its current state where farm management is among the whitest professions, farm labor is predominantly Brown and exploited, and people of color disproportionately live in food apartheid neighborhoods and suffer from diet-related illness, this system is built on stolen land and stolen labor, and needs a redesign. (2018, 5)

Our food system and the inequities it produces, in other words, are the afterlife of slavery—the ways the "past" extends beyond a fixed position or time period to extend into the present day (Hartman 2007, 6). In this afterlife, one in which the racial calculus devalues Black life, inequities and injustices are not accidental but the result of deeply entrenched systemic processes: the fruit that is produced from a capitalist economic system for which the expendability of Black life is not tertiary but central.

The implications for those of us who study food is that it is not enough to simply examine race in the food system. We must also consider how the food system is part of larger structures that, by design, were never created for Black survival (Lorde 1997; Costa Vargas 2010). In this way, food inequities are one manifestation of the afterlife of slavery. Rasheed Salaam Hislop connects food justice explicitly to racial justice, defining it as "the struggle against racism, exploitation, and oppression taking place within the food system that addresses inequality's root causes both within and beyond the food chain" (2014, 19). Working from the premise that anti-Blackness is "pervasive as climate" and operates as a precondition for the expendability of Black lives (Sharpe 2016, 106), in her book *Black Food Geographies: Race, Self-Reliance, and Food Access in Washington, D.C.*, Ashanté Reese argues that examining both the specificity and the mundaneness of anti-Blackness "opens up possibilities for us to reconsider and imagine constraint and possibility, harm and care, and destruction and community building" (2019, 4). We frame this edited volume in similar ways to Hislop, adding the specificity of anti-Blackness that Reese (2019) offers with the hope that within the chapters, we may witness seedlings of resistance and refusal. As the chapters in this volume demonstrate, we are talking about not only racial disparities that Black people experience in the food system but the conditions that produce those disparities. The "contested landscape" (Twitty 2017, 6) in which Black people shop for, grow, distribute, and consume food is multidimensional. Redlining in housing and supermarkets, nefarious practices of discrimination and exclusionary lending, and ongoing forms of institutionalized discrimination and circuits of capital exacerbate deeply entrenched inequalities and poverty. This is the context from which many food justice movements have taken up the call to provide or fight for healthy, accessible food for all. Intermingled with these contexts, Black communities maintain vibrant Black food cultures that draw from Black history and shift into contemporary variations.

Weaving together the contexts of vibrant Black food cultures and the need to incorporate racial justice into the food justice movement, *Black Food Matters* brings together authors who examine production, distribution, and consumption through the lens of (anti-)Blackness to explore themes of fugitivity and disposability, the consumability of Blackness and Black food culture, and the everyday resistances that are produced in the making of Black food geographies. Some scholars and activists have pointed to the brokenness of our food system, while others have suggested that there is nothing broken, that the inequities it produces are functions of how it should work, as the push to maximize production and consumption while devaluing labor are integral to capitalist production. This volume operates from the latter assumption. We presume that many of the solutions offered—particularly those related to combatting the so-called obesity epidemic and those that stem from the "food desert" framing—are antithetical to rather than supportive of Black life. Rather than offer solutions to brokenness, these chapters provide some insight into how Blackness is contested even within food justice work, the challenges that emerge when different perspectives of "healthy" emerge, or how Black people imagine otherwise.

In particular, the authors collectively grapple with questions of Black agency and leadership, (hyper)visibility of Black people as targets for food justice interventions, and how geography influences the particularities of how food resources and food justice efforts unfold in different spaces. We illuminate how Black people are in the midst of their own struggles for justice within the mainstream food justice movement (White 2018). Though food insecurity (or the threat of it) is a thread that runs throughout the chapters, one of the main arguments of this volume is that food and the fugitive practices Black people employ around food comprise a lens through which we can explore anti-Blackness and Black life. The chapters explore individual and community values, the influence of history, and the everyday ways that institutions and communities reflect an ongoing struggle to not only meet needs but affirm Black life (see also Smart-Grosvenor 1970, 1972). The chapters in this volume reflect what pioneering food anthropologist Sidney Mintz (1996) urged those who research food to do:

to see food as a reflection of sociopolitical relations that are much broader than what is on our plates. Even in their recognition of a food system that, by design, ensures that Black people and Black spaces are not adequately resourced, many of the chapters still grapple with possibility, challenging popular notions that the only way to understand Black people's relationships with food and food institutions is through lack.

What Survives: Reading Black Life, Refusal, and Self-Determination in Food

In 2017, at the Young Farmers Conference held at the Stone Barns Center for Food and Agriculture in New York, chef Nadine Nelson asked keynote speaker Mark Bittman a question after he and Ricardo Salvador finished their joint presentation on racism and land reform: "How do you hold yourself accountable to communities of color, and vulnerable communities . . . to the things you say that you aspire to change?" Bittman did not directly answer her question, first saying that he did not know what she meant by "hold [yourself] accountable to" before moving on to field additional questions. Later, North Carolina–based farmer Dallas Robinson declared that Bittman's dismissal of the question was hurtful and that what was needed was for white men like him to share power and listen to people of color. The National Black Food and Justice Alliance (NBFJA) publicly applauded chef Nadine and others, declaring that

> Black and Brown people have always been the life force of the food movement. From national formations created and led by Black leaders such as the National Black Food and Justice Alliance, to local formations such as Detroit Black Community Food Security Network, groups are organizing and thus positioning themselves in rightful leadership within the food movement. Continuously portraying the leadership of the food movement almost exclusively in the body of white men is not only inaccurate and harmful, but a dated form of hegemony. (NBFJA 2017)

This moment, albeit brief, illustrates ongoing tensions within food movements: Who has the power to name and define? Who is creating policy? In what ways are Black and other people of color framed as the recipients of aid but rarely the theorists, creators, and experts, even though there is a long history of Black, Indigenous, and other people of color–led community-based activism that forms the crux of contemporary food justice movements? It also calls to mind refusal as a strategy for navigating inequity, for holding (white) people in powerful positions accountable, and for creating everyday lives. Audra Simpson (2007, 2014) has developed the notion of "refusal" in the context of the anthropological study of Indigenous communities as a way of pushing back against particular forms of power and sovereignty that do not align with the needs and identities of a particular group. In some cases, this includes refusing to participate in ethnographic projects or refusing definitions created by outsiders. We build upon and extend this understanding of refusal to think through the ways Black communities use forms of refusal to assert what is at stake and what matters deeply in our lives.

In this volume, we theorize how Black food culture—whether at the level of cultivation or consumption—reflects refusals, fugitive food practices, and the desire for Black self-determination: the ability to imagine, define, determine, and create sustainable worlds free of anti-Blackness and its accompanying oppressions. We document the myriad ways in which the nation-state in which we live does not provide for or protect Black people and, more often than not, causes direct and indirect harm. From systematically withholding financial support from Black farmers, to histories of redlining and racist lending practices for Black homeowners and businesses, to categorizing Black neighborhoods as violent and "deserts" devoid of food worth eating, various state and institutional actors have contributed to the food inequities these chapters grapple with. Those who uphold Black food culture, who insist on our right to grow, buy, sell, trade, and consume the foods that we are historically and culturally connected to regardless of how other groups see these practices, are prominently featured in this volume.

In an effort to examine self-determination and self-reliance, some food scholars have highlighted the ways that neoliberalism shapes the contours of food justice organizing and funding (Alkon and Guthman 2017; Sbicca 2018). The neoliberal turn in food studies in particular has demonstrated, for example, how access to funding and capital create opportunities and constraints for even the most radical food justice organizations and have shown little evidence of having an effect on the root causes of food inequities. In this volume, however, we ask the question, What is possible when we root self-determination and self-reliance in cultural and historical practices that are not solely the product of neoliberal logics? Offering collective agency as a theoretical framework, Monica White (2018) argues that history and commitment to communally produced solutions are a manifestation of self-reliance and self-determination and Reese (2018) argues that the "self" in these articulations is less about the individual and more about the ways the community itself can produce alternatives, though they may be limited in scope and sustainability.

This is a tension we explore in this volume, as the inclination of Black communities toward forms of self-reliance and self-determination articulates more with the food sovereignty movement, which is grounded in "the people's right to determine their own agricultural and food policies" (McMichael 2008, quoted in Carney 2012). For some Black communities, this turn to self-determination is not only a response to a food system that fails them; it is also built upon a long-standing distrust of the state (see Gillian Richards-Greaves's chapter in this volume). While efforts to take control of food production and consumption are rarely permanent solutions, in their efforts people feel they are able to do something tangible rather than waiting for the U.S. government to solve the food problem (see Pulido 2016). In many Black communities, it has been accepted that rather than solely depending on the state to alleviate structural inequalities and violence, Black people must instead take care of our own needs, even if that includes food production and distribution, such as through informal cookshares or rideshares (see Reese's chapter). This volume builds on germinal texts in the African American food canon that established the significance of food in the study of Black political, social, and cultural life. The chapters in this volume are not overly celebratory and they acknowledge the limitations inherent in the work that each explores. At the same time, they demonstrate the possibilities that can emerge when people are not positioned as social or political risk objects but are responding to and pushing against white supremacy in institutional and everyday ways.

Considering self-reliance and self-determination and Black food cultural production, this also leads us to ask: What are the particular geographic components that factor into the production, distribution, and consumption of food in Black communities? Specifically, what additional questions does a Black geographical lens applied to food ask us to consider and what knowledge is produced at that intersection? Each chapter in this volume grapples with these questions. Bringing together chapters that explore Black food cultural production and justice in Los Angeles, Detroit, Memphis, South Carolina, the rural South, Miami, and Washington, D.C., *Black Food Matters* presumes the significance of spatial food practices. Specifically, we challenge the tendency to treat Black neighborhoods and communities as blank slates in need of guidance or structure. Rather, epistemologically and methodologically, we concern ourselves with examining how a "Black sense of place" that does not reduce Black people or Blackness to countable objects (McKittrick and Woods 2007; McKittrick 2011) emerges through how Black people produce, navigate, resist, and read their food landscapes. Margaret Marietta Ramírez (2015, 749) argues that food justice organizations often overlook these Black geographies, demonstrating how deeply rooted contemporary practices are based on racialized processes dating back to the plantation. Similarly, Reese (2019) suggests that the Black food geographies that unfold are not simply a response to contemporary restraints but are grounded in personal and communal histories as well as desires to build community; and Priscilla McCutcheon (2015) and Naya Jones (2018) turn to how these personal and communal histories intersect with an embodied experience of navigating food inequities. In their works, both McCutcheon and Jones illustrate that food access is not solely about the location of food and food consumption is not purely about individual choice or taste. Authors in this volume all grapple with this in different ways: exploring the choices and decisions residents make to protect or change their food landscapes, alternative food distribution mechanisms, the role of legal proceedings in protecting farmland, and, as in the case of Billy Hall's and Judith Williams's chapters in particular, gentrification's role in creating the conditions under which Black food geographies are threatened.

In addition, we see the chapters included here as part of a longer continuum that explores the changes in and preservation of Black food culture and institutions. For some of the chapters, this means thinking deeply about the ancestral knowledge that was brought to the Americas in the seeds and practices of those enslaved. What does that knowledge look like in the contemporary sense? What remains? As Jessica Harris and Michael Twitty have both demonstrated, Black food culture is tied to histories of enslavement and diaspora connections, and the knowledge of cultivating, processing, and preparing foods was not only brought to the Americas but also incorporated into everyday life (Harris 2003; Twitty 2017; see also Carney 2001, 2010; Miller 2013). Food cultures were carried in the wake of slavery, transformed by contact and hybridities that reverberated and, in some cases, carried over into contemporary Black food culture. Exploring enslavement and the related movement of foods and people is one way of considering how everyday food consumption patterns reflect fugitivity. Across the volume, and in particular in Williams's and Reese's chapters, we are challenged to consider the ways that people employ fugitive practices, to meet their or community food needs, challenging us to consider the possibility that these practices, too, can fly under the banner of food justice. By fugitive here we mean an ongoing refusal to accept standards imposed from elsewhere: "fugitivity, then, is a desire for and a spirit of escape and transgression of the proper and the proposed. It's a desire for the outside, for a playing or being outside, an outlaw edge proper to the now always already improper voice or instrument" (Moten 2018, 336). Building on Tina Campt (2014) and Audra Simpson (2016), who both theorize refusal as a creative practice or set of practices that undermine dominant authorities and logics, Damien Sojoyner argues that Black fugitivity is "based on the disavowal of and disengagement from state-governed projects that attempt to adjudicate normative constructions of difference through liberal tropes of freedom and democratic belonging" (2017, 516). Rather than being static or historical acts that happened in the past, Black fugitivity is a central and ongoing part of envisioning other ways of being and relating. In other words, Black fugitivity is and perhaps always has been part of the work taken up by those who survive in spite of constant attacks on Black life. These fugitivity practices, in fact, may be the reasons for survival. In this volume, we think and write about what is possible when we examine food through this lens.

Appropriating Black Food

Amid Black fugitivity and refusal, Black food culture has remained a source of cultural production and community building in spite of ongoing threats to its very existence. The African American food studies canon has carefully documented the erasure of Black cooks and their culinary knowledge from the history of American food more generally (Whitehead 1992; Bower 2007; Opie 2008; Harris 2011; Miller 2013; Wallach 2015, 2019; Zafar 2019). As Toni Tipton-Martin (2015) demonstrates, Black cooks, usually women, were the creators of the many kinds of delicacies and traditional dishes coming out of early American kitchens. Linked to this idea, as Saidiya Hartman notes, "the systematic violence needed to conscript black women's domestic labor after slavery required locking them out of all other sectors of the labor market, a condition William Patterson (1982) described as economic genocide. Race riots, the enclosure of the ghetto, the vertical order of human life, and the forms of value and debt promulgated through emergent forms of racism, what Sarah Haley terms 'Jim Crow modernity,' made it impossible for black women to escape the white household" (Hartman 2016, 170; see also Patterson 1982; Haley 2016). Whether under chattel slavery or as underpaid domestic labor, Black women's culinary knowledge and practices were stolen by white cookbook authors, absconded by white housewives, and absorbed into a white-washed American cuisine, erasing the Black foundations of our food system. While authors like Tipton-Martin have painstakingly demonstrated the centrality of Black cooks in our history despite the limited number of cookbooks published by them, it is still not commonly accepted that Black culinary practices form a critical foundation of all-American food culture. Furthermore, if we turn our attention to this history, we can clearly see the fallacy of the notion that Black people's food preferences and culinary practices have always been the stereotypical "soul foods" that Black people created as a way to make "something out of nothing" (Tipton-Martin 2015, 7). Instead we find that there is a whole lesser-known history of teaching "industry and self-reliance" in the kitchen, using fresh fruits and vegetables and maintaining a variety of nutrients in Black cuisine "that shunned frying or dependence upon fatback seasoning" (Opie 2008, quoted in Tipton-Martin 2015, 7). As Psyche Williams-Forson's (2006, 2012) work shows, the devaluation of Black foodways and pigeonholing of it into one narrow type of food is a common misconception built upon the clichés and stereotypes of advertisers who portrayed Black people as dim-witted, incapable, and useful only as "the docile servant who was always ready to serve" (Kern-Foxworth 1994, quoted in Tipton-Martin 2015, 8). While consumption is key, Black food culture is also deeply intertwined with global systems of food production and distribution. Indeed, one troublesome narrative of Black foodways is that the foods we eat were the trash and scraps that white people threw at us and we made something out of nothing. While that can be an uplifting story of overcoming adversity, a deeper look at Black food culture tells us that it is simply not true.

The culinary and agricultural knowledge of Black people, some of which was stolen and appropriated, was fundamental to the economic development of the United States and further supported the global economic dominance of European colonizing countries for centuries (see Robinson 1983). Black people were brought to the Americas with extensive knowledge of cooking and agriculture and came together to produce a rich diasporic Black culture

(Carney 2001, 2010). Not only have Black people been cultivating, processing, and preparing Black food for hundreds of years, but this quintessential Black knowledge also forms the basis of many cuisines thought to be just "American," where Blackness has been erased—such as southern food (Franklin 2018). Still, while Black knowledge and skill have long been key to Black food culture, oppressive and restrictive systems of food distribution have hampered and limited food access and threatened Black food culture.

Amid the many Black cultural forms that are celebrated, commoditized, and highly sought after by Black and non-Black people alike, such as music, clothing styles, hairstyles, ways of speaking, and so on, Black food cultures span the range of popular acceptance—from being devalued to seeing a "renaissance" in cities like Oakland (Nettles-Barcelón 2012). By turning our attention to the richness of Black food culture across the diaspora and its history, we can help illuminate how Blackness is so much more than merely making something out of the scraps of white folks, more than histories of shucking and jiving as Black hands processed massive amounts of corn. That said, Black people in the United States and the broader African diaspora have been incredibly adept at responding to and improving on the conditions of inequity in which so many Black people live. This ability to make and build Black communities in this way is a strength, and is not merely the outgrowth of whiteness or the use of what is rejected by white people (Lewis 1976; Franklin 2018). Black food culture is in fact the inverse, and Blackness is a foundation upon which American food culture was built.

While all kinds of people consume and enjoy foods that are culturally Black, the appropriation of those foods means that members of a dominant or privileged group in society adopt or lay claim to the production of and profits from Black food culture. This sometimes leads to stereotypes that are entrenched in the marketing of some foods. As Williams-Forson (2006) details, images of the Black cook, servant, slave, and mammy have been used by large corporations to sell food products since at least the late nineteenth century. For instance, in the 1880s, "Aunt Jemima materialized as a product of commercial advertising inspired by blackface routines" (Tipton-Martin 2015, xi; see also Turner 1994; Kwate 2019). These kinds of advertisements draw from imagined docile Black (often maternal) figures, equate "simple" with blackness, and disparage Black intelligence and culinary skills while simultaneously erasing the Black contribution to American food.

The brief history we detail here is tied up with our deliberate move to use *Black food culture* in this volume rather than *African American food culture*. We use *Black* in multiple ways to indicate Black people, those who are the descendants of African slaves brought to the United States against their will, and those who claim other ties to the African diaspora, such as through the Black Caribbean (as in Williams's chapter in this volume). We also engage Blackness here as a theoretical concept and political stance. Drawing on W. E. B. Du Bois, Cedric Robinson and Elizabeth Robinson argue that "Black people" did not always exist in the Americas since the slave trade. They assert: "The 'Negro' was in place; that is, his docility, ignorance, beastality, child-like inferiority, that was in place. But a strata was emerging in conflict with that, to contest it" (Robinson and Robinson 2017, 6). For Du Bois, making a claim on Black identity was taking a strong stance against the degradation of Black people. The assertion of Blackness, the naming of *Black* people, was staking a claim that "we are a people, we have achieved cultures, we have left a mark on the world, we have a past and we can have a future . . . Black Sovereignty!" (Robinson and Robinson 2017, 6).

These ways of reclaiming Blackness were also taken up by related movements, like the Black Power movement. Although the Black Power movement was vilified as a form of violence and tyranny, Analena Hope Hassberg's chapter documents that Black Power was and continues to be misunderstood (see also White 2018). We draw from the understanding of Black Power as a way of productively channeling Black rage into Black consciousness "built on the twin pillars of racial pride and unity," which "sought to foster black self-respect and redefine blackness by reclaiming and venerating black history and culture" (Davies 2017, 1). A focus on Black food culture thus allows us to illuminate the variety of ways in which Black cultural forms come up against other dominant (white) culture, analyzing why Black ways of being are sometimes degraded and at other times celebrated. Food allows that entry point into understanding the complexities of Blackness.

Positionality and the Politics of Studying Black Food Culture

As interest in food justice (and the related concept of food sovereignty) has grown, so too have questions about methodological, theoretical, and ethical concerns about studying racialized communities that bear the weight of food inequities. Questions of food justice are fundamentally about the production, distribution, and consumption of food. In the process of envisioning a more equitable and sustainable food system, however, we must also contend with the epistemological lenses and frameworks from which we theorize ways forward. *Black Food Matters* was compiled based on the belief that it is imperative to center Black ways of knowing and being as a place from which to understand not only the constraints produced by anti-Blackness but the possibilities that Black people innovate and create in the wake of these constraints.

We (the editors of this volume) developed the ideas for this volume over the course of two panels at the American Anthropological Association annual meetings, the first in Denver in November 2015 and the second in Washington, D.C., in November 2017. Following these two panels, in May 2018, we brought together six scholars, included in this volume, to present publicly on our work at the University of California, San Diego, and engage in a weekend-long writing and thinking workshop. As part of the workshop, we each read each other's chapters, provided feedback on them individually, and then discussed the themes that cut across each of them. While we would have preferred to have all the contributors be part of this workshop, limited funding meant we had to make strategic decisions. We chose to invite those with whom we had not had extensive engagement in other venues.

We mention this workshop here because as we conceptualized this volume, we were intentional and clear that we wanted to model the type of collaborative work that many of us write about, knowing that collaboration is not always easy, nor is it clear-cut. We also wanted to bring together these scholars, the majority of whom identify as Black, to discuss the various tensions and contradictions we see and experience as Black people mainly writing about other Black people in a field in which most of those who are writing about Black people are not Black. We include this here to call attention to the number and diversity of Black scholars, particularly those who work from a social science perspective, engaging in food work, and note that other scholars have complicated the notion that one can have automatic or permanent "insider" status (Zavella 1993; Jacobs-Huey 2002; Yelvington et al. 2015). With this approach, we take up another aspect of Williams-Forson's call for food studies to take intersectionality more seriously: what does that look like when we apply it to research participants and communities but also turn that lens on ourselves—the ones doing the studying? Black feminist anthropologists have long argued that to decolonize our disciplines, who produces knowledge and how it is produced matters, especially when Black scholars see ourselves and our own liberation bound up with those with whom we conduct research (McClaurin 2001; Rodriguez 2003; Harrison 2008; E. Williams 2013; B. Williams 2018). In an interview with *Savage Minds,* Faye Harrison articulates this in terms of vulnerability and care in the context of ethnographic work.

When we do it right the fact [is] that we immerse ourselves in everyday lives and demands of ordinary people all over the world. We humble ourselves to being sort of re-socialized and enculturated, which means you show your vulnerabilities . . . when you do it right. And to the extent that we go beyond those models of fieldwork which are really based on what I call the mining and the extraction of data as though it's a raw material that needs to be then refined and created into some other sort of commodity. If we can get away from that model which is consistent with basically a market, a capitalist market, commodification, competitive individualism, hierarchies and whatever, and realize that the people who make our research possible are much like us. (Harrison 2016)

In this volume, we bring together a group of scholars whose work has been motivated by deep engagements with the communities of study and to the extent possible has moved away from extractivist research, which are characteristics of research that embodies a Black feminist approach.

The majority of the work included here comes from a social scientific or ethnographic approach, and the authors write from perspectives that reflect Harrison's assertion that there are ways to do this work that do not reify colonialist approaches to "the other." In this way, we build on the work that forms the base of the African American foodways canon, much of which has analyzed food from historical, literary, and other humanistic perspectives. Most of the chapters in this volume draw upon empirically rich, historically grounded ethnographic data to document the food-related practices and the everyday lives of Black people. While we build upon the foodways literature, we have moved away from using the term *foodways* in favor of *food culture*. The term *foodways,* often connected to "folk culture," connotes an essentializing gaze on the food-related practices of marginalized communities. We want to move away from the assumption that American food means white middle class and that everything else is "ethnic" or marginal in some way.

Across the chapters, the volume works to illuminate how Black food culture is experienced in the everyday lives of Black and non-Black people. We center lived experience as a way to demonstrate how Black food culture is not fixed but instead an emergent and vibrant phenomenon. We also deliberately include noncanonical works on African American and Black foodways here. The work of writers such as Michael Twitty and Toni Tipton-Martin has made significant intellectual contributions to our understanding of Black food culture, and we acknowledge that in our work. We draw upon these tools as a platform for rethinking and retheorizing the social, economic, and political dimensions of American food culture beyond the unstated but assumed white middle-class perspective. We assert that food studies should always include multiple forms of Black food culture and the various ways in which food matters in Black communities.

Black food culture and Black life are varied and ever changing; they are not monolithic. Yet the surveillance of Black bodies, Black lives, and Black communities as unruly and uncontrolled is pervasive and often results in outside efforts to control Black practices through our food, our health, our bodies, and our communities. In her remarks after one of our panels at the American Anthropological Association annual meetings, Williams-Forson was reminded of an important 1903 Du Bois quote: "How does it feel to be a problem?" The fact that we are still asking this question, that we must still defend Black life as legitimate, vibrant, and beautiful, is part of what makes this volume so crucial right now.

Overview of the Book

Black Food Matters enters two conversations at once: one that concerns the persistent threats to Black life and another that concerns problems produced by the increasingly global and corporatized food system. The chapters do not posture absolute solutions to either. Instead, we offer epistemological and theoretical perspectives that place these two conversations in the same frame to grapple with *what survives* (Sharpe 2016) when threats to Black life are endemic to our food system. This volume examines Black food culture and food justice from several distinct but complementary angles. In the first chapter, Ashanté M. Reese grounds the volume in Black agency with ethnographic research on how residents of Washington, D.C., "(re)inhabit and (re)imagine" Black food culture through self-reliance, entrepreneurship, and artistic impressions. Reese anchors these local forms of food work within the broader frame of "wake work" that we find to be central to the resilience of many Black communities and cultural forms.

The connections between histories of food production, Black fugitivity, and food culture as a site of resistance and practice of self-reliance are then further illuminated in chapter 2 by Gillian Richards-Greaves, whose inquiry moves us from the urban to a small town in South Carolina. Residents of Cool Spring, part of Carolina low country, are descendants of enslaved Africans with ties to the coastal Gullah-Geechee community. Gullah-Geechee food culture, as Twitty has said, "came from an 'African culinary grammar' in which 'methods of cooking and spicing, remembered foods, ancestral tastes' defined the flavor of the dishes and the people who created them" (Joyner 1984, 91, quoted in Twitty 2017, 183; see also Beoku-Betts 1995). Richards-Greaves documents the agricultural and animal husbandry practices of this community, which plants crops year-round with an explicit praxis of exchanging with or selling to local neighbors and friends. Richards-Greaves's sharp analysis reveals that these food production practices are "a deliberate means of maintaining self-ownership, self-sufficiency, and personal security in post-emancipation America," arising from "political uncertainty" and fear of a potential "world war three." This community draws on hundreds of years of Black knowledge and agricultural skill to protect itself against further incursions or new forms of political violence.

In a similar vein, Analena Hope Hassberg's chapter centers on the role of the Black Panther Party's food work as part of its "survival programs." Hassberg analyzes how food provisioning was central to the Panther mission as a way to ensure that Black folks stayed alive because "hungry people cannot effectively organize for freedom." Hunger and malnutrition in Black communities were and continue to be one of the greatest forms of oppression in the United States. The Black Panther Party's food work also served to shift attention away from the negative image of the Panthers as too radical and violent. The chapter not only reveals that food was central to the Panther mission but also shows that this program was critical in shaping the early food justice movement in South Los Angeles.

Hanna Garth's chapter picks up on these tensions through an explicit analysis of the forms of "justice" and resulting forms of anti-Blackness that emerge from the work of several food justice organizations in Los Angeles. Garth examines Community Services Unlimited Inc. (CSU), which is the present-day continuation of the nonprofit arm of the Black Panther Party detailed by Hassberg. In addition to CSU, the chapter analyzes the work of several Los Angeles nonprofits and the Los Angeles Food Policy Council. Garth reveals how food justice work can operate in a wide variety of ways, from a radical grassroots orientation that supports Black communities, to orientations that try to fit Black life into dominant white legal and political structures, to those that serve only to protect white social and political interests. This chapter forces us to ask, Who does food justice serve and why?

In a related interrogation of food justice, Andrew Newman and Yuson Jung flip the approach from Garth's focus on food justice to look at the role that food has played in (re)imagining Detroit as a vibrant majority Black city. Newman and Jung "look beyond the food justice movement as it is typically formulated and examine how individuals within these movements are contesting and reworking the moral meaning of economic exchange itself, especially within Black communities." The authors point out the tensions in the positioning of food, which is sometimes cast as part of the foodie frontier of repurposing urban space and thus paving a path for the emergent forms of gentrification that others want to ward off. The authors analyze this as part of a competing moral economy of "good food" that is differentiated and organized by race, racism, and Detroit's history of Black politics in symbolic and tangible ways. Newman and Jung reveal that differing moral beliefs and commitments can produce schisms concerning what is good food, not simply because of the food items themselves but because of the social relations that are embedded in them.

Building on the tensions that are apparent in both trying to define food justice at the intersection of Blackness and exploring the limitations of food justice efforts, Billy Hall's chapter takes us to Miami's Overtown community, formed in 1896, which has endured a long history of racism. Today Overtown faces yet another racialized project as "economic development" paves the way for gentrification and the removal of Black people. Hall demonstrates how food becomes central to the racialized project of gentrification by carefully documenting the ways Overtown is sometimes cast as an unsafe, blighted "food desert" and other times as a culturally vibrant, racial heritage and soul food destination-in-the-making. Beyond just Overtown, this sort of labeling of Black communities in this way allows for the justification of ongoing forms of policing, removal, and subsequent "investment" and "development" of Black areas. These forms of "heritage" tourism not only elide histories of anti-Black racism and ongoing forms of structural violence but also erase the centrality of Black history, Black practices, and Black knowledge that built those places.

As Kimberly Kasper's chapter on Memphis illuminates, the contributions of Black people to American BBQ practices are often ignored, particularly as BBQ is taken up by younger hipster foodies in the Nashville scene. Brad Weiss (2016) has documented a similar phenomenon in North Carolina, focusing on the rise of local hipster foodies' whole hog BBQ practices in the local food movement. Richards-Greaves's chapter in this volume documents the connections of contemporary practices of whole hog BBQ in South Carolina to histories of Black animal husbandry and BBQ knowledge intricately connected with a large system of Black food culture. The erasure of Black cultural significance from these food histories is a form of anti-Blackness in and of itself, and it facilitates an extension of this anti-Blackness into tangential aspects of Black life. Additionally, as Garth's chapter points out, when the important Black cultural connection is removed from a dish, foods such as macaroni and cheese are rendered as merely unhealthy, fatty foods commonly consumed by Black people, allowing for people to slip into the anti-Black logics about the consumption of unhealthy, undignified foods within Black communities.

Kasper's chapter on BBQ demonstrates how Black food culture is also a central force in cohesion and collective effervescence within Black communities. Black food culture thus becomes critical to resistance, fighting institutionalized racism, and the development of alternative, community-based approaches around food justice. The thread of resistance runs through Monica M. White's chapter as she explores how Black women activists participate in urban agriculture to reclaim their cultural roots connected to food cultivation as well as power over their food supply. Along similar lines as Richards-Greaves's chapter, White argues that through building community, Black women enact agency and self-determination. White's chapter provides a critical analysis of gender and uses an ecofeminist perspective to connect Black food culture, women's resistance, and the environment. The activists in White's chapter "construct the farm as a community safe space, which operates as a creative, public outdoor classroom where they nurture activism and challenge the racial and class-based barriers to accessing healthy food" in ways that align with the work of the Black Panther Party as detailed in Hassberg's chapter and its continuation as CSU as described in Garth's chapter.

One of the fundamental problems with agriculture and urban gardening in Black communities is the lack of land ownership, which is tied to racist histories of redlining and systematic prevention of Black land ownership. Willie J. Wright, Tyler McCreary, Brian Williams, and Adam Bledsoe's chapter argues that rural land ownership has been associated with "cultural retention, desire to till and tend to the earth, self-determination, personal and mental health, and intergenerational transfer of wealth" (citing Salamon 1979). Yet they explain that "Black farmers represent just under 50,000 of the nation's 3.5 million farm operators" (citing Census of Agriculture 2017). Wright, McCreary, Williams, and Bledsoe analyze *Pigford et al. v. Glickman* (1999), then the largest class-action lawsuit levied against the U.S. government. This case found that agents within the USDA's county-level programs deliberately and unjustly denied Black applicants much-needed financial and agricultural assistance. The case resulted in more than $500 million in payments to Black farmers who could prove they were discriminated against by the USDA. Given this context, how do we understand food justice as serving the real needs of Black communities? Wright and his coauthors reexamine this case through the lens of the politics of recognition, asking us to reconsider the ways that acknowledgment and validation by the state can thwart radical visions for a more equitable distribution of resources. They refuse to accept financial compensation for dispossession as an end goal of struggle, which would "normalize commodified social relations and foreclose more radical visions of Black liberation." They argue that a "radical Black agrarian politics must look beyond the teleological finality of compensation" and move toward the "goal of agrarian struggle being land restitution and the development of communal forms of Black land use and ownership."

Finally, akin to the histories of land dispossession and denial of access to financing, Judith Williams documents the ways that ongoing forms of food appropriation strip Black chefs and food producers of their livelihoods and potential business growth as outsiders commodify and capitalize on the trendiness of "ethnic food" in South Florida. Centering on Little Haiti, Little Havana, and other "ethnic food" enslaves, Williams frames her analysis around Cedric Robinson's theory of racial capitalism, where "the function of the laboring classes was to provide privileged classes with the material and human resources needed for their maintenance and further accommodations of power and wealth" (Robinson 1983, 21). Williams argues that chefs who appropriate the culture and cuisine of nonwhite people, specifically to profit off it, are consuming and reproducing the Other within a racial hierarchy. This chapter clearly delineates the boundaries of liberal forms of multiculturalism, demonstrating the privileging of whiteness, the erasure of Black knowledge and histories as culinary practice, and the boundless pursuits of racial capitalism. We draw the volume to a close with an afterword by Psyche Williams-Forson, whose 2006 book, *Building Houses out of Chicken Legs,* shifted the field of food studies broadly and African American food studies in particular. For well over a decade, Williams-Forson has pushed our fields toward more critical and thoughtful engagement with race and intersectionality, emphasizing the need to focus on power dynamics rather than simply the aesthetics of food (Williams-Forson and Wilkerson 2011). Reflecting on both the volume and the state of the field itself, Williams-Forson draws together the themes of the volume and underscores how Black food culture is an intellectual and political centerpiece of food studies debates and scholarship more broadly.

In this contemporary moment, we see the need and urgency for more work that enters the conversation about food inequities and justice from perspectives that understand that there is no shifting local or national food system without understanding food within broader contexts. *Black Food Matters* is our response to this need. From gathering several of the authors in the same place to think, write, eat, and share space together to the various ways each of us grapple with aspects of contemporary Black food life, one of the common threads in this volume is that Black people are deeply invested in food and justice and produce ways of being that demonstrate those investments in spite of the ongoing threats to Black life. Though seemingly simple, the declaration that Black people are deeply invested in and making space for protecting and providing food is one that cannot be overstated. This volume, we hope, contributes to epistemic shifts in the study of Black food and justice because there is much at stake — much more than the arguments that emerge in popular media every few years about soul food; much more, too, than simply adding grocery stores to Black neighborhoods. What wake work as an analytic offers us moving forward is an opportunity to grapple with how the "past" shows up continuously in the present; how food is part of the same anti-Black climate that produces and reinforces the carceral state that extends beyond prisons and jails and into our homes; and how, even under these conditions, something survives. People survive. We offer this book as one entry point into thinking about the hows and the whys.

Note

1. To read the full report on food insecurity in the United States, see USDA, "Key Statistics & Graphics," accessed February 18, 2020, https://www.ers.usda.gov.

Bibliography

Alkon, Alison Hope, and Julie Guthman, eds. 2017. *The New Food Activism: Opposition, Cooperation, and Collective Action.* Berkeley: University of California Press.

Beoku-Betts, Josephine A. 1995. "We Got Our Way of Cooking Things: Women, Food, and Preservation of Cultural Identity among the Gullah." *Gender & Society* 9 (5): 535–55.

Bower, Anne, ed. 2007. *African American Foodways: Explorations of History and Culture.* Urbana: University of Illinois Press.

Campt, Tina. 2014. "Black Feminist Futures and the Practice of Fugitivity." Helen Pond McIntyre '48 Lecture, Barnard College, October 7. http://bcrw.barnard.edu.

Carney, Judith. 2001. *Black Rice: The African Origins of Rice Cultivation in the Americas.* Cambridge, Mass.: Harvard University Press.

Carney, Judith. 2010. "Landscapes and Places of Memory: African Diaspora Research and Geography." In *The African Diaspora and the Disciplines,* edited by Tejumola Olaniyan and James H. Sweet, 101–18. Bloomington: Indiana University Press.

Carney, Megan. 2012. "'Food Security' and 'Food Sovereignty': What Frameworks Are Best Suited for Social Equity in Food Systems?" *Journal of Agriculture, Food Systems, and Community Development* 2 (2): 71–88.

Census of Agriculture. 2017. "Race/Ethnicity/Gender/Profile." https://www.nass.usda.gov.

Costa Vargas, João H. 2010. *Never Meant to Survive: Genocide and Utopias in Black Diaspora Communities.* Lanham, Md.: Rowman & Littlefield.

Davies, Tom Adam. 2017. *Mainstreaming Black Power.* Berkeley: University of California Press.

Franklin, Sara B. 2018. *Edna Lewis: At the Table with an American Original.* Durham, N.C.: Duke University Press.

Gottlieb, Robert, and Anupama Joshi. 2010. *Food Justice.* Cambridge, Mass.: MIT Press.

Haley, Sarah. 2016. *No Mercy Here: Gender, Punishment, and the Making of Jim Crow Modernity.* Chapel Hill: University of North Carolina Press.

Harris, Jessica B. 2003. *Beyond Gumbo: Creole Fusion Food from the Atlantic Rim.* New York: Simon & Schuster.

Harris, Jessica B. 2011. *High on the Hog: A Culinary Journey from Africa to America.* New York: Bloomsbury.

Harrison, Faye V. 2008. *Outsider Within: Reworking Anthropology in the Global Age.* Urbana: University of Illinois Press.

Harrison, Faye V. 2016. "Decolonizing Anthropology: A Conversation with Faye V. Harrison, Part I." *Savage Minds,* May 2. http://savageminds.org.

Hartman, Saidiya. 2007. *Lose Your Mother: A Journey along the Atlantic Slave Route.* New York: Farrar, Straus and Giroux.

Hartman, Saidiya. 2016. "The Belly of the World: A Note on Black Women's Labors." *Souls* 18 (1): 166–73.

Hislop, Rasheed Salaam. 2014. "Reaping Equity: A Survey of Food Justice Organizations in the U.S.A." PhD diss., University of California, Davis.

Jacobs-Huey, Lanita. 2002. "The Natives Are Gazing and Talking Back: Reviewing the Problematics of Positionality, Voice, and Accountability among 'Native' Anthropologists." *American Anthropologist* 104 (3): 791–804.

Jones, Naya. 2018. "'It Tastes Like Heaven': Critical and Embodied Food Pedagogy with Black Youth in the Anthropocene." *Policy Futures in Education* 17 (7): 905–23.

Joyner, Charles. 1984. *Down by the Riverside: A South Carolina Slave Community.* Urbana: University of Illinois Press.

Kern-Foxworth, Marilyn. 1994. *Aunt Jemima, Uncle Ben, and Rastus: Blacks in Advertising, Yesterday, Today and Tomorrow.* New York: Praeger.

Kwate, Naa Oyo A. 2019. *Burgers in Blackface: Anti-Black Restaurants Then and Now.* Minneapolis: University of Minnesota Press.

Lewis, Edna. 1976. *The Taste of Country Cooking.* New York: Knopf.

Lorde, Audre. 1997. *A Litany for Survival: The Collected Poems of Audre Lorde.* New York: W. W. Norton.

McClaurin, Irma, ed. 2001. *Black Feminist Anthropology: Theory, Politics, Praxis, and Poetics.* New Brunswick, N.J.: Rutgers University Press.

McCutcheon, Priscilla. 2015. "Food, Faith, and the Everyday Struggle for Black Urban Community." *Social & Cultural Geography* 16 (4): 385–406.

McKittrick, Katherine. 2011. "On Plantations, Prisons, and a Black Sense of Place." *Social & Cultural Geography* 12 (8): 947–63.

McKittrick, Katherine, and Clyde Woods, eds. 2007. *Black Geographies and the Politics of Place.* Cambridge, Mass.: South End.

McMichael, Philip. 2008. "Food Sovereignty, Social Reproduction, and the Agrarian Question." In *Peasants and Globalization: Political Economy, Rural Transformation and the Agrarian Question,* edited by A. Haroon Akram-Lodhi and Cristobal Kay, 288–311. London: Routledge.

Miller, Adrian. 2013. *Soul Food: The Surprising Story of an American Cuisine, One Plate at a Time.* Chapel Hill: University of North Carolina Press.

Mintz, Sidney. 1996. *Tasting Food, Tasting Freedom: Excursions into Eating, Culture, and the Past.* Boston: Beacon Press.

Moten, Fred. 2018. *Stolen Life.* Durham, N.C.: Duke University Press.

Myers, Ana McCormick, and Matthew A. Painter. 2017. "Food Insecurity in the United States of America: An Examination of Race/Ethnicity and Nativity." *Food Security* 9 (6): 1419–32.

National Black Food and Justice Alliance (NBFJA). 2017. "NBFJA State-ment: Land Justice Is Essential to Food Justice." December 21. https://www.blackfoodjustice.org.

Nestle, Marion. 2002. *Food Politics: How the Food Industry Influences Nutrition and Health.* Berkeley: University of California Press.

Nettles-Barcelón, Kimberly. 2012. "California Soul: Stories of Food and Place from Oakland's Brown Sugar Kitchen." *Boom: A Journal of California* 2 (3): 18–24.

Opie, Frederick. 2008. *Hog and Hominy: Soul Food from Africa to America.* New York: Columbia University Press.

Patterson, Orlando. 1982. *Slavery and Social Death: A Comparative Study.* Cambridge, Mass.: Harvard University Press.

Penniman, Leah. 2018. *Farming while Black: Soul Fire Farm's Practical Guide to Decolonizing Land, Food, and Agriculture.* Hartford, Vt.: Chelsea Green.

Pulido, Laura. 2016. "Geographies of Race and Ethnicity II: Environ-mental Racism, Racial Capitalism and State-Sanctioned Violence." *Progress in Human Geography* 41 (4): 524–33.

Ramírez, Margaret Marietta. 2015. "The Elusive Inclusive: Black Food Geographies and Racialized Food Spaces." *Antipode* 47 (3): 748–69.

Reese, Ashanté M. 2018. "'We Will Not Perish; We're Going to Keep Flourishing': Race, Food Access, and Geographies of Self-Reliance." *Antipode* 50 (2): 407–24.

Reese, Ashanté M. 2019. *Black Food Geographies: Race, Self-Reliance, and Food Access in Washington, D.C.* Durham, N.C.: University of North Carolina Press.

Robinson, Cedric J. 1983. *Black Marxism: The Making of the Black Radical Tradition.* Chapel Hill: University of North Carolina Press.

Robinson, Cedric J., and Elizabeth P. Robinson. 2017. "Preface." In *Futures of Black Radicalism,* edited by Gaye Theresa Johnson and Alex Lubin, 1–8. New York: Verso.

Rodriguez, Cheryl. 2003. "Invoking Fannie Lou Hamer: Research, Ethnography and Activism in Low-Income Communities." *Urban Anthropology and Studies of Cultural Systems and World Economic Development* 32 (2): 231–51.

Salamon, Lester, M. 1979. "The Time Dimension in Policy Evaluation: The Case of the New Deal Land Reform Experiments." *Public Policy* 27 (2): 130–83.

Sbicca, Joshua. 2018. *Food Justice Now! Deepening the Roots of Social Struggle.* Minneapolis: University of Minnesota Press.

Sharpe, Christina. 2016. *In the Wake: On Blackness and Being.* Durham, N.C.: Duke University Press.

Simpson, Audra. 2007. "On Ethnographic Refusal: Indigeneity, 'Voice' and Colonial Citizenship." *Junctures: The Journal for Thematic Dialogue,* no. 9: 67–80.

Simpson, Audra. 2014. *Mohawk Interruptus: Political Life across the Borders of Settler States.* Durham, N.C.: Duke University Press.

Simpson, Audra. 2016. "Consent's Revenge." *Cultural Anthropology* 31 (3): 326–33.

Smart-Grosvenor, Vertamae. 1970. *Vibration Cooking: Or, The Travel Notes of a Geechee Girl.* Athens: University of Georgia Press.

Smart-Grosvenor, Vertamae. 1972. *Thursdays and Every Other Sunday Off: A Domestic Rap by Verta Mae.* New York: Doubleday.

Sojoyner, Damien M. 2017. "Another Life Is Possible: Black Fugitivity and Enclosed Places." *Cultural Anthropology* 32 (4): 514–36.

Tipton-Martin, Toni. 2015. *The Jemima Code: Two Centuries of African American Cookbooks.* Austin: University of Texas Press.

Turner, Patricia A. 1994. *Ceramic Uncles and Celluloid Mammies: Black Images and Their Influence on Culture.* Charlottesville: University of Virginia Press.

Twitty, Michael W. 2017. *The Cooking Gene: A Journey through African American Culinary History in the Old South.* New York: Amistad / HarperCollins.

Wallach, Jennifer Jensen. 2015. *Dethroning the Deceitful Pork Chop: Rethinking African American Foodways from Slavery to Obama.* Fayetteville: University of Arkansas Press.

Wallach, Jennifer Jensen. 2019. *Getting What We Need Ourselves: How Food Has Shaped African American Life.* Lanham, Md.: Rowman & Littlefield.

Weiss, Brad. 2016. *Real Pigs: Shifting Values in the Field of Local Pork.* Durham, N.C.: Duke University Press.

White, Monica M. 2018. *Freedom Farmers: Agricultural Resistance and the Black Freedom Movement.* Chapel Hill: University of North Carolina Press.

Whitehead, Tony L. 1992. "In Search of Soul Food and Meaning: Culture, Food, and Health." In *African Americans in the South: Issues of Race, Class, and Gender,* edited by Hans A. Baer and Yvonne Jones, 94–110. Athens: University of Georgia Press.

Williams, Bianca C. 2018. *The Pursuit of Happiness: Black Women, Diasporic Dreams, and the Politics of Emotional Transnationalism.* Durham, N.C.: Duke University Press.

Williams, Erica Lorraine. 2013. *Sex Tourism in Bahia: Ambiguous Entanglements.* Urbana: University of Illinois Press.

Williams-Forson, Psyche. 2006. *Building Houses out of Chicken Legs.* Chapel Hill: University of North Carolina Press.

Williams-Forson, Psyche. 2012. "Other Women Cooked for My Husband: Negotiating Gender, Food, and Identities in an African American/Ghananian Household." In *Taking Food Public: Redefining Foodways in a Changing World,* edited by Psyche Williams-Forson and Carole Counihan, 138–54. New York: Routledge.

Williams-Forson, Psyche, and Abby Wilkerson. 2011. "Intersectionality and Food Studies." *Food, Culture, and Society* 14 (1): 7–28.

Yelvington, Kevin A., Alisha R. Winn, E. Christian Wells, Angela Stuesse, Nancy Romero-Daza, Lauren C. Johnson, Antoinette T. Jackson, Emelda Curry, and Heide Castañeda. 2015. "Diversity Dilemmas and Opportunities: Training the Next Generation of Anthropologists." *American Anthropologist* 117 (2): 387–92.

Zafar, Rafia. 2019. *Recipes for Respect: African American Meals and Meaning.* Southern Foodways Alliance Studies in Culture, People, and Place. Athens: University of Georgia Press.

Zavella, Patricia. 1993. "Feminist Insider Dilemmas: Constructing Ethnic Identity with 'Chicana' Informants." *Frontiers: A Journal of Women Studies* (13) 3: 53–76.

1

IN THE FOOD JUSTICE WORLD BUT NOT OF IT

Everyday Black Food Entrepreneurship

Ashanté M. Reese

• • •

There has been a proliferation of interdisciplinary critical food studies scholarship. From unequal access to supermarkets (Eisenhauer 2001; Kwate et al. 2009; Russell and Heidkamp 2011; Zhang and Ghosh 2016), to investigating the extent to which poor and Black residents pay more for groceries, some of which are inferior in quality (Alwitt and Donley 1997; Chung and Myers 1999; Alkon et al. 2013), to whiteness permeating mainstream alternative food movements (Slocum 2007; Alkon and McCullen 2011; Guthman 2011), and to unequal access to the means required to build food and farming infrastructure (Grim 1993), scholars have continuously demonstrated the extent to which the food system follows a racial order fundamentally built on willful and systematic anti-Black racism. In this way, anti-Blackness is, as Christina Sharpe (2016, 106) suggests, as pervasive as climate, in part shaping people's relationships with the environment, resources, and each other.

However, the constraints produced by anti-Blackness are only part of the story about how Black people access and create food-related infrastructure. Elsewhere, I have argued that Black food geographies are as shaped by memory, visions for self-reliance, and understandings of Black history as they are by supermarkets and restaurants (Reese 2019). Others have also pointed to the everyday but sometimes obscured ways Black people meet their food needs through a variety of strategies and lenses that are about both food and other important factors such as faith, self-determination, land justice, and rights to public space (McCutcheon 2015; White 2018; Jones 2019). This is not to say that unequal access to food and its attending infrastructures is moot. On the contrary, it is both a burden to residents and a social problem that threatens the well-being of whole communities. However, theoretically and methodologically, food studies inquiries focused on Black lives or Black spaces are often disconnected from the everyday lived experiences of those who are the subjects of the study. This is particularly salient for Black and low-income communities, as social scientists have often rendered those who bear the heaviest weight of inequities as agentless, which is evident in deficit models that fail to interrogate or meaningfully consider the various assets or ingenious ways Black people navigate systematic inequalities (Cox 2015; Hunter and Robinson 2016; Hunter and Robinson 2018). This lack of agency ascribed to Black people precludes or neglects opportunities to see individual and community-based assets that could be leveraged to create a more racially, economically, and food just world.

In Washington, D.C., where most of my ethnographic research has taken place, there is little doubt that racial inequities impact the lives of residents spatially, communally, and individually. The city itself is racially and economically segregated, with the majority of the city's poor and working-class Black residents living in wards 7 and 8. Among the 150,000 residents in wards 7 and 8, the average household incomes of $39,165 and $30,910 fall far below the city's median income of $70,848.[1]

While 23.6 percent of families in ward 7 and 35.3 percent of families in ward 8 lived below the poverty line, the D.C. average was 14.3 percent. Detailed analyses of the roots of these inequities are beyond the scope of this chapter, but documented housing redlining, the removal of Black communities in Georgetown, and white and middle-class flight in the mid-twentieth century undergird continued segregation that is deeply entrenched in the city's geography (Prince 2016). This is reflected in the city's food infrastructure. At the time of writing, wards 7 and 8 have three supermarkets total (two in ward 7 and one in ward 8) for their 150,000 residents, down from seven (four in ward 7 and three in ward 8) in 2010.[2] In addition, east of the Anacostia River also lacks sit-down restaurants, and mobile food delivery services are limited. During my fieldwork, I became very familiar with Denny's, because despite documented abuses against Black customers, it was the only sit-down restaurant in ward 7 at the time.[3]

Yet, even within these constraints, Black organizations and residents have figured out ways to meet their needs or, to borrow from Black southern vernacular, *to make a way outta no way.* As the late Clyde Woods (2017, 257) noted, one of the consequences of overly deterministic hegemonic narratives about urban revitalization and deviance is the possibility of missing traditions of "resistance, affirmation, and development," particularly in Black working-class spaces. In the context of food, some of these strategies go unnoticed, despite the attention given to food access, in favor of replicating models in which Black people are almost solely seen as the recipients of education and aid (Jones 2019). Theorizing from a framework that positions the food system as a function of anti-Black racism, this chapter contends with the question, What possibilities emerge when we turn to the everyday ways people *make a way outta no way* and theorize Black ways of distributing food under structural constraints? In this chapter, I focus on Black entrepreneurs who operate mobile food services. While Black restaurants, grocery stores, and other service-based businesses have been the subject of much academic inquiry (see Manning 1998 and Mullins 2008 for more detailed discussions of entrepreneurship and economics in Black neighborhoods and Cooley 2015 and Opie 2017 for histories of restaurants), there has been less of a focus on mobile services. Access to capital has, historically, been a significant barrier to entrepreneurship for Black people, resulting in varied approaches to developing and running businesses: sometimes out of individual homes, sometimes in shared spaces, and— as is the focus of this chapter—sometimes opting into providing mobile services. During and immediately after enslavement, Black people who entered the commercial economy as producers often did so in ways that capitalized on their ability to move, however constrained, to sell their goods, especially food (Westmacott 1992; Williams-Forson 2006, 17).

While significant in terms of providing a much-needed resource for Black communities, these entrepreneurs' role extends beyond commodity exchange. Sociologists offer Black placemaking as a way to understand how public space is transformed by its inhabitants, reflecting cultural priorities through creating "sites of endurance, belonging and resistance" in spite of social stratification (Hunter et al. 2016, 32). These sites have cultural meanings and geographic resonance, as they often emerge in spaces that outsiders may not understand as life giving—if they see them at all beyond their potential for capitalist gains. Alesia Montgomery (2016) argues that Black placemaking in gentrifying cities is sometimes exploited and used as a tool to attract white people back to the neoliberal city. In response, Black residents in gentrifying cities enact spatial agency, "the ability to be in, act on or exert control over a desired part of the built-and-natural environment—for example, the ability to use, make or regulate a public space," to claim spaces as their own (Montgomery 2016, 777). The ability to control parts of the environment emerges within specific sociohistorical contexts—in this case, deepening race–class divisions and conflicts in a city that is growing less and less hospitable to poor and working-class Black families and native Washingtonians while also using "diversity" as a strategy for gentrifying the city (Summers 2015). This, combined with Black geographical thought that contends that place is always political and the specific contexts in which Black lives unfold are important for understanding the restraints and resistances that emerge (McKittrick and Woods 2007; Hawthorne and Meché 2016; Bledsoe et al. 2018), form the basis on which this chapter proceeds.

Drawing from ethnographic fieldwork conducted in Washington, D.C., this chapter grapples with how Black residents (re)see, (re)inhabit, and (re)imagine food through mobile food entrepreneurship and ingenuity (Sharpe 2016), treating these entrepreneurs as not only food distributors but also place makers who stake claim to a changing city. This is not to position Black entrepreneurship as a definitive solution to food inequities. On the contrary, it could also, intentionally or otherwise, contribute to maintaining a status quo. However, through the examples provided in this chapter, I expand on the notion of Black food geographies by examining agency through the lens of Black entrepreneurship.

Black Entrepreneurship and Food in Historical Context: Hucksters

At the end of the nineteenth century and the beginning of the twentieth century, many U.S. cities were growing quickly, and they faced the challenges that come with rapid growth: failing infrastructures, concerns about public health and safety, and unclear paths forward in terms of expectations for and regulations of public space. Food retail, vending on city streets in particular, was a particularly important point of contention, as street vendors (mostly immigrants and people of color) were often considered nuisances, unsafe, unclean, and unhealthy (Wessel 2017). In Savannah, Georgia, ordinances in 1917 established daily public markets, set required fees for vendors, and established times for which produce could be sold outside market hours. In San Francisco, a 1914 ordinance banned the sale of food from carts and wagons. It also made it illegal to produce and sell food from one's home.[4] In Washington, D.C., huckster regulations appeared as early as 1853. According to the census, "huckster" was an official occupation and referred to a person who grew food and sold it at markets from stalls or on the street from wagons.[5] The regulations that governed their movement through the city included requiring a license (for which there was a fee) and the use of scales and measures at one's stall or in their wagon. Notably, the ordinance also specifically named free Black people, giving them permission to sell but also binding them to the consequences that would incur if they did not have a permit.

> Sec.5. And be it enacted, That the Mayor be and he is hereby authorized to issue licenses to free negroes and mulattoes, whether resident or non-resident, under the provisions of this act, any law

of this Corporation to the contrary notwithstanding; and all the provisions, requirements, fines, penalties, and forfeitures prescribed by this act shall apply to and govern such free negroes or mulattoes in the same manner as they apply to and govern all others engaged in the business of huckstering.[6]

I offer this brief history of city ordinances related to street vending because it is the context in which Black hucksters in Washington, D.C., operated. In predominantly Black neighborhoods, the fight for equal resources has been a constant struggle. So, too, has the impetus to create Black spatial practices that respond to structural inequities and affirm Black people's senses of place and community. In *Chocolate Cities,* Marcus Anthony Hunter and Zandria Robinson argue that chocolate cities not only are spaces in which Black people live, or scrape by to live, but are also primary sites of freedom struggles—both well-known, nationally organized ones and the daily, everyday ways that Black folks found to resist white supremacy, racial segregation, persisting economic inequalities, and, generally, the assault on Black life. They write:

> Chocolate cities are a perceptual, political, and geographic tool and shorthand to analyze, understand, and convey insights born from predominantly Black neighborhoods, communities, zones, towns, cities, districts, and wards; they capture the sites and sounds Black people make when they occupy place and form communities. Chocolate cities are also a metaphor for the relationships among history, politics, culture, inequality, knowledge, and Blackness. (Hunter and Robinson 2018, xiii)

Bearing the nickname "Chocolate City," Washington, D.C., is an ideal place to understand how Black food geographies unfold. The businesses that develop and the entrepreneurial spirit that moves through D.C.'s Black neighborhoods reflect opportunities to explore nuances in agency and power and entrepreneurs' role in community making. While entrepreneurship reflects a central tenet of the "American Dream," for Black businesses in segregated neighborhoods, these pursuits are often seen as means for individual and familial economic security, opportunities for self-definition (Williams-Forson 2006), and communal stability (Boyd 2008).

Bobby Wilson (2012, 962–63) dates the "black economy" as far back as enslavement, when freedmen sold goods and labor in segregated parts of northern and southern cities, creating opportunities to distinguish themselves as a separate class. Postenslavement, sharecropping created conditions under which Black people were exploited and cheated out of their land and labor while also actively encouraged to engage in the consumer side of the market, even if they were not able to sell their goods or services for a competitive price. For those living in the South, this was, in part, a reason for increasing moves to urban centers primarily in midwestern and northern cities during the Great Migration. The concentration of Black people in urban centers meant developing their own "social, cultural, and economic space from the very space that was designed to thwart them" (Wilson 2012, 966).

Food was essential to this development, and contemporary food entrepreneurship in Washington, D.C., is connected to a history of the entrepreneurial efforts within these segregated spaces. An oral history study conducted by Washington, D.C.–based historian Ruth Ann Overbeck in the 1980s revealed that both brick-and-mortar grocery stores and mobile entrepreneurs like hucksters were a significant component of the food landscape in northeast Washington, D.C. in the first half of the twentieth century. These Black men and women sold produce from carts or wagons that would drive through segregated Black neighborhoods, supplementing what residents purchased from grocery stores or grew themselves. Part of the local economy of northeast Washington, D.C., hucksters were largely supported by community buy-in as well as by the interpersonal relationships that developed between buyer and seller (Westmacott 1992, 192). These hucksters—who were most often men or young boys accompanying older men— sometimes came from other nearby cities to sell their produce, fish, and other wares.

In ethnographic interviews I conducted with elder residents who had grown up in D.C. prior to the 1960s, it was not uncommon for them to remember hucksters as part of their everyday lives. In one such instance, a resident recalled:

> They would come through on the wagons. They would bring fish here. They brought vegetables, watermelon . . . I mean, especially before the Safeway and of course, when the Safeway came through that sort of cut into their [business] . . . But yeah, I had forgot about the hucksters . . . the vendors who would come through with their horses. . . . Yeah, I know all about the hucksters. Yeah, the vendors that would come through with their horses and eventually, I think, there probably were trucks that came through.

In a literal sense, the food provided by these mobile vendors provided sustenance. Beyond the body, the social relationships and community built through and around the food geographies hucksters created were integral to the maintenance of neighborhoods. As place makers, these mobile food entrepreneurs played triple roles. They produced and provided food. They were neighbors and community members. They were also the backs on which the state's failures to provide equal and adequate resources for Black communities rested.

Yet, as this participant's narrative indicates, the scope and longevity of these entrepreneurial practices were limited. Growth of corporate supermarkets, changing (and growing) U.S. American consumer appetites, and, as Wilson noted, white businesses marketing to Black consumers challenged the viability of hucksters. In nearby Baltimore, for example, the tradition of Black men selling from horse-drawn wagons endured longer and was still a visible neighborhood fixture as late as 2017. In 2018 the *Baltimore Sun* reported that the mobile vendors faced threats due to new city ordinances and safety concerns (Rodricks 2018). In 2015 the stable where several vendors kept their horses was closed down by health officials, and the vendors were charged with animal cruelty, an offense for which they were found not guilty. They lost their horses and wages as a result of this ordeal (Rodricks 2018). I note Baltimore as an example here to highlight the ways contemporary city ordinances and laws echo similar problems as those at the turn of the twentieth century. Over the past decade, restrictions on mobile vending have increased, in part because of complaints from brick-and-mortar businesses about competition and issues framed as public health concerns (Wessel 2017). These regulations and the criminalization of street vending have a longer history than what can be shared here.[7] What is clear, however, is what Kathleen Dunn (2017, 53) argues: that the regulation of street vending is one way to control public space and intersects with the ways state actors attempt to regulate people of color, immigrants, and poor people. In the context of anti-Black racism, city ordinances and concerns for public health and safety become one way in which public place-making strategies are criminalized. Persisting residential segregation and economic inequalities, however, continue to create conditions under which Black entrepreneurs are interested in filling both food and economic gaps in Black neighborhoods. In the following two sections, I explore two mobile entrepreneurial pursuits that made up part of the food geographies in northeast D.C. as examples of how entrepreneurs attempted to fill food gaps and in the process exerted spatial agency in a city in which Blackness is marketable even as Black people are displaced (Summers 2015).

Black Entrepreneurship in Contemporary Context: Danny's Ice Cream–Turned–Food Truck

Almost everything about it signaled ice cream truck: its location in front of the recreation center where peewee football was happening, its boxy shape, the window opening through which a man served each person standing in line. However, each ice cream photo on the outside of the truck was marked out with a giant black X. I stepped up to talk to a second man, who sat in the driver seat. We exchanged names and I gave the customary spiel, "I'm a researcher studying food and community in the neighborhood." Danny pulled blue gloves from a box, commenting that he always uses a fresh pair before serving someone. I had to wonder if the performance of drawing the fresh pair of gloves, if the decision to serve me through the truck's front door rather than let me wait in line with the others, had anything to do with my researcher identity. So, while others stood in line, waiting to be served by the man at the window, Danny gave me VIP service, fixing up two half-smokes with chili and cheese for less than seven dollars. Sometimes described as a cross between a hot dog and a sausage, a half-smoke is a staple in Black neighborhoods in D.C. Like mambo sauce, an elusive condiment made of ketchup, barbeque sauce, hot sauce, and other ingredients, half-smokes serve as a barometer of authenticity. Recognizing them signals that you know something about the "real" D.C.

I had heard about this truck prior to my first visit. A research participant described Danny as the local "ice cream man" who sold chips, ice cream, hot foods, and noodles. Speaking to Danny's flexibility, he continued to say that he also provided food for parties and church events and made deliveries. In the fall, he parked at the recreation center to sell snacks and nachos during the flag football games. The only thing he did not sell, the participant lamented, was chicken wings and fries—the perfect accompaniment for mambo sauce.

Though my research at the time was narrowly focused on supermarkets and urban agriculture, I made note of Danny's truck and casually asked about it while hanging out with participants, conducting interviews, and volunteering at the neighborhood recreation center. I thought of Danny's truck as a novelty in the neighborhood, but the more I talked to others, the more it became clear that many residents saw his service as a necessary intervention in a neighborhood that had very few food options. Danny parked his truck outside the recreation center, a central gathering point in the neighborhood, two to three times a week, especially during the fall, to offer food during football games and rec center events. His prices were reasonable, he himself was a familiar figure in the neighborhood, and, since his business was mobile, his location was convenient. Danny's truck filled a void for those who frequented the recreation center and beyond because of the inequities outlined in the opening of this chapter. During my fieldwork, the recreation center hosted activities on a daily basis. With no food outlets immediately surrounding the center, Danny's truck provided food for patrons. When not at the recreation center, Danny's truck could be seen driving the streets of Deanwood, stopping to sell food to students after school, or parked in front of another location.

Food systems researchers and activists have paid little attention to entrepreneurs like Danny and the role they play in neighborhood food systems or Black food geographies more broadly (Short, Guthman, and Raskin 2007). Instead, the focus is largely on the presence or absence of large retail grocers or alternative means for food production like community gardens and farmers markets (Short, Guthman, and Raskin 2007; Markowitz 2008; Widener, Metcalf, and Bar-Yam 2012; Alkon et al. 2013). One of the reasons may be the emphasis on fresh fruits and vegetables because of their association with healthiness (Pearson et al. 2005; Befort et al. 2006; Morland and Filomena 2007; Bodor et al. 2008; McGee et al. 2008). A second reason may be that Danny's truck could be considered another form of fast food. A third reason may be an issue of (in)visibility. Geographic information system (GIS) mapping of food availability, community food surveys, or phone directory searches may not adequately account for mobile food outlets like Danny's, unless they are located in cities that require GIS tracking as part of the permitting process (assuming, of course, that they have obtained permits).

Yet food trucks like Danny's are integral to both food distribution and the continued cultural identities of neighborhoods, performing cultural place-making work that grocery stores, urban farms, and farmers markets do not do. Positioning food trucks as distinctly postmodern, Julian Agyeman, Caitlin Matthews, and Hannah Sobel (2017) argue that they not only provide food but demonstrate the extent to which food truck operators claim a right to the city by developing spatial practices that support everyday life. Further, in her work with Black-owned food trucks around the country, Ariel Smith (2019) has shown that the operators often have larger visions of their purpose beyond making money and have interests in investing in communities. As a spatial practice, Danny's food truck—especially its challenge to the visual aesthetics of the increasing number of gourmet trucks in the United States that bear fancy signage and often bright colors—stakes a claim to a neighborhood that is simultaneously disenfranchised in terms of food access and undergoing gentrification after a combination of public and private partnerships have sought to address more than four decades of disinvestment. Lenore Lauri Newman and Katherine Alexandra Newman (2017, 257) argue that the reemergence of food trucks in Vancouver reinforces the branding of it being a "livable city," is used to "tame" urban spaces, and promotes diversity, contributing to gentrification. Though the violent displacement of people and the destruction of places are the necessary predecessor to the emergence of these new, marketable amenities (Summers 2015), the excitement and anticipation surrounding the cultural demands produced through food trucks (Lemon 2017) obscure these processes. Thus, through his truck, Danny claims his neighborhood, claims his right to be there; and in these claims, he supports and reinforces cultural practices around food and sociality in his neighborhood.

Operating in his neighborhood was no small feat. If he had obtained a permit, then Danny had made significant yearly financial investments to operate. According to a study funded by the U.S. Chamber of Commerce Foundation, to start and maintain the requirements for a food truck in the United States, operators, on average, were required to complete forty-five different mandated procedures and spent approximately $28,276 on permits and licenses. The report also included indexes that ranked twenty cities based on the ease of completing the process to acquire a permit, complying with restrictions, and having the funds to operate a food truck. On all three indexes, Washington, D.C., landed in the bottom five, making it one of the most difficult cities in which to operate a food truck.[8] If he was operating without a permit, then Danny's choice to operate his truck was even riskier because of the expensive fines incurred if caught without one. In either case, his choice of Deanwood meant he could serve his community. It also meant that, perhaps, Danny was able to operate more freely in ward 7 than in other parts of town where food trucks may have been more heavily surveilled and policed (like around the national mall, for example). In turn, what may be considered constrained movement was an opportunity. Danny's truck intersected with the daily routines of ward 7 residents as a part of the social landscape.

Black Entrepreneurship in Contemporary Context: Derek's Mobile Food Delivery

Before there was Uber Eats, there was Derek's mobile food delivery. Derek, a lifetime resident of the neighborhood, was a forty-something-year-old director of a nonprofit. By his own account, he was civically minded, taking cues from his parents, who had served the neighborhood association and helped create a community economic development plan for the neighborhood. When I met him, Derek was serving as the president of the neighborhood civic association. This informed the mobile food delivery service he had cocreated with a friend and neighbor three years prior to our meeting. The food delivery service, intended to fill a gap in the neighborhood's food system, particularly concerning access to diverse and healthier restaurant options, was not well received by funders. After coauthoring an economic development plan with other ward 7 residents, Derek and his partner pitched the idea for a food delivery service that would pick up food from select restaurants in other parts of the city and deliver it to people in the community. If businesses were not going to come to ward 7, they were determined to bring the business to their neighbors. In an interview with me, Derek was clear that he was interested in using the food business as a way to provide opportunities for others and to provide a service to the community.

> We were doing food delivery for the community. We used a social enterprise model for our young people. If anybody drove for us, we paid for the deliveries, but they also got paid for commissions for any business that they created. They could actually become their own business owner. The reason why we started the business was because we couldn't get food over here. We created relationships with about one hundred restaurants that we could deliver for, at a modest profit for our business. More importantly, it

provided a service to the community, and it provided income for a community that needed jobs. We needed money. We put the business on hold, but it's still there.

Derek relayed several important aspects of what it meant for him to run a business in his neighborhood. On the one hand, he valued providing this service for the community. On the other hand, he distinguishes this service from other businesses by referring to it as a social enterprise, which Janelle Kerlin defines as "market-based approaches to address social issues" (2006, 247). For Derek, providing this service was about more than delivering food. It also provided an opportunity to employ neighborhood youth and supply entrepreneurial training. This, coupled with Derek's community-based advocacy through the neighborhood association, reflected his interest in and commitment to racial uplift ideologies and practices that emphasize the strengths and responsibility of Black residents as a mechanism to maintain Black space and sustain Black life. This, too, reflected Derek's class-based approach to fixing a social problem. Not unlike men and women who were early residents of his neighborhood (Nannie Helen Burroughs was one), Derek emphasized pursuing education and engaging in social endeavors that concerned themselves with addressing the problems of (mostly lower-class) Black people. Thus, when he talked about his neighbors who lived in nearby public housing, he framed them less as neighbors and more as examples of the effects of not only structural changes but also familial and interpersonal ones.

Derek's model was different from that of large, mainstream delivery services. As late as 2018, the *Washington Post* reported that while Uber Eats had expanded food possibilities in D.C., that expansion stopped at the Anacostia River (Carmen 2018). Just as residents were plagued with grocery store and restaurant inequities, so too did the neighborhood experience mobile delivery disparities as no delivery company provided adequate service to the predominantly Black part of D.C. Prompted by a petition started by Latoya Watson of ward 7, Postmates and Caviar announced that they were expanding their services to include wards 7 and 8

(Nania 2018). Derek's approach to developing mobile food delivery reflected what Simon Teasdale (2010, 4) refers to as a "social business," one that has a clear social goal but is still striving to be economically viable. The two goals were not easily integrated with each other, as balancing the social and economic goals presents significant challenges for social entrepreneurs, particularly those who are operating within neighborhoods that have continuously been neglected by both public and private sectors (Teasdale 2010). Derek describes this tension, particularly concerning financial constraints and community support:

> It's amazing. Somebody else came in, a Virginia firm, and saw the vision immediately and invested in it; put in about $40,000 and invested in it. They replicated our model exactly, with better branding, because they had money. They're doing it now, in the northwest, which was critical really for our expansion. We just [*pause*] we'll overtake them. It's only going to happen, if our people support it. Let me tell you a story, about business . . . [our neighbors] don't want to do it. If you understood the greater good, you would. It takes time to build a business. I run a nonprofit. . . . A couple years ago, my house was robbed in a home robbery. When I finally got the organization fully funded . . . [*pause*] I just haven't been able to recover from it financially. I've got these two businesses, the food and Washington tours and transportation. They're all designed to teach history and preserve the culture of our community, and make money doing it. Food is the biggest aspect of the business. I was interested in that.

By folding in history and storytelling, Derek's business model was one that was invested in profit while also preserving the neighborhood culture. However, in his attempts to build an entrepreneurial pursuit that would meet a need in the community, Derek inevitably had to contend with forms of precarity that are not uncommon for Black businesses owners, regardless of their interests in social justice. In Derek's case, the social and economic goals he put forth for his business were in tension, which he expresses through his assertions that building a business is hard and takes the support of the community. Though frustrated with the lack of community support, Derek firmly believed in community-grown businesses and the potential success of them, later adding, "If we decide we are going to collectively do it, we can make it work."

Conclusion

In this chapter, I have offered Black food entrepreneurship as a vital aspect of understanding contemporary Black food geographies in segregated Black neighborhoods, particularly in urban areas. As Danny's ice cream–turned–food truck and Derek's food delivery service demonstrate, some services provided by Black residents to their neighbors may be overlooked in neighborhood studies of food, particularly those that focus on supermarkets and urban agriculture. Though great strides have been taken to understand that the food system does not operate separately or apart from other manifestations of racism such as redlining, economic disparities, and a so-called color-blind free market system, the legacy of social science research that focuses on what's wrong instead of what is happening (Chin 2001), positioning Black people as risk objects (Boholm 2003; Jones 2019) that are acted upon rather than having an agency themselves, persists.

Challenging this notion, Danny's and Derek's services contribute to sustaining Black life in the midst of inequities and demonstrate the complexities of Black food geographies. When placed in this context—one that recognizes Black agency and the limits of the state—Danny's truck and Derek's food delivery are examples of the creative, everyday maneuvering that occurs in Black spaces. Rather than wait for systematic change, they created opportunities that impacted the neighborhood foodscape. The everydayness of their businesses met food needs. As place makers, Danny and Derek exhibit the types of spatial agency that happens in urban areas, even when taking into account the varied ways anti-Blackness and inequalities influence access.

There are countless other examples, large and small, of Black place makers who use food as a mechanism in their communities: Renaissance Community Cooperative in Greensboro, North

Carolina; Gangers to Growers in Atlanta, which employs formerly incarcerated youth and provides urban agriculture training; and informal exchanges and economies (cookshares, rideshares, etc.) in Black spaces all over the country. This work is about food but also speaks to intersecting needs and experiences that expand beyond it. It is not without its challenges. As Derek hinted, the success of his business (and others like it) depended on community support. That was just one concern. With stringent city ordinances, increasing competition from the rapidly growing number of food trucks, some of which were parked weekly at a government building less than a mile from the recreation center, and an ever-expanding technological world that now includes food delivery services like Uber Eats, it is unclear how businesses like Danny's and Derek's can or will be able to thrive. Perhaps ironically, the segregated nature of D.C. functioned as a protective mechanism for these entrepreneurial pursuits. However, as D.C. race and class demographics and food landscapes change, the future of businesses like those discussed in this chapter is tenuous, particularly since city ordinances had a negative impact on Black-owned businesses in other, gentrifying parts of town (Hyra and Prince 2015; Hyra 2017; Summers 2019). They may, as their huckstering forefathers and mothers, be near the end of their lifelines. And, as has been demonstrated through this lineage, perhaps there are other forms of entrepreneurship waiting to emerge. What is clear is that despite how pervasive anti-Blackness is and continues to be, Black entrepreneurs play an important role in both resisting anti-Blackness and contributing to the distinct cultural fabrics of the communities they serve.

This chapter has offered just one way of examining how Black people have developed systems to address structural food violence in their neighborhood. It also offers, however, a broader challenge to food justice advocates and researchers. Through examinations of food entrepreneurs in and around Black communities, food scholars can begin to contend with the dearth of scholarship that foregrounds Black agency in the context of food justice. Though definitions of food justice vary, with access to healthy, affordable food being central to most, who produces or provides this food is critical to the conversation of food justice. This is not only a question of access; it is also a question of methods and epistemology: Who do we not see when we do not include these locally grown entrepreneurial pursuits? What narratives are ignored or erased? By widening our frame to understand various and sometimes obscured ways individuals and communities meet their needs, this not only highlights the "making a way out of no way"; it also offers a more nuanced understanding of how deeply entrenched food inequities are and opens opportunities for thinking about more just ways of improving the food system that include everyday efforts on the ground.

Notes

1. District of Columbia, "Annual Economic Report 2016," https://does.dc.gov.

2. For comparison, ward 2 and ward 3—the wealthiest and whitest wards in the district—had seven and nine grocery stores, respectively, in 2016. For a full breakdown of grocery stores by ward, income, and race, see D.C. Hunger Solutions, "Closing the Grocery Store Gap in the Nation's Capital," spring 2016, http://www.dchunger.org.

3. A sample of headlines covering Denny's and its treatment of Black people across the United States includes "Blacks, Not Whites, Told to Pay before Dining. Now Federal Way's Denny's Workers Are Jobless (*News Tribune* [Tacoma, Wash.], October 1, 2017); "Secret Service Agents Allege Racial Bias at Denny's" (*Washington Post,* 1993). In 1994 Denny's paid $54 million in race bias lawsuits.

4. I originally learned of this ordinance through communication with Erica J. Peters on July 17, 2019. She used it in a public presentation and gave me permission to use it in this chapter. The ordinance reads in part:

ORDINANCE NO. 2917 (New Series).

Approved September 22, 1914.

Regulating the Manufacture, Handling, Care and Sale of Foodstuffs Within the City and County of San Francisco.

Be it Ordained by the People of the City and County of San Francisco as follows:

Section 1. On and after the passage of this Ordinance it shall be unlawful for any person, firm or corporation to engage in the handling, manufacture or sale of foodstuffs intended for human consumption, or after six (6) months from the date of passage of this Ordinance to continue in said business, or businesses, except in compliance with the conditions hereinafter specified.

Section 2. It shall be unlawful for any person, firm, corporation or their servants or employees to maintain or operate within any building, room, apartment, dwelling basement, or cellar, a bakery, confectionery, cannery, packing house, candy factory, ice cream factory, restaurant, hotel, coffee and chop house, grocery, meat market, sausage factory, delicatessen store, or other place in which food is prepared for sale, produced, manufactured, packed, stored, or otherwise disposed of, or to vend or peddle from any wagon or other vehicle, or from any basket, hand steamer, street stand, any food product whether simple or compound, or a mixture, which is sold, or otherwise disposed of for human consumption within the City and County of San Francisco, without having first obtained a certificate, issued by the Board of Health and signed by the Health Officer, of said City and County, that first, the premises are in a sanitary condition, and that all proper arrangements for carrying on the business without injury to the public health have been complied with, and second, that the provisions of all Ordinances, or regulations made in accordance with Ordinances, for the conduct of such establishments have been complied with. Said certificate when issued shall be kept displayed in a prominent place on the premises of the establishment, stand, vehicle, wagon or peddler for which or whom it is issued and is not transferable without the consent of the Board of Health. . . .

Section 5. The certificate provided for in Section 2, of this Ordinance, shall be valid for one (1) year from date of issue.

5. In some more contemporary contexts, "huckster" is used as synonymously with "peddler" or "swindler" in a pejorative way, especially in politics. That is not how it is being used in this chapter. As early as 1850, "huckster" was listed as an occupation that required a license to legally sell on the city's streets. These licenses were issued to both white and free Black people, though early newspapers like the *Georgetown Courier* alluded to the idea that most hucksters were Black. Residents in northeast D.C. who I interviewed did not use "huckster" as a pejorative term. In fact, when they were brought up, residents referred to them as a more desirable form of business than the local supermarket that failed to meet their needs.

6. For the complete regulations of hucksters in D.C., see Sheahan 1853.

7. See Agyeman, Matthews, and Sobel 2017 for a collection of essays, many of which explore histories of city ordinances. See also Morales 2000; Wasserman 2009.

8. To read the full report, see U.S. Chamber of Commerce Foundation, "Food Truck Nation," March 2018, https://www.foodtrucknation.us/wp -content/themes/food-truck-nation/Food-Truck-Nation-Full-Report.pdf.

Bibliography

Agyeman, Julian, Caitlin Matthews, and Hannah Sobel. 2017. *Food Trucks, Cultural Identity, and Social Justice: From Loncheras to Lobsta Love.* Cambridge, Mass.: MIT Press.

Alkon, Alison Hope, Daniel Block, Kelly Moore, Catherine Gillis, Nicole DiNuccio, and Noel Chavez. 2013. "Foodways of the Urban Poor." *Geoforum* 48: 126–35.

Alkon, Alison Hope, and Christie Grace McCullen. 2011. Whiteness and Farmers Markets: Performances, Perpetuations . . . Contestations?" *Antipode* 43 (4): 937–59.

Alwitt, Linda F., and Thomas D. Donley. 1997. "Retail Stores in Poor Urban Neighborhoods." *Journal of Consumer Affairs* 31 (1): 139–64.

Befort, Christie, Harsohena Kaur, Nicole Nollen, Debra K. Sullivan, Naiman Nazir, Won S. Choi, Laurie Hornberger, and Jasjit S. Ahlu-walia. 2006. "Fruit, Vegetable, and Fat Intake among Non-Hispanic Black and Non-Hispanic White Adolescents: Associations with Home Availability and Food Consumption Settings." *Journal of the American Dietetic Association* 106 (3): 367–73.

Bledsoe, Adam, LaToya Eaves, Brian Williams, and Willie Jamaal Wright. 2018. "Introduction." *Southeastern Geographer* 900: 1–18.

Bodor, J. Nicholas, Donald Rose, Thomas Farley, and Christopher Swalm. 2008. "Neighbourhood Fruit and Vegetable Availability and Con-sumption: The Role of Small Food Stores in an Urban Environment." *Public Health Nutrition* 11 (4): 413–20.

Boholm, Åsa. 2003. "The Cultural Nature of Risk: Can There Be an Anthropology of Uncertainty?" *Ethnos* 68 (2): 159–78.

Boyd, Michelle R. 2008. *Jim Crow Nostalgia: Reconstructing Race in Bronzeville.* Minneapolis: University of Minnesota Press.

Carmen, Tim. 20018. "D.C. Has Never Had More Food Delivery Options. Unless You Live across the Anacostia River." *Washington Post,* April 2.

Chin, Elizabeth. 2001. *Purchasing Power: Black Kids and Consumer Culture*. Minneapolis: University of Minnesota Press.

Chung, Chanjin, and Samuel L. Myers. 1999. "Do the Poor Pay More for Food? An Analysis of Grocery Store Availability and Food Price Disparities." *Journal of Consumer Affairs* 33 (2): 276–96.

Cooley, Angela Jill. 2015. *To Live and Dine in Dixie: The Evolution of Urban Food Culture in the Jim Crow South*. Athens: University of Georgia Press.

Cox, Aimee Meredith. 2015. *Shapeshifters: Black Girls and the Choreography of Citizenship*. Durham, N.C.: Duke University Press.

Dunn, Kathleen. 2017. "Decriminalize Street Vending: Reform and Social Justice." In *Food Trucks, Cultural Identity, and Social Justice: From Loncheras to Lobsta Love*, edited by Julian Agyeman, Caitlin Matthews, and Hannah Sobel, 47–66. Cambridge, Mass.: MIT Press.

Eisenhauer, Elizabeth. 2001. "In Poor Health: Supermarket Redlining and Urban Nutrition." *GeoJournal* 53 (2): 125–33.

Grim, Valerie. 1993. "The Politics of Inclusion: Black Farmers and the Quest for Agribusiness Participation." *Agricultural History* 69 (2): 257–71.

Guthman, Julie. 2011. "'If They Only Knew': The Unbearable Whiteness of Alternative Food." In *Cultivating Food Justice: Race, Class and Sustainability*, edited by Alison Hope Alkon and Julian Agyeman, 263–82. Cambridge, Mass.: MIT Press.

Hawthorne, Camilla, and Brittany Meché. 2016. "Making Room for Black Feminist Praxis in Geography: A Dialogue between Camilla Hawthorne and Brittany Meché." *Society & Space,* September 13. https://www.societyandspace.org.

Hunter, Marcus Anthony, Mary Pattillo, Zandria F. Robinson, and Keeanga-Yamahtta Taylor. 2016. "Black Placemaking: Celebration, Play, and Poetry." *Theory, Culture & Society* 33 (7–8): 31–56.

Hunter, Marcus Anthony, and Zandria F. Robinson. 2016. "The Sociology of Urban Black America." *Annual Review of Sociology* 42: 385–405.

Hunter, Marcus Anthony, and Zandria F. Robinson. 2018. *Chocolate Cities: The Black Map of American Life*. Berkeley: University of California Press.

Hyra, Derek. 2017. *Race, Class, and Politics in the Cappuccino City*. Chicago: University of Chicago Press.

Hyra, Derek, and Sabiyha Prince, eds. 2015. *Capital Dilemma: Growth and Inequality in Washington*. New York: Routledge.

Jones, Naya. 2019. "'It Tastes Like Heaven': Critical and Embodied Food Pedagogy with Black Youth in the Anthropocene." *Policy Futures in Education* 17 (7): 905–23.

Kerlin, Janelle A. 2006. "Social Enterprise in the United States and Europe: Understanding and Learning from the Differences." *Voluntas* 17 (September): 246–62.

Kwate, Naa Oyo A., Chun Yip Yau, Ji Meng Loh, and Donya Williams. 2009. "Inequality in Obesigenic Environments: Fast Food Density in New York City." *Health and Place* 15 (1): 364–73.

Lemon, Robert. 2017. "The Spatial Practices of Food Trucks." In *Food Trucks, Cultural Identity, and Social Justice: From Loncheras to Lobsta Love,* edited by Julian Agyeman, Caitlin Matthews, and Hannah Sobel, 169–88. Cambridge, Mass.: MIT Press.

Manning, Robert D. 1998. "Multicultural Washington, DC: The Changing Social and Economic Landscape of a Post-Industrial Metropolis." *Ethnic and Racial Studies* 21 (2): 328–55.

Markowitz, Lisa. 2008. "Produce(ing) Equity: Creating Fresh Markets in a Food Desert." *Research in Economic Anthropology* 28: 195–211.

McCutcheon, Priscilla. 2015. "Food, Faith, and the Everyday Struggle for Black Urban Community." *Social & Cultural Geography* 16 (4): 385–406.

McGee, Bernestine B., et al. 2008. "Perceptions of Factors Influencing Healthful Food Consumption Behavior in the Lower Mississippi Delta: Focus Group Findings." *Journal of Nutrition Education and Behavior* 40 (2): 102–9.

McKittrick, Katherine, and Clyde Woods. 2007. *Black Geographies and the Politics of Place.* Toronto: Between the Lines Press.

Montgomery, Alesia. 2016. "Reappearance of the Public: Placemaking, Minoritization and Resistance in Detroit." *International Journal of Urban and Regional Research* 40 (4): 776–99.

Morales, Alfonso. 2000. "Peddling Policy: Street Vending in Historical and Contemporary Context." *International Journal of Sociology and Social Policy* 20 (3/4): 76–98.

Morland, Kimberly, and Susan Filomena. 2007. "Disparities in the Availability of Fruits and Vegetables between Racially Segregated Urban Neighbourhoods." *Public Health Nutrition* 10 (12): 1481–89.

Mullins, Paul R. 2008. "Marketing in a Multicultural Neighborhood: An Archaeology of Corner Stores in the Urban Midwest." *Historical Archaeology* 42 (1): 88–96.

Nania, Rachel. 2018. "Petition Hopes to End Food Delivery Desert East of Anacostia River." *WTOP,* April 16.

Newman, Lenore Lauri, and Katherine Alexandra Newman. 2017. "Scripting the City: Street Food, Urban Policy, and Neoliberal Redevelopment in Vancouver, Canada." In *Food Trucks, Cultural Identity, and Social Justice: From Loncheras to Lobsta Love,* edited by Julian Agyeman, Caitlin Matthews, and Hannah Sobel, 243–62. Cambridge, Mass.: MIT Press.

Opie, Frederick Douglass. 2017. *Southern Food and Civil Rights: Feeding the Revolution.* Mt. Pleasant, S.C.: Arcadia.

Pearson, Tim, Jean Russell, Michael J. Campbell, and Margo E. Barker. 2005. "Do 'Food Deserts' Influence Fruit and Vegetable Consumption?—A Cross-Sectional Study." *Appetite* 45 (2): 195–97.

Prince, Sabiyha. 2016. *African Americans and Gentrification in Washington, DC: Race, Class and Social Justice in the Nation's Capital.* New York: Routledge.

Reese, Ashanté M. 2019. *Black Food Geographies: Race, Self-Reliance, and Food Access in Washington, D.C.* Chapel Hill: University of North Carolina Press.

Rodricks, Dan. 2018. "Baltimore's Arabbers are Struggling to Keep the Tradition Alive. Here's How the City Can Help." *Baltimore Sun,* April 10.

Russell, Scott E., and C. Patrick Heidkamp. 2011. "'Food Desertification': The Loss of a Major Supermarket in New Haven, Connecticut." *Applied Geography* 31 (4): 1197–1209.

Sharpe, Christina. 2016. *In the Wake: On Blackness and Being.* Durham, N.C.: Duke University Press.

Sheahan, James W., ed. 1853. *Corporation Laws of the City of Washington, to the End of the Fiftieth Council.* Washington, D.C.: Printed by Robert A. Waters.

Short, Anna, Julie Guthman, and Samuel Raskin. 2007. "Food Deserts, Oases, or Mirages? Small Markets and Community Food Security in the San Francisco Bay Area." *Journal of Planning Education and Research* 26 (3): 352–64.

Slocum, Rachel. 2007. "Whiteness, Space and Alternative Food Practice." *Geoforum* 38 (3): 520–33.

Smith, Ariel D. 2019. "Black Food Trucks as Agents of Change." *Cuisine Noir,* January 29. https://www.cuisinenoirmag.com.

Summers, Brandi Thompson. 2015. "H Street, Main Street, and the Neoliberal Aesthetics of Cool." In *Capital Dilemma: Growth and Inequality in Washington, DC,* edited by Derek Hyra and Sabiyha Prince, 299–314. New York: Routledge.

Summers, Brandi Thompson. 2019. *Black in Place: The Spatial Aesthetics of Race in a Post-Chocolate City.* Chapel Hill: University of North Carolina Press.

Teasdale, Simon. 2010. "How Can Social Enterprise Address Disadvantage? Evidence from an Inner City Community." *Journal of Nonprofit & Public Sector Marketing* 22 (2): 89–107.

Wasserman, Suzanne. 2009. "Hawkers and Gawkers: Peddling and Markets in New York City." In *Gastropolis: Food and New York City,* edited by Annie Hauck-Lawson and Jonathan Deutsch, 156–59. New York: Columbia University Press.

Wessel, Ginette. 2017. "Relaxing Regulatory Controls: Vendor Advocacy and Rights in Mobile Food Vending." In *Food Trucks, Cultural Identity, and Social Justice: From Loncheras to Lobsta Love,* edited by Julian Agyeman, Caitlin Matthews, and Hannah Sobel, 23–45. Cambridge, Mass.: MIT Press.

Westmacott, Richard. 1992. *African-American Gardens: Yards in the Rural South.* Knoxville: University of Tennessee Press.

White, Monica M. 2018. *Freedom Farmers: Agricultural Resistance and the Black Freedom Movement.* Chapel Hill: University of North Carolina Press.

Widener, Michael, Sarah Metcalf, and Yaneer Bar-Yam. 2012. "Developing a Mobile Produce Distribution System for Low-Income Urban Residents in Food Deserts." *Journal of Urban Health* 89 (5): 733–45.

Williams-Forson, Psyche. 2006. *Building Houses out of Chicken Legs: Black Women, Food, and Power.* Chapel Hill: University of North Carolina Press.

Wilson, Bobby M. 2012. "Capital's Need to Sell and Black Economic Development." *Urban Geography* 33 (7): 961–78.

Woods, Clyde. 2017. *Development Drowned and Reborn: The Blues and Bourbon Restorations in Post-Katrina New Orleans.* Athens: University of Georgia Press.

Zhang, Mengyao, and Debarchana Ghosh. 2016. "Spatial Supermarket Redlining and Neighborhood Vulnerability: A Case Study of Hartford, Connecticut." *Transactions in GIS* 20 (1): 79–100.

2

THE INTERSECTION OF POLITICS AND FOOD SECURITY IN A SOUTH CAROLINA TOWN

Gillian Richards-Greaves

• • •

On a hot Sunday afternoon in 2016, my sons and I drove about sixteen miles from our home in Conway, South Carolina, to the Cool Spring community to visit Glindian, a middle-aged African American woman and former student of mine.[1] Glindian, referred to as "Nookie" by relatives and friends, was born in South Carolina but migrated north with her family when she was about four years old. However, Glindian spent her summers in South Carolina with her grandmother and later resettled in Cool Spring when she was in high school. As we pulled into Cool Spring, I was first struck by the vast, open landscape decorated by green leafy vegetables and other crops. We made our way into Glindian's home and were greeted by the smell of rotisserie chicken and other delicious foods. After we had eaten, we went into her large garden, where my sons picked cabbage and other vegetables. That Sunday became the first of many days I would spend with Glindian in and around the Cool Spring community, eating locally grown foods, harvesting crops, and having in-depth conversations with members of the community.

Cool Spring is a diverse, unincorporated community in Horry County, South Carolina. With a population of approximately five thousand people, Cool Spring is frequently overlooked or lumped into the larger neighboring town of Aynor (Benjamin 1979, 3). Based on the 2010 census, Cool Spring is composed of (in order of population size) white people (88.1 percent), Black people (9.2 percent), Hispanic and Latinx people (2.4 percent), Native American people (0.6 percent), mixed-raced individuals (1.2 percent), other (unlisted) races (0.7 percent), and Chinese people (0.1 percent).[2] Even though the Black population is only a small percentage of the larger community, prominent Black people, such as the Dixons, the Fores (Fords), and the Gerralds, have lived and farmed in the area for several generations, dating back to the mid-nineteenth century.

Although most of the Cool Spring population is employed outside the home, a sizeable portion of the community also practices horticulture, animal husbandry, fishing, and foraging.[3] When driving through the streets of Cool Spring, it is common to see neat rows of cabbage or other leafy vegetables, legumes, herbs, fruit trees, and tubers such as potatoes. Coops, filled with chickens, ducks, and other domesticated birds, along with rabbits and pigs, are also a familiar sight. On the surface, Cool Spring seems like the average South Carolina town, where residents have resided for centuries on land that has been passed down from one generation to the next, but the narratives of this small community are much more complex and multilayered, and the town includes longtime residents, re-migrants and their children from other parts of the country, and relatively new settlers.[4]

Cool Spring falls within the geographic boundaries of the Gullah Geechee Cultural Heritage Corridor, and many Black residents are descendants of Gullah Geechee people, who moved to the mainland and maintained the horticultural practices of their foreparents as a means of subsistence and economic advancement. The Gullah Geechee people live along the coastal areas of Florida, Georgia, North Carolina, and South Carolina (Pollitzer 2005; Cross 2008; Joyner 2009). This community emerged during slavery in large part due to their relative immunity to malaria and isolation from the mainland United States. These enslaved Africans were captured from rice-growing regions on the continent of Africa and transplanted to the southern United States (Pollitzer 2005,

198). Their work on rice plantations, which were infested with malaria-carrying mosquitoes, afforded them relative autonomy, since enslavers often stayed away from the plantations during the summer months, leaving Black overseers in charge of the enslaved, who were immune to malaria (Pollitzer 2005, 13–20, 70). In this relatively autonomous environment, the Gullah Geechee were able to maintain more of their African heritage, particularly food values (Robinson 2007; Joyner 2009, 58; Jenkins 2010, 7). It is in the Gullah Geechee community that many of the southern cuisines categorized as "Black food" or "soul food" emerged and developed. William Pollitzer states, "The language and culture that developed in the sea islands were . . . a creative synthesis. . . . With it all, people preserved an indomitable spirit that was never crushed by labor or lash, by property or prejudice" (2005, 200). The cuisines, as well as processes of preparation, reflected the blending of cultures (acculturation), with notable African continuities, such as one-pot communal meals like gumbo and hoppin' john (Singleton 1991; Thurman 2000; Mintz 2009, 182). Although Black Cool Spring residents generally do not self-identify as Gullah Geechee— partly because of long-held negative stereotypes of the Gullah Geechee being "backward"—many maintain the cultural traditions of their ancestors, particularly regarding food.

This chapter illuminates the multifaceted role that food plays for many Black Cool Spring residents. More specifically, this chapter examines the ways that residents of this South Carolina town supplement their income, diversify their diet, create newer cuisines, and maintain a sense of community through horticulture and animal husbandry. Ultimately, this chapter interrogates the intersections of politics and food security by articulating the tactics Cool Spring residents use to safeguard against the impending food scarcity that will result from an inevitable civil war or world war.

Cool Spring has always been a farming community where its members supplement their diet and income through local projects like foraging, farming, and animal husbandry. While residents from every ethnic group engage in similar subsistence strategies, this chapter focuses on the Black residents, for whom these practices constitute a preemptive strike against food insecurity. As Psyche

Williams-Forson argues, "Food, including what it is, who prepares it, and sometimes how and when it is consumed, is intensely
personal. Powerfully symbolic in its ability to communicate, food
conveys messages about where we come from, who we are as individuals, and how we think and feel at any given moment" (2012,
139). For Black Cool Spring residents, food is not just a source of
income and nourishment but also the preparation for a literal and
figurative fight.

Very often, residents discuss the undercurrents of civil war
that are currently raging, due to a country that is sharply divided
along racial lines and rigidly entrenched in disparate political views.
Even worse, many Americans seem to be willing to kill or be killed
to defend their racialized political views, as observed in the June 17,
2015, murders of nine parishioners at the Emanuel African Meth-
odist Episcopal Church in Charleston, South Carolina, and the
vehicular homicide that resulted from confrontations between pro-
testors at a Charlottesville, Virginia, rally on August 11–12, 2017.
Every time political bile spills into the public discourse via the
media or the actions of common citizens, Black residents regard
such developments as an indication of things to come and recom-
mit themselves to self-sufficiency. When political discord is underscored by racial strife, which it often is, it further validates the
urgency for self-protection through food security and food sovereignty in the Black community. Thus, police shootings of unarmed
Black people, the use of racial epithets by political leaders and
other elected officials, and the proposals of bills and the passage
of laws that seek to limit or eliminate subsidies ("entitlements")
cause dis-ease in the Black community and compel them to continue the struggle for self-protection. Moreover, for many, these
forms of racialized violence are reminiscent of how food was used
to undermine the civil rights movement of the 1960s and 1970s and
prevent Blacks from voting (Williams-Forson 2012) and humili-
ate them in other sociopolitical spheres (Cooley 2015, 206). Many
Black residents view the values of the Republican Party as antithetical to their continued success and their very existence. They
often equate the current Republican Party to twentieth-century
Dixiecrats who sought to disenfranchise them of their basic human

rights by enacting laws that limit or eliminate their ability to develop themselves or advance economically. Whether the issue of concern is voting rights, police brutality, or redlining districts, the Republican Party is often viewed by many Black residents as the source of their disenfranchisement. Even though they generally discuss issues privately within the community, their proactive stance on food security loudly articulates their positions on sociopolitical developments in the country.

While the Republican Party is seen as rooted in values antithetical to their own, many Black residents view President Donald Trump's rhetoric, particularly on immigration and race, as crucial to the current divisive climate in the country. His continued caustic language toward political allies and foes around the world further creates political toxicity and fosters insecurity on the part of Black residents. For many, also, a particularly troubling aspect of the current president's behavior is his apparent obsession with President Barack Obama, particularly his apparent need to "Otherize" him and trivialize his accomplishments. Some contend that the current president's rhetoric toward people of color and immigrants, in tandem with the power to enforce those values through laws and executive orders, can adversely affect their lives. It is the presence of what many residents view as impending and tangible danger that causes many to actively safeguard their own food source.

Over the course of a year, I conducted an ethnographic study of the subsistence patterns of Black Cool Spring residents. This research began informally through conversations with Glindian and expanded to include dozens of other Cool Spring residents. Frequently, casual conversations with Glindian resulted in extensive show-and-tell activities that required me to drive to the homes of her relatives and neighbors to explore their crops and livestock. Although I generally spent the time documenting my experiences with photos and videos, in some instances, residents asked or compelled me to "put down the camera" and participate in the harvesting of crops, the gathering of eggs, or other subsistence activities. Subsequently, through casual conversations, formal and informal interviews, and participant observation with residents,

I was able to gain firsthand experiences and collect a wealth of data that provided crucial insight into the role of food in Cool Spring and, by extension, historical Black communities in the American South. While research primarily focused on the Black residents of Cool Spring, I also had many fruitful conversations and interactions with non-Black residents whose personal lives and subsistence activities intersected with members of the Black community.

Horticulture

In Cool Spring, food production and consumption continue to be the principal means by which Black residents articulate and maintain autonomy and tradition and safeguard against what they view as impending detrimental changes in the larger American society. I became interested in the role of food production, broadly speaking, within the Black community of Cool Spring after casual conversations with Glindian's relatives, friends, and neighbors revealed the crucial yet multifaceted role that food played in the social structure and continuity of the community. For many, horticulture is their only source of income; thus, while they may share their harvest with relatives and neighbors, they also often sell their produce to earn a living wage.

Glindian has a large kitchen garden, the length of about half a city block, where she varies her crops seasonally. In the early spring, beginning in January, she plants white potatoes, garden peas, onions, broccoli, and spinach; in the late spring, she plants vegetables, including tomatoes, beans, and okra; and from late summer into early fall, she plants her winter garden, which includes broccoli, collards, mustard, turnips, and onions. Like many Cool Spring residents, Glindian also often gleans crops from her neighbors' gardens when she needs specific crops, when she has not planted a specific crop for the season, or when her neighbors have excess produce. Cool Spring residents have an unspoken culture of crop sharing, but this is generally limited to relatives, close friends, and neighbors; thus, it would be frowned upon for non-residents or individuals who do not have a close relationship or established agreement to harvest crops from each other's gardens.

Unlike Glindian, Tony, a law enforcement officer with a large extended family and deep roots in the community, tends his farm and raises animals in addition to his regular job. Tony has two gardens: a small one in his backyard as well as a larger one about the length of a city block across the street from his home. When I visited Tony's garden in the fall of 2017, it had several vibrant rows of eggplant, cabbage, peppers, potatoes, and many other vegetables. What was striking to me was the fact that his garden across the street was not fenced in, which potentially gave anyone access to his crops. In fact, he informed me that neighbors and friends often harvested some of his crops, and he was fine with that, even though he planted them for his personal use. The day I visited Tony with Glindian, he gave us permission to harvest cabbage and other greens. Tony also raises pigs in his backyard, close to the smaller garden and a pond in which he keeps fish.

In addition to providing a financial support system for Cool Spring residents, farming has also become a means of diversifying their diet, allowing them to obtain a balanced diet year-round.

Figure 2.1. Glindian in Tony's garden, discussing diverse uses for cabbage leaves, including making wraps. Cool Spring, South Carolina, December 2017.

Because of the climate, the South has a relatively long growing period, and residents often produce more food than they can personally use, gift, or sell, forcing many to employ diverse preservation methods, such as canning, drying, fermenting, freezing, pickling, and smoking meats and vegetables for future use. For instance, a quick survey of Glindian's home revealed mason jars of okras, peppers, greens, and even meats. When she has excess cabbage, collards, and other green leafy vegetables, Glindian blanches them, cools them, and stores them in freezer bags. Preserving foods in these manners ensures that she has greens for most of the year, even when she does not plant specific crops. Even though the South has a long history of preserving foods using these techniques, especially during national crises such as the Civil War (Benjamin 1979, 31; Weigl 2014, 1–3), many Black Americans would have learned some of these preservation methods from their West African ancestors, who used them long before the advent of the Atlantic slave trade (Farnsworth and Wilkie 2006, 58; Covey and Eisnach 2009). During slavery, Blacks drew on their knowledge of preservation techniques to ensure they always had food, and after emancipation, the continued canning, pickling, and other forms of food preservation (Bennett 1973).

Procuring Meats in Cool Spring

Cool Spring residents also supplement their diet by raising domestic animals, hunting game, fishing, and obtaining meat donations from neighbors and relatives. Glindian, for instance, raises ducks and chickens for meat and eggs. Additionally, from late fall through winter, when her white neighbors go hunting, they often bring her whole deer and other wild game, which she shares with relatives and friends. When Glindian kills chickens or receives donations of pork, deer, raccoons ("coons"), or other animals, she uses the meats to make soups, stews, and other cuisines. Recently, Glindian purchased a pig from one of her neighbors and named it Henrietta. After she slaughtered Henrietta, she made barbecued pork, sausages, hog-head cheese, and other delicious cuisines she shared with family and friends. Like Glindian, most residents eat diverse meats, but the slaughter and cooking of pigs seem to be an affair that brings together more members of the community to work and eat. It is not uncommon to see residents cooking (barbecuing) an entire pig while other members of the community eat, drink, and chat. In *Real Pigs*, Brad Weiss points out a similar phenomenon among white farmers in North Carolina, where pigs are a source of income, community building, education, and placemaking. As they do for to the residents of Cool Spring, pigs create that linkage between "cuisine and heritage" (Weiss 2016, 155), linking particular tastes to that geographic location and their heritage at large. Many residents preserve excess meats for later use by placing them into large storage bags, labeling them, and packing them in freezers according to their content. Some Cool Spring residents also dry and smoke meats to cure them. While Cool Spring residents may diversify their diet to accommodate visiting relatives, personal cravings, or an insufficient quantity of a specific kind of food item, the underlying influence continues to be an abundance of locally grown foods and relatively easy access to them.

Figure 2.2. Glindian displays some of her frozen meats. Cool Spring, South Carolina, 2018.

More recently, my sons and I visited Glindian to help her harvest green onions, peas, and potatoes. On that same day, her uncle Sam, who lives across the street from her, was doing a whole-hog barbecue. We stopped by, engaged in humorous conversation, and even got our own to-go container of barbecue pulled pork. The meals that neighbors distribute help strengthen the community by providing sustenance for those in need, particularly the elderly, and giving others a reprise from cooking. As there is often an abundance of crops and meat, sharing meals with the community is also a means of combating waste that can result from having excess crops or meals.

Regardless of what is on the menu, however, members of the community, particularly the older ones, often provide commentary and feedback on the spices, preparation methods, and every aspect of the cuisines, as a way of simultaneously policing the boundaries of authenticity and articulating ethnic identity. In one of my numerous conversations with Glindian, for instance, she discussed the many methods of properly obtaining and cooking "coons." Displaying a large freezer bag with a frozen raccoon, she explained: "If you don't shoot your coon yourself, you never take a coon from anybody or purchase a coon from anybody without the feet being intact . . . because that way [without the feet] you can't tell a coon from a dog. I mean, this could be any animal without a feet or tail or head" (personal conversation, March 2018). Several other residents I spoke with discussed various cuisines and the lengths to which they go to ensure that it is "just like mama used to make it" or like an established standard. Thus, producing their own foods allows Black Cool Spring residents to maintain Black foodways by reducing or eliminating the scarcity that results from seasonal crops or insufficient finances and ensuring some degree of authenticity.

Disruptions to Horticulture and Animal Husbandry

Not all Cool Spring residents practice self-sufficiency through horticulture and animal husbandry. Some individuals find it difficult to maintain Black foodways because of the scarcity that results from their separation from the land (farming) and the food values that sustained Cool Spring for generations. According to Sidney Mintz and Christine Du Bois, "Like all culturally defined material substances used in the creation and maintenance of social relationships, food serves both to solidify group membership and to set groups apart" (2002, 109). Thus, for instance, some re-migrants and their children often experience difficulty (re)integrating themselves into the community, partly because some still view farming as a stigma that connects them to slavery and servitude (Allen 2013, 49). This disconnect has resulted in increased incidents of theft, particularly by young people who desire food but lack the diligence or skill necessary to produce it.

In addition to maintaining cultural traditions, many Cool Spring residents also use the abundance of crops to create newer cuisines. Some of these newer cuisines are inspired by existing ones, but many others are created because of individual tastes or convenience. Many of my conversations with Glindian were fueled with fried cassava and other tubers, deer meat and potatoes on mustard greens, and greens sautéed with strips of pork or other meats, a practice common in the Black community before and during slavery (Benjamin 1979, 27–36). Glindian also uses green leafy vegetables in innovative ways to make soups, stews, and wraps, and to garnish other cuisines. One evening, after a long day in the garden, she wanted a quick snack and decided to make a burrito-like wrap using cabbage leaf, poached eggs, cheese, tomatoes, vegetables, and seasonings. She placed a leaf of cabbage in a few ounces of boiling water and allowed it to simmer until it was a bit soft. She then cracked an egg on the cabbage leaf and added salt, black pepper, diced tomatoes, and other spices. She poached the egg by systematically basting it with hot water from inside the frying pan. When the egg was almost cooked, she placed a slice of pepper jack cheese on top of the egg and wrapped the contents in the cabbage leaf, which was fully steamed by that time. As we enjoyed our healthy green wrap, it was not lost on us that all the ingredients of the snack came from Glindian's yard and were underscored by years of socialization of seasoning food and making something from nothing. More importantly, the stereotype of

Black foods being fatty and unhealthy is undermined in communities like Cool Spring, where residents practice horticulture and animal husbandry and prepare healthy meals.

Glindian also uses parts of plants and their roots to add color and flavor to her meals or to create entirely new meals. For instance, she uses blossoms from the onion plant, which smell and taste like onions, to flavor and garnish vegetable salads and soups. Glindian also actively forages for edible plants and roots and the fruit of the edible pindo palm, and, combining these other common fruits, makes gallons of fruit juices and homemade wines. During the fall months, she also forages for sassafras roots, which she uses to make teas. The use of available or excess crops to create newer cuisines that many regard as equally soulful or down-home cooking, as well as established Black cuisines, demonstrates that Black food culture is not just "traditional" (stuck in the past) but dynamic.

The practice of horticulture and animal husbandry continues today, as it did in the past, to create and maintain a sense of community among Cool Spring residents, who assist each other with food production. Frequently, younger or more able-bodied residents plant their gardens first, and then assist their elderly or sick relatives and neighbors to plough, plant, and reap their produce. When neighbors render assistance to healthy, able-bodied individuals, the favor is often repaid in kind later. By helping each other plant, the residents practice a sort of crop rotation, whereby they vary the crops planted on each other's lands (gardens) as a means of obtaining a more bountiful and diverse harvest. It was not uncommon to hear Glindian say, for instance, "I didn't plant snow peas this time, but 'Mr. McDonald' did, so I'll get some from him." This communal work is not limited to crops but also includes the slaughtering and dressing of animals. Every few weeks, members of the community who raise chickens kill the mature birds, often coordinating their "killing time" to ensure they have as many available hands as possible for the dressing. During hunting season, this is important because white neighbors who hunt with firearms often donate deer, raccoons, and other game when their freezers are full or when they have enough animals for their personal use. By assisting each other plant and harvest crops or slaughter animals, Cool

Spring residents secure the future goodwill of others and add to their food storage by gaining access to each other's gardens when the need arises.

The Place of Food in the Black Community

Black foodways, particularly in the southern United States, are shaped by diverse factors, including an African past, enslavement, and sustained interactions with other ethnic groups in the New World (Harris 2003, 2–3; Marks 2015, 80–81). According to Kelly Wisecup, "What makes African American cuisine distinctive is the blending of techniques, ingredients, and consumption patterns that developed through the Columbian exchange and the intertwined process of colonization and slavery: specifically, the combination of African, European, and Native American foodways—exchanges that occurred not only within the southern United States, but also in Africa and the Caribbean" (2015, 17–18). Before the Atlantic slave trade, Africans on the continent had their own unique food production and consumption practices that served as crucial markers of ethnic and social divisions in society. Whether it was planting rice (Carney 2001, 3, 120), harvesting yams (Pollitzer 2005, 139), pounding fufu (Covey and Eisnach 2009, 42), or cooking and eating one-pot communal meals (Singleton 1991), food on the African continent served a pivotal role in the social constructions of and divisions within pre–Atlantic slave trade Africa. Slavery disrupted Indigenous "traditional" African foodscapes of enslaved populations by physically separating them from their ancestral farmlands and the familiar flora and fauna that were crucial to the production of African cuisines, disrupting food communities, and significantly eroding food knowledge banks (Carney 2001, 42). Despite the gastronomic, physical, and psychological trauma that resulted from slavery, however, displaced Africans in the Africa diaspora continued to draw on the embodied knowledge that survived the Middle Passage and slavery, as well as those acquired through acculturation, to continue to produce African-influenced crops and cuisines (Mintz 1996, 36; Hughes 1997, 272; Covey and Eisnach 2009, 43, 211). For enslaved African Americans, especially in the southern United States, food (production and consumption) was uniquely instrumental in shaping individual lives and communities, and many of those food influences and values are observable even today. As Warren Belasco states, "Agriculture remade the world, both physically and culturally, transforming landscapes and geography, subsidizing soldiers and poets, politicians and priests" (2008, 1).

During slavery, food crops like sugar and rice were major cash crops in the United States, so much so that by 1850, rice was the major cash crop in South Carolina (Carney 2001, 1; Farrish 2015, 152) and "257 plantations along ten rivers of the state produced an astounding 159,930,613 pounds or nearly 80,000 tons of rice. At its peak 150,000 acres of swamp and tidal marshes were under cultivation" (Pollitzer 2005, 94). The strategic enslavement of peoples from rice-growing regions in Africa—such as Sierra Leone and The Gambia, where the *Oryza glaberrima* strain of rice was planted—was crucial to the development of the rice industry in southern states like South Carolina (Littlefield 1981). According to Pollitzer: "Rice, the crop that dominated and characterized South Carolina from the late eighteenth to the mid-nineteenth century, illustrates the debt to Africans, for they were imported for their experience in growing the grain" (2005, 196). Though food production, specifically farming, was largely done under duress, the enslaved exchanged ideas that demonstrated their embodied knowledge (memory) and acquired knowledge and reaffirmed their shared sense of community (Joyner 2009, 89).

Slavery was instrumental in shaping food values and cuisines in the African American community and the African diaspora at large. This is partly because during slavery, enslavers used food instrumentally, to feed, punish, reward, or bribe slaves (Douglass 1846, 76; Covey and Eisnach 2009, 196; Farrish 2015, 156). Enslavers fed the slaves to keep them alive and working, but the food the slaves ate was in large part inexpensive, like peas (Albala 2007, 117, 126–28), substandard in quality and rejected by the planter class (Bowen 1992; Fountain 1995). Thus, for instance, "leftover ears, tails, feet, fat, ribs, tripe chicken feet, heads, tongues, and innards" (Covey and Eisnach 2009, 97), which enslavers rejected, became staples of the slave diet (Cusick 1995; Yentsch 2007). Food was, therefore, a means of control, through which enslavers determined what slaves ate, how much they ate, and, in some instances, if they ate (Olmsted 1863, 108; Farrish 2015, 156–57). The control of slaves' diet through rationing of food affected the social structure of the enslaved community and reinforced the elevated status of enslavers, who enjoyed bountiful high-protein meals, and a stratified Black community that faced uncertainty and lack in its diet. According to Christopher Farrish, "The monotonous diet of the enslaved may have filled one's stomach, but it did not stave off pellagra and other diseases associated with a nutrient-poor diet" (2015, 156; see also McCandless 2014). In places like South Carolina, poor nutrition among the Black population resulted in pica, an eating disorder that involves the consumption of nonfood items, such as clay (Pollitzer 2015, 69–85). This is not to suggest that slaves totally lacked agency with regard to their diet but to emphasize how a gross imbalance of power during slavery facilitated food and nutrition insecurity and, in tandem with other factors, inadvertently gave rise to Black food culture often labeled "soul food" (Henderson 2007). In his well-regarded book *Hog and Hominy: Soul Food from Africa to America,* Frederick Douglass Opie defines the concepts of "soul" and "soul food" in the following manner: "Soul is the style of rural folk culture. Soul is black spirituality and experiential wisdom. And soul is putting a premium on suffering, endurance, and surviving with dignity. . . . [Soul food] is the intellectual invention and property of African Americans" (2008, xi). The term *soul food* was said to have emerged in the North and became popular when commentators like Amiri Baraka (LeRoi Jones) "began valorizing it as an expression of pride in the cultural forms created from and articulated through a history of Black oppression" (Witt 1999, 80). As Christine Marks argues, "Today, pig chitterlings are a staple dish of African American cuisine, another testament to the creative power of Black cooks who managed to turn discarded parts of animals into dishes that are now consumed throughout the nation" (2015, 85). Cool Spring residents continue to draw on many of the food values of the past to prepare some of the same meals they often refer to as "that good down-home cooking," "soul food," "real food," and similar descriptions.

Despite the culinary restrictions imposed during slavery, African Americans were able to exercise agency through horticulture and animal husbandry (Otto and Burns 1983; Morgan 1998). During slavery, many African Americans kept kitchen gardens or larger plots of land where they cultivated greens, vegetables, and even rice, which they used to supplement their diet (Moore 1989; Rivers 2000; Whit 2007, 48–49; Carney and Rosomoff 2009). In many instances, also, slaves gained income by selling their surplus produce to other members of the Black community and to enslavers (Otto and Burns 1983, 191; Covey and Eisnach 2009, 76). Their subsistence strategies also enabled them to diversify their diet and achieve a degree of food security, "a condition in which all individuals have regular access to sufficient food to satisfy their nutritional and energy needs," and maintain food sovereignty, "a population's ability to determine the best ways to fulfill their sustenance requirements" (Cooley 2015, 202; see also Alkon and Agyeman 2011, 121, 126).

While the process of slavery facilitated acculturation and the subsequent rise of creolized cuisines, many of the foods enslaved Blacks prepared were "African retentions" or "African continuities" that were brought from the African continent (Covey and Eisnach 2009, 62). As Mintz notes, foods eaten "have histories associated with the pasts of those who eat them; the techniques employed to find, process, prepare, serve, and consume the foods are all culturally variable, with histories of their own (Mintz 1996, 7). Thus, raw food items like okra (Hughes 1997, 242; Harris 2003, 12), black-eyed peas (Albala 2007, 3), and rice (Stanonis 2015), and cuisines like gumbo (Hughes 1997, 272; Harris 2003, 2–3) and red rice (Singleton 1991), are all influenced by an African heritage. African American cooking methods are also undergirded by African values, such as communal eating, particularly of one-pot meals, which required fewer cooking utensils, utilized leftovers, and took less time to feed more individuals (Singleton 1991). For many, the quintessential African practice of making "something from nothing" as a technique of adaptation also became crucial in

African American foodways. Thus, enslaved African Americans continued to draw on the knowledge and techniques they cultivated during slavery to craft unique foodways that were simultaneously unique, intersectional, and functional (Marks 2015, 80). While African Americans in the southern United States have carved a unique foodscape—where African influences as well as creolization and acculturation are simultaneously visible—the Gullah Geechee have been particularly instrumental in creating and propagating cuisines categorized as "soul food."

In fact, many Black Cool Spring residents mainly plant crops and raise animals that are integral to cuisines that fall under the umbrella of "soul food," which serves as "a form of self-identification and of communication" (Mintz 1996, 13). While the culinary traditions many refer to might be regarded in their larger context as "southern food" (Hoffman 2015, 67; Wallach 2015, 178), beneath the surface, many Black residents credit their enslaved ancestors with bringing the knowledge from the African continent, creating the cuisines during slavery, and propagating them with Whites and other ethnic groups with whom they shared geographic spaces (Pollitzer 2005, 198; Mintz 2009, 182). Thus, for instance, William Van Deburg argues, "Although collard greens, black-eyed peas, hush puppies, deep-fried chicken, and catfish may have appeared on both white and black tables in the antebellum South, it seemed to take a black hand in the kitchen before any recipe could be considered 'soulful'" (1993, 203). Therefore, ethnic cuisines once associated with poverty and low status (Kalcik 1984, 40) are now crucial markers of Black and southern authenticity.

Intersections of Food and Religion

While oral narratives, hands-on experiences through enculturation, and cookbooks (Witt 1999; Chatelain 2015, 32–33; Stanonis 2015, 103) have been important media for the transmission of Black food culture from one generation to the next, the church has been particularly crucial in the establishment and propagation of the food values in the Black community, and this continues to be true for Black residents of Cool Spring. Before the civil rights movement and long after, the church was the only space in the United States where the Black community was afforded relative autonomy to address economic, political, and social issues (Lincoln and Mamiya 1990). The church was also a place that nourished—literally and figuratively—political leaders and the larger Black community with cuisines classified as "soul food" (Stanonis 2015, 94). Anthony Stanonis argues:

> Understanding the religious context for soul food helps us understand the aims of the African American community in later championing their foodways under the phrase. The significant role of Christian churches and ministers in providing the faithful with solace while also energizing support for civil rights mirrored the comfort and sustenance offered by soul food dishes that allowed African Americans to resist the dehumanizing effects of segregation. (2015, 95)

In the Cool Spring community, the church continues to occupy a crucial space where members receive religious instruction, are in fellowship with each other, and address the complex social issues affecting the Black community. Every church has a kitchen, which is used at least once per week (usually on Sundays), to nourish community members. As Glindian puts it, "The church is the community's home kitchen." While some form of food is available each Sunday, "soul food" is put on full display when the community comes together on special occasions to celebrate or to mourn. Thus, the collard greens, macaroni and cheese, and other stereotypically Black foods are prepared in abundance during weddings, funerals, Mother's Day services (when men cook for the women), Father's Day services (when women prepare meals for men), and Friends Day, when guests are invited to church. Consuming food with other community members in the context of church provides opportunities for Cool Spring residents to reaffirm, transmit, evaluate, and comment on established Black food values.

Through food, gendered values in the church and the larger Black community were also put on display, as it was the women who would cook hearty meals to nourish the congregation at the end of services. Carole Counihan argues, "Food is a powerful voice, especially for women, who are often heavily involved with food acquisition, preparation, provisioning, and cleanup" (2004, 1). During these gatherings, which were almost always fueled by food, it is often the church mothers and other women who bore the responsibility for feeding the community (Lincoln and Mamiya 1990, 44–45). Even today, women continue to "hold down" the kitchen, often while service is actively in session. In fact, many churches have begun installing closed-circuit monitors in the kitchens, enabling women to "participate" in the service while preparing meals for after-service fellowships. Jon Holtzman states that "food can be an important vehicle through which we may understand the extent to which memory, as a more general process, is more closely tied to gender than we may typically acknowledge" (2006, 176). Cooking as a female gendered expression of love continues today in just about every sphere of the Black community and is exemplified in various forms of media, such as George Tillman's 1997 film *Soul Food* (Bower 2007, 3). Glindian argued that even though the men in the church may prepare meals for the women on special occasions like Mother's Day, cooking in the Black church continues to be a largely female enactment because "women's nature is to nurture."

Food Justice and Self-Defense

Even more important than maintaining community, food is a means of safeguarding the future of the Black community. Mary Douglas argues, "If food is treated as a code, the message it encodes will be found in the pattern of social relations being expressed. The message is about different degrees of hierarchy, inclusion and exclusion, boundaries and transactions across the boundaries. . . . Food categories therefore encode social events" (1971, 61). For many Black residents of Cool Spring, food is encoded with economic and sociopolitical messages about their perceptions of the United States and their continued survival. Many of these residents are old enough to have experienced sharecropping, Jim Crow, and other neoslavery systems in the United States, and many recount narratives of food scarcity transmitted by foreparents, as a way of reminding themselves to continue to "work the land." On several occasions, for instance, Glindian explained, "I'm getting old and tired. I'm not going to plant anymore." Then, almost instinctively, she would begin discussing what she would plant the next season. The angst surrounding food security and food sovereignty in the Black community is tangible and stems from a distant and recent history where food was used in political tactics to control or disenfranchise Blacks, even those who produced their own food. As Angela Jill Cooley notes, "During the civil rights era, white landowners and public officials took advantage of black food insecurity and white control over the region's sustenance to disrupt voting campaigns" (2015, 205–6). For many Black residents, horticulture and animal husbandry is a "bondage" they embrace because it prevents them from becoming enslaved again.

Over the past few years, horticulture and animal husbandry have become active strategies for ethnic boundary maintenance and protection for many Black Cool Spring residents. This subsistence strategy is not a new concept in the Black community, but due to recent political developments in the United States, it has taken on renewed importance, particularly in farming communities like Cool Spring. Those who actively farm have begun doing so with renewed fervency in response to what they regard as political incorrectness, which they view as detrimental to their continued safety and security, particularly their ability to sustain themselves. Many who receive government aid, such as Medicare, Medicaid, or food stamps, regard these support systems as endangered and actively work to secure newer safety nets. Many reside in homes and on lands that were inherited from relatives and thus have some degree of lodging security; however, even when they do not own their lands or residences, controlling their food source seems to be of paramount importance to their self-ownership and security. The dis-ease expressed by many Blacks is caused by what they perceive to be a divisive sociopolitical climate wrought by current political structures.

Black residents often complain that the toxic social and political climate in the country will inevitably result in a civil war, which will in turn cause the disruption of food sources in the country, affecting the lives of those who depend on the government for assistance and those who do not produce their own foods. Some also argue that a civil war would result in forced servitude of Blacks, just as it did during the Civil War and other disruptions in the country, when Blacks were forced to be sharecroppers or leave their farms to prepare food for others (Hurt 2016, 66, 150). One of the women I spoke with argued that the young people will suffer the most during a war because they are lazy and entitled and thus unprepared for uncertainty and hardships. She further explained that the young people, particularly the young men, prefer to spend their days engaging in frivolous activities instead of returning to the land and earning their meals the way their ancestors did. Some residents have also begun to arm themselves because they are convinced that a civil war will result in food shortages, which will cause young people and those who do not farm to steal from those who do. Glindian often said, "I have to get me a shotgun because when things get hard, they're going to come raid my barn for food." As they work to ensure food security and food sovereignty, Black Cool Spring residents keep in mind that a preparation for civil war must be multifaceted and account for conflicts within and without the community.

Black Cool Spring residents' fear of an impending civil war is often exacerbated by fears of all-encompassing World War III. Their concern was particularly heightened when President Trump and North Korea's supreme leader, Kim Jong-un, began trading insults, and some lamented that "Trump is going to get us killed." Black residents' dis-ease increased further when the president began breaking alliances with allies, canceling international agreements, and forming friendships with geopolitical foes. Among themselves, they reasoned that a third world war would impose difficulties on the Black community and particularly on their ability to feed themselves (Wiliams-Forson 2006). Moreover, a third world war would expose the entire country, and specifically the Black community, to the increased possibility of agroterrorism, the "biological attacks against the nation's food supply" (Halloran 2015, 215). Thus, while they may not be able to resist a military draft or other international calamities brought on by elected officials, many regard food production as a means of remaining independent of overarching political systems in the country.

As they engage in horticulture and animal husbandry, Cool Spring residents remain committed to diversifying their crops and their storage sites to ensure maximum independence and security (Wallach 2015, 178–79). While each family may be able to plant only so many diverse crops, by alternating the types of crops they plant, and by sharing the harvest, they are able to increase the overall food supply they accumulate each season. Thus, over the course of a year, residents eat and store diverse types of meats and vegetables, removing the limitations from the types of cuisines they prepare. Some residents also go to extreme lengths to limit their supermarket purchases because every item they purchase makes them potentially indebted to someone else. As they strive toward food security and food sovereignty, however, many understand that the dangers they work to combat through horticulture and animal husbandry come from within and without the community.

Conclusion

The Black community, broadly construed, actively draws upon its shared African heritage, values cultivated during slavery and transmitted to future generations, and diverse factors that work in tandem with each other to create a unique food culture that persists today.

The Black residents of Cool Spring, South Carolina, uniquely demonstrate the ways that contemporary Black communities straddle the past and present to create food values that are both "traditional" and dynamic. Thus they use the crops and meats they produce to prepare cuisines categorized as "soul food," as well as more innovative meals. Food production and consumption serve multifaceted roles in Cool Spring, including nourishing their bodies, supplementing their income, and facilitating a sense of community. However, among Black residents, food is a uniquely potent yet seemingly muted voice that allows residents to articulate history, hopes, and fears in contradistinction to the racialized political discourse in the United States. More importantly, for residents of Black Cool Spring, food is a principal strategy for resistance during what they perceive as an impending civil war or World War III and the aftereffects.

The dedicated practice of horticulture and animal husbandry in Cool Spring reflects the tangible fear and distrust that many Black residents have of the racialized political systems in the United States. Their feelings are informed by personal experiences with bigotry and discrimination, which began when they were very young and continue in various forms today. Many of the older residents discussed the trauma of growing up in a segregated country where they were constantly reminded publicly and privately that they were second-class citizens. Those who experienced de jure (legally sanctioned) discrimination during the Jim Crow era are uniquely aware of how state-sanctioned discrimination can quickly result in disenfranchisement, violence, and even death. Moreover, the literal and figurative gastronomic pains that resulted from these traumatic life experiences compel the Black community of Cool Spring to keep working, even when its members become aged or feel emotionally exhausted. For these residents, food production provides them with a degree of self-protection from the possible physical and psychological harm that comes from dependency on a government that might reverse course on food subsidies or their basic humanity.

The angst that compels Black Cool Spring residents to continue to produce their own food is also informed by oral narratives transmitted to them over several generations. In addition to their personal experiences, many rehearse the traumatic stories and experiences of their parents, grandparents, and other older community members, who experienced a segregated American society that affected how and what they ate. In their reported speech, many of the residents told the narratives of foreparents who faced food and nutrition insecurity because of merchants who refused to sell them food items, customers who refused to pay, and racially motivated political tacticians who sought to secure votes before providing them with governmental assistance. Because many residents see the bad experiences of previous generations repeated, they surmise that the prejudicial practices that undergird the political system and affect their basic human rights will continue to threaten their very existence. By passing on the narratives of food and nutrition insecurity, Black Cool Spring residents promote heightened awareness among younger generations while also safeguarding their food source.

Ultimately, food production among Black Cool Spring residents is underscored by their convictions of impending civil war or World War III, fueled by the sociopolitical climate in the United States. Wars, many opine, will result in a variety of hardships, including food scarcity or agroterrorism. These residents view their community, and the larger Black community, as being at risk of annihilation if the country were to face agroterrorism or other war-related food disruptions. Thus they actively farm and store food because they regard food sovereignty as a means of survival, even if other processes in the country are interrupted, for as Mintz notes, "Being starved by someone else . . . is a more dramatic—and demoralizing—way to discover hunger's terrible power" (1996, 5). For Cool Spring residents, the drudgery of planting crops and raising animals may bind them to the land year after year, but that bondage diminishes the chance of them becoming enslaved again. Ultimately, food is a vehicle that enables the Black residents of Cool Spring to simultaneously engage mainstream America and live on the margins of society by providing a certain degree of autonomy and independence.

Notes

1. While the official name of the town is Cool Spring, residents refer to it as Cool Springs, with an "s."

2. The category "Hispanic or Latinx" encompasses individuals who also self-identify with other racial (ethnic) groups, such as Black and white. U.S. Census 2010, accessed September 27, 2018, https://data.census.gov.

3. "Cool Spring Demographics," accessed September 27, 2018, https://www.point2homes.com.

4. I use the term *re-migrants* to refer to individuals who migrated to the North and then returned to the South.

Bibliography

Albala, Ken. 2007. *Beans: A History.* New York: Berg.

Alkon, Alison Hope, and Julian Agyeman, eds. 2011. *Cultivating Food Justice: Race, Class, and Sustainability.* Cambridge, Mass.: MIT Press.

Allen, Will. 2013. *The Good Food Revolution: Growing Healthy Food, People, and Communities.* New York: Gotham Books.

Belasco, Warren. 2008. *Food: The Key Concepts.* Oxford: Berg.

Benjamin, Mary Kate Jones (Mrs. Ludy). 1979. "Cool Springs." *Independent Republic Quarterly* 13 (3): 1–36.

Bennett, Lerone, Jr. 1973. "Money, Merchants, Markets: The Quest for Economic Security." *Ebony* 29 (1): 72–82.

Bowen, Joanne. 1992. "Faunal Remains and Urban Household Subsistence in New England." In *Art and Mystery of Historical Archaeology: Essays in Honor of James Deetz,* edited by Anne E. Yentsch and Mary E. Beaudry, 267–81. Boca Raton, Fla.: CRC Press.

Bower, Anne, ed. 2007. *African American Foodways: Explorations of History and Culture.* Urbana: University of Illinois Press.

Carney, Judith. 2001. *Black Rice: The African Origins of Rice Cultivation in the Americas.* Cambridge, Mass.: Harvard University Press.

Carney, Judith, and Richard Nicholas Rosomoff. 2009. *In the Shadow of Slavery: Africa's Botanical Legacy in the Atlantic World.* Berkeley: University of California Press.

Chatelain, Marcia. 2015. "Black Women's Food Writing and the Archive of Black Women's History." In *Dethroning the Deceitful Pork Chop: Rethinking African American Foodways from Slavery to Obama,* edited by Jennifer Jensen Wallach and Lindsay R. Swindall, 31–46. Fayetteville: University of Arkansas Press.

Cooley, Angela Jill. 2015. "'Freedom Farms': Activism and Sustenance in Rural Mississippi." In *Dethroning the Deceitful Pork Chop: Rethinking African American Foodways from Slavery to Obama,* edited by Jennifer Jensen Wallach and Lindsay R. Swindall, 199–213. Fayetteville: University of Arkansas Press.

Counihan, Carole. 2004. *Around the Tuscan Table: Food, Family, and Gender in Twentieth-Century Florence.* New York: Routledge.

Covey, Herbert C., and Dwight Eisnach. 2009. *What the Slaves Ate: Recollections of African American Foods and Foodways from the Slave Narratives.* Santa Barbara, Calif.: Greenwood Press.

Cross, Wilbur. 2008. *Gullah Culture in America.* Winston-Salem, N.C.: John F. Blair.

Cusick, Heidi Haughy. 1995. *Soul and Spice: African Cooking in the Americas.* San Francisco: Chronicle Books.

Douglas, Mary. 1971. "Deciphering a Meal." In *Myth, Symbol, and Culture,* edited by Clifford Geertz, 61–82. New York: W. W. Norton.

Douglass, Frederick. 1846. *The Narrative of the Life of Frederick Douglass, an American Slave.* Dublin: Webb and Chapman, Gt. Brunswick-Street.

Farnsworth, Paul, and Laurie A. Wilkie. 2006. "Fish and Grits: Southern, African, and British Influences in Bahamian Foodways." In *Caribbean and Southern Transnational Perspectives on the U.S. South,* edited by Helen A. Regis, 34–72. Athens: University of Georgia Press.

Farrish, Christopher. 2015. "Theft, Food Labor, and Culinary Insurrection in the Virginia Plantation Yard." In *Dethroning the Deceitful Pork Chop: Rethinking African American Foodways from Slavery to Obama,* edited by Jennifer Jensen Wallach, 151–63. Fayetteville: University of Arkansas Press.

Fountain, Daniel L. 1995. "Historians and Historical Archaeology: Slave Sites." *Journal of Interdisciplinary History* 26 (1): 67–77.

Halloran, Vivian N. 2015. "Food Security, Urban Agriculture, and Black Food Citizenship." In *Dethroning the Deceitful Pork Chop: Rethinking African American Foodways from Slavery to Obama,* edited by Jennifer Jensen Wallach, 215–28. Fayetteville: University of Arkansas Press.

Harris, Jessica B. 2003. *Beyond Gumbo: Creole Fusion Food from the Atlantic Rim.* New York: Simon & Schuster.

Henderson, Laretta. 2007. "'Ebony Jr!' and 'Soul Food': The Construction of Middle-Class African American Identity through the Use of Traditional Southern Foodways." *MELUS* 32 (4): 81–97.

Hoffman, Gretchen L. 2015. "What's the Difference between Soul Food and Southern Cooking? The Classification of Cookbooks in American Libraries." In *Dethroning the Deceitful Pork Chop: Rethinking African American Foodways from Slavery to Obama,* edited by Jennifer Jensen Wallach and Lindsay R. Swindall, 61–78. Fayetteville: University of Arkansas Press.

Holtzman, Jon. 2006. "The World Is Dead and Cooking's Killed It: Food and the Gender of Memory in Samburu, Northern Kenya." *Food and Foodways* 14 (2/3): 175–200.

Hughes, Marvalene H. 1997. "Soul, Black Women, and Food." In *Food and Culture: A Reader,* edited by Carole Counihan and Penny van Esterik, 272–80. New York: Routledge.

Hurt, R. Doulas. 2016. *Food and Agriculture during the Civil War.* Santa Barbara, Calif.: Praeger.

Jenkins, Charlotte. 2010. *Gullah Cuisine: By Land and Sea.* Charleston, S.C.: Evening Post Publishing.

Joyner, Chares W. 2009. "Come by Here, Lord." In *Down by the Riverside: A South Carolina Slave Community,* 141–71. 25th Anniversary Edition. Urbana: University of Illinois Press.

Kalcik, Susan. 1984. "Ethnic Foodways in America: Symbol and the Performance of Identity." In *Ethnic and Regional Foodways in the United States: The Performance of Group Identity,* edited by Linda Keller Brown and Kay Mussell, 37–65. Knoxville: University of Tennessee Press.

Lincoln, C. Eric, and Lawrence H. Mamiya. 1990. *The Black Church in the African American Experience.* Durham, N.C.: Duke University Press.

Littlefield, Daniel C. 1981. *Rice and Slaves.* Baton Rouge: Louisiana State University Press.

Marks, Christine. 2015. "Creole Cuisine as Culinary Border Culture: Reading Recipes as Testimonies of Hybrid Identity and Cultural Heritage." In *Dethroning the Deceitful Pork Chop: Rethinking African American Foodways from Slavery to Obama,* edited by Jennifer Jensen Wallach, 79–92. Fayetteville: University of Arkansas Press.

McCandless, Peter. 2014. *Slavery, Disease, and Suffering in the Southern Lowcountry.* Cambridge: Cambridge University Press.

Mintz, Sidney W. 1996. *Tasting Food, Tasting Freedom: Excursions into Eating, Culture, and the Past.* Boston: Beacon.

Mintz, Sidney W. 2009. "Memory Dishes of the African Diaspora." In *In the Shadow of Slavery: Africa's Botanical Legacy in the Atlantic World,* edited by Judith A. Carney and Richard Nicholas Rosomoff, 177–86. Berkeley: University of California Press.

Mintz, Sidney W., and Christine M. Du Bois. 2002. "The Anthropology of Food and Eating." *Annual Review of Anthropology* 31: 99–119.

Moore, Stacy Gibbons. 1989. "Established and Well-Cultivated: Afro-American Foodways in Early Virginia." *Virginia Cavalcade* 39: 70–83.

Morgan, Phillip D. 1998. *Slave Counterpoint.* Chapel Hill: University of North Carolina Press.

Olmsted, Frederick Law. 1863. *A Journey in the Black Country.* New York: Mason Brothers.

Opie, Frederick Douglass. 2008. *Hog and Hominy: Soul Food from Africa to America.* New York: Columbia University Press.

Otto, John Solomon, and Agustus Marion Burns III. 1983. "Black Folks and Poor Buckras: Archaeological Evidence of Slave and Overseer Living Conditions on an Antebellum Plantation." *Journal of Black Studies* 14: 185–200.

Pollitzer, William. 2005. *Gullah People and Their African Heritage.* Athens: University of Georgia Press.

Rivers, Larry Eugene. 2000. *Slavery in Florida: Territorial Days to Emancipation.* Gainesville: University Press of Florida.

Robinson, Sallie Ann. 2007. *Cooking the Gullah Way, Morning, Noon, and Night.* Chapel Hill: University of North Carolina Press.

Singleton, Theresa A. 1991. "The Archaeology of Slave Life." In *Before Freedom Came: African American Life in the Antebellum South,* edited by Edward D. C. Campbell Jr. and Kym S. Rice, 155–75. Charlottesville: University Press of Virginia.

Stanonis, Anthony. 2015. "Feast of the Mau Mau: Christianity, Conjure, and the Origins of Soul Food." In *Dethroning the Deceitful Pork Chop: Rethinking African American Foodways from Slavery to Obama,* edited by Jennifer Jensen Wallach, 93–106. Fayetteville: University of Arkansas Press.

Thurman, Sue Bailey. 2000. *The Historical Cookbook of the American Negro.* Boston: Beacon.

Van Deburg, William. 1993. *New Day in Babylon: The Black Power Movement and American Culture, 1965–1975.* Chicago: University of Chicago Press.

Wallach, Jennifer Jensen. 2015. "Dethroning the Deceitful Pork Chop: Food Reform at the Tuskegee Institute." In *Dethroning the Deceitful Pork Chop: Rethinking African American Foodways from Slavery to Obama,* edited by Jennifer Jensen Wallach and Lindsay R. Swindall, 165–180. Fayetteville: University of Arkansas Press.

Weigl, Andrea. 2014. *Pickles and Preserves: A Savor the South® Cookbook.* Chapel Hill: University of North Carolina Press.

Weiss, Brad. 2016. *Real Pigs: Shifting Values in the Field of Local Pork.* Durham, N.C.: Duke University Press.

Whit, William C. 2007. "Soul Food as Cultural Creation." In *African American Foodways: Explorations of History and Culture,* edited by Anne L. Bower, 45–58. Urbana: University of Illinois Press.

Williams-Forson, Psyche. 2006. *Building Houses out of Chicken Legs: Black Women, Food, and Power.* Chapel Hill: University of North Carolina Press.

Williams-Forson, Psyche. 2012. "Other Women Cooked for My Husband: Negotiating Gender, Food, and Identities in an African American/ Ghanaian Household." In *Taking Food Public: Redefining Foodways in a Changing World,* edited by Psyche Williams-Forson and Carole Counihan, 138–54. New York: Routledge.

Wisecup, Kelly. 2015. "Foodways and Resistance: Cassava, Poison, and Natural Histories in the Early Americas." In *Dethroning the Deceitful Pork Chop: Rethinking African American Foodways from Slavery to Obama,* edited by Jennifer Jensen Wallach and Lindsay R. Swindall, 3–16. Fayetteville: University of Arkansas Press.

Witt, Doris. 1999. *Black Hunger: Food and the Politics of U.S. Identity.* New York: Oxford University Press.

Yentsch, Anne E. 2007. "Excavating the South's African American Food History." In *African American Foodways: Explorations of History and Culture,* edited by Anne L. Bower, 59–98. Urbana: University of Illinois Press.

3

NURTURING THE REVOLUTION

The Black Panther Party and the Early Seeds of the Food Justice Movement

Analena Hope Hassberg

• • •

What never became clear to the public, largely because it
was always deemphasized in the media, was that the armed
self-defense program of the Party was just one form of what
Party leaders viewed as self-defense against oppression. . . .
The Panther means for implementing its concept of self-defense
was its various survival programs . . . [and] it was these
broad-based programs, including the free food programs where
thousands of bags of groceries were given away to the poor
citizens of the community, that gave the Party great appeal to
poor and Black people throughout the country.

—Huey P. Newton, "War against the Panthers"

The Black Panther Party (BPP) gained notoriety in popular American memory and imagination after the infamous 1967 march on the state capitol in Sacramento to protect its members' Second Amendment right to bear arms and surveil police activity. For the last five decades, mainstream media images of Black men and women marching through city streets with beret-capped afros and loaded shotguns have obscured the true motives of the Black Panther Party and the Black Power movement more broadly. In a strategic move to reclaim the narrative, the Panthers intentionally shifted their focus away from the armed resistance that had brought them much bad press and developed simple yet radical "survival programs" to help sustain Black communities in the face of racism, state-sanctioned violence, poverty, and starvation. Despite this shift, many still believe that the Black Panthers were violent racial separatists whose politics and praxis were a far cry from the nonviolent legacy of the civil rights movement. In truth, the Black Panthers were a direct outgrowth of civil rights organizations like the Student Nonviolent Coordinating Committee (SNCC) and the Lowndes County Freedom Organization (LCFO).[1] Additionally, while their militancy garnered them national attention, it was their community health institutions and food programs that helped the Black Panthers gain traction and build lasting rapport in Black communities across the United States (Seale 1991; Jones 1998; Joseph 2007). This chapter examines the Panthers' commitment to liberating oppressed Black people and building more just and equitable societies through community-based food and health programs. I suggest that the subversive revolutionary organizing tools put forth by the Panthers are important templates for the twenty-first-century food justice efforts that exist in their wake.

Food, Health, and Freedom Struggles

Huey P. Newton and Bobby G. Seale developed the Black Panther Party for Self-Defense in response to police brutality in Black urban communities in 1966 while they were students at Merritt College in Oakland, California. By 1968 the party had dropped the term *self-defense* from its title and rearticulated the notion of self-defense as that which strengthens community health (Joseph 2006). As Alondra Nelson writes, "Health was a site where the stakes of injustice could be exposed and a prism through which struggles for equality could be refracted" (2011, 5). Although there have been national efforts to alleviate hunger and poverty, neither state nor federal governments have ever provided adequate protections, resources, or services for Black communities. To the contrary, Black Americans have historically been enslaved, exploited, disenfranchised, segregated, policed, and poisoned by toxic industrial processes (Du Bois 1935; Robinson 1983; Bullard 1994). The long-term neglect and abuse of Black urban communities (which has persisted despite important civil rights achievements) galvanized the Black Panther Party and its social service agenda. It was an explicit intervention into the failures of the state to protect the most vulnerable populations from the effects of American poverty, like malnutrition, inadequate health care, and substandard education (Newton 1972; Joseph 2006). The Panthers organized oppressed communities, offering tangible survival strategies for a people under siege, with food as a primary tool of liberation.

Food and land have always been central to Black freedom struggles, but the Black Panthers were among the first to frame the peculiar relationship between race, advanced capitalism, food access, and health outcomes in the urban core (Heynen 2009; Potorti 2017). They recognized hunger as one of the greatest forms of oppression in the United States and feeding people—especially Black and poor children—as a central tenet of liberation (Hilliard 2008). As evidenced throughout this volume, food is at the same time social, spiritual, performative, and political, with deep significance beyond edible meals. In virtually all cultures and regions of the world, food is part of how human beings come to know ourselves, our kin, and our place. Jennifer Jensen Wallach explains, "Food habits are always markers of identity and can be decoded to reveal much about the eater's social, environmental, and cultural world" (2014, 29). Unlike many other cultures, Black people's relationship to food has been repeatedly fractured by generations of forced migration, acute racial terror, and lasting psychological trauma. And yet, despite the atrocities of slavery, Jim Crow segregation, poverty, and lasting structural racism, there is still a shared sense of humanity, custom, culture, and cosmology that links African diasporic peoples throughout the world in what Cedric Robinson (1983) calls a "black radical tradition." Robinson argues that the global project of colonization (and its concomitant placement of Europe as the center of civilization) required that Africans be rendered less human: depicted as a barbaric species that has made minimal contributions to the world. The negation of Black food culture is part of this destructive global project, rooted in a long legacy of genocide, omissions, falsehoods, and distortions.

Black diasporic food culture(s), though rich and varied, are regularly dismissed as little more than scraps from the proverbial master's table, which lack any real cultural or nutritive value (Witt 2004). Or they are reduced to discussions of unhealthy and stereotypical "soul food" dishes that are high in animal fat, sodium, and sugar—ingredients that have been shown to produce adverse health outcomes when eaten regularly (Davis and Melina 2000; Dunn-Emke, Weidner, and Ornish 2001; Schlosser 2012). When decoded, however, it becomes clear that Black food cultures are the cuisine of a stolen, hybridized people and thus must be traced in multiple ways to tell the full story.[2] Although traditional African diets are plant based and sustainable, enslavement deeply impacted Black foodways and eating habits (Covey and Eisnach 2009; Cooley 2015). The institution of slavery relied on Africans' deep knowledge of agriculture for the cultivation of everything from cash crops to medicinal herbs and supplementary gardens, so the enslaved worked from sunup to sundown caring for plants, raising animals, and nursing children—their own and those of the slaveholding class (Whit 2007; Penniman 2018). They cooked succulent meals that they dared not eat for fear of violence as their own families suffered severe vitamin and nutrient deficiencies and high rates of infant mortality (Penniman 2018). Renowned abolitionist Frederick Douglass even recounts the way that food was routinely weaponized against enslaved communities who were alternately starved and forced to binge on food and alcohol during holidays to keep them in a drunken stupor (Douglass 1851).

Much work has been done to redeem and decolonize Black foodways and delink them from the stigmas of slavery and soul food. For instance, Anne Yentsch (2007, 16) argues that "real" soul food is actually a uniquely American fusion of African, European, and Native American cooking methods. Additionally, William Whit posits that "virtually all Africans who came to the United States, whether before or after the formation of the Republic, came from what were food-growing societies," and thus their cultural foods and food practices are diverse and heterogeneous (2007, 47). Moreover, even when enslaved, Africans regularly maintained gardens to supplement their diets with vegetables of all kinds (47).[3]

In his documentary *Soul Food Junkies* (2012), filmmaker Byron Hurt explores the impact of soul food on Black bodies and culture, suggesting that industrial food systems and fast food (including fast soul food) are the real culprits behind disproportionately high rates of preventable illnesses in Black communities. Similarly, chef Bryant Terry offers healthy new plant-based recipes for old soul food favorites (such as collard greens and corn bread) and evokes culinary traditions from across the African diaspora (Terry 2009, 2014). Meanwhile, Black vegan Breeze Harper (2010) suggests that precolonial soul food was plant based and holistic and that such a diet today could help heal racialized physical, emotional, and spiritual ailments.

The twentieth century brought increases in large-scale, capital-intensive production, new farming technologies, and new complex modes of processing and distributing food that were exclusionary to small family farmers (particularly Black and/or poor farmers), who could not afford to expand their enterprises. Chapter 9 of this volume explores how discriminatory practices by the United States Department of Agriculture (USDA) and the rise of multinational and transnational agribusiness corporations led to the further decline of small farmers and caused a 98 percent loss of Black farm operations between 1900 and 1997 (Green, Green, and Kleiner 2011; Allen 2012; Penniman 2016). Facing personal and institutional discrimination, landlessness, and racial terror in the South, rural Black people migrated north and west in droves, lured by the wartime prospect of shipyard jobs and hopes of a new beginning (Litwack 2010; Wilkerson 2011). Consequently, the Black population in California nearly quadrupled during the 1940s, with most migrants tracing their roots to the American South, particularly Texas and Louisiana (Dodson and Diouf 2004). Even Black Panther Party cofounder Huey P. Newton came to Oakland, California, from Monroe, Louisiana, in 1943 (Wilkerson 2011).

More than just a geographical shift from rural to urban, this exodus was also an ideological turn away from the provincial in favor of modernity and development. The physical relocation of Black people altered Black American relationships to land, food, and health. As "urban" became synonymous with "modern," agricultural work became stigmatized as unsophisticated. New urban environments were often characterized by a lack of space for gardens, colder climates, and new cooking technologies like modern stoves, all of which led to new eating practices among Black migrants and workers (Opie 2010). Industrialization also brought the mechanization and processing of food, which has had a lasting impact on food purchasing and preparation in Black urban communities.[4] Many Black migrants found work in food-product canning and processing plants and increasingly purchased these canned and processed foods to eat and feed to their families (Poe 2013). Newly urbanized Black people also ate fewer vegetables because the physical landscape had changed drastically as well—there was suddenly ubiquitous concrete in place of fertile soil and smog where there was once clean air. For people with a rich agricultural history both in the United States and throughout the African diaspora, the migration to urban environments created a (still widening) chasm between Black people, land, and food and severely impacted Black health outcomes and livelihood (Finney 2014).

Survival Pending Revolution

Although the West Coast symbolized a reprieve from Southern repression and hardship, transplanted Black people in cities like Los Angeles and Oakland quickly learned that the frameworks of structural racism, poverty, and exploitation in fact existed across the nation (and the world) (Flamming 2005; Costa Vargas 2006; Widener 2009). The Black Panther Party and its survival programs were born from a desire to meet the basic needs of Black urban communities that had long been neglected by the state (Abron 1998). The party developed dozens of free programs, including armed "cop watches" to monitor and curb racially motivated police brutality, health clinics and sickle cell anemia testing services, community schools, ambulatory services, legal aid, a commissary for incarcerated people, escort services for senior citizens, and food programs for poor families and children (Holder 1990; Alkebulan 2007). The survival programs were explicitly anticapitalist, but they required material goods to operate, so the Panthers sought volunteer labor, food donations, and monetary contributions from local businesses (Broad 2016). The first and arguably the most popular of the survival programs was Free Breakfast for School Children, which began in Oakland and was quickly implemented in party chapters nationwide. It is estimated that the breakfast programs served between fifteen thousand and thirty thousand hungry children across the country on a daily basis (West 2010; Seale 2018).

According to former Panther Joan Kelly-Williams, it was difficult to organize Black people in Los Angeles when the Southern California Chapter of the Black Panther Party first took root in 1968 because many Black Angelenos were suspicious that the Panthers were "just another gang coming on the set" (KPFA Radio 1970). However, the Panthers' organized presence actually reduced gang violence in South Los Angeles, and community wariness was quickly replaced with enthusiasm when the Southern California Chapter implemented its first breakfast program at the University Seventh-Day Adventist Church on Budlong Avenue in April 1969—respectfully titled the "John Huggins Hot Breakfast for Children Program" in honor of the slain deputy minister of information John Huggins (Hilliard 2008). The breakfast program filled Black children (and adults) with far more than just food (Murch 2010). For the Panthers, food was a medium to politicize Black communities about the limits and failures of capitalism and the merit and praxis of revolution. Their survival programs provided tangible resources, cultivated racial pride and self-determination, and functionally challenged power structures that exploit, dominate, and control Black bodies (Self 2005). It was common knowledge that the state did not deliver basic protections to Black people but the Panthers did. As Panther Marshall "Eddie" Conway writes:

> One group was beating and killing them and the other group was trying to feed and protect them, the choice was not rocket science, it was the choice between being beaten or being fed. . . . Seeing hundreds of people emerge from our centers with food and not empty promises, serves to educate the people as to who is really concerned about their future. (2009, 35)

Beyond meeting basic needs, survival also hinges upon an understanding of oneself in the world, and the context of the conditions in which one lives. Joy Ann Williamson explains that the "Panthers believed that exploited and oppressed people deserved an education that provided them with the tools to critically examine the capitalist structure, understand their reality as Blacks in America, and then plot a course for change" (2005, 138). Although feeding hungry Black children did help them concentrate better in school, it did not fundamentally transform the American education system, which has historically failed to teach students of color in accurate and culturally competent ways. In response, the Panthers developed "liberation schools" in tandem with their free breakfasts to provide a space for Black children (and adults) to learn about their true heritage through songs, games, and cartoons (Alkebulan 2007). Having learned to make sense of structural inequality by studying Frantz Fanon and Malcolm X, and taking cues from Mao Tse-Tung, Karl Marx, and Che Guevara to build their framework and ten-point platform, the political education that accompanied the Panthers' food was deliberately designed to develop a revolutionary consciousness (Cleaver 1998; Broad 2016).

In a methodological departure from the civil rights movement, the Panthers did not promote sit-ins at restaurants and other establishments where Blacks were unwelcome. Instead, they created tangible alternatives to shopping with avaricious businessmen and did not hesitate to call for boycotts of franchises that did not support Black people. The Panthers also supported other groups and organizations that were confronting racialized systemic oppression (Cleaver 1998).[5] For instance, they stood with the United Farm Workers (UFW) during the Delano grape strike, which protested grape workers' low pay and abhorrent working conditions. Los Angeles Panthers joined picket lines, educated shoppers about the boycott, created a "motor pool" to provide transportation to other grocery stores, and stood up to police on behalf of UFW protesters (Pulido 1996). Conversely, the UFW was mutually and reciprocally supportive of the BPP during the 1969 police raids on L.A. Panther offices, immediately offering its moral and strategic support.[6] This relationship opened up new and important dialogues within Black communities about food production, pesticides, and labor rights, and the political power of both organizations was strengthened considerably (Araiza 2009).

Providing critical services that were otherwise unavailable in poor Black neighborhoods humanized the Panthers and endeared them to the people. As the party gained traction and rapport in Black communities, so intensified a repressive state backlash, spearheaded by the Federal Bureau of Investigation (FBI). The Black Panther Party quickly became the central target of the FBI's Counter Intelligence Program (COINTELPRO), a secret, illegal operation that intended to dissolve, quell, and neutralize a growing Black revolutionary consciousness. As early as 1967, infiltrators and provocateurs were employed to plant seeds of dissent within the group and create discord between the Panthers and other Black radical organizations.[7] Claims of poisoned food in the breakfast programs and child abuse in the liberation schools were published and aired through syndicated media outlets to incite fear and discourage participation in Panther programs (Newton 1980). Police were dispatched to raid and ransack clinics and kitchens. Local Panther offices were burned, and their files stolen or destroyed (Churchill and Vander Wall 2002). In a desperate attempt to thwart the rising credibility of the Panthers, several party members were viciously beaten, imprisoned (some still to this day), and savagely murdered, a testament to "the extent to which the BPP and the Black Power Movement of which it was a part, succeeded in eroding black consensus to U.S. sovereignty" (Keeling 2007, 78).

As demonstrated in a number of seething memos from FBI director J. Edgar Hoover to his regional offices, the breakfast programs for schoolchildren and their "insidious poison" were a particularly sharp thorn in the side of the state (Churchill 2014). But what was so intimidating about feeding hungry children? After all, there was a larger national effort to end hunger and malnutrition among children coinciding with and preceding the Panthers' survival programming. For instance, the National School Lunch Program was established by the USDA in 1946, and the 1966 Child Nutrition Act established the pilot School Breakfast Program, which provided low-cost or free breakfast to children in public schools.[8] However, Susan Levine (2011) and Mary Potorti (2017) maintain that the National School Lunch Program was primarily a way to address agricultural surpluses by feeding them to schoolchildren, and the Federal Breakfast Program was met with political resistance and funding constraints, so it gained momentum slowly and did not always meet community needs. Moreover, neither program was particularly concerned with Black children living in inner-city urban communities. By the time the Panthers began serving meals in 1969, it was clear that federal food programs were not sufficiently relieving hunger among those most impacted. Geographer Nik Heynen argues that the Panther breakfast programs were "both the model and impetus for all federally funded school breakfast programs in existence within the United States today" (2009, 411). In California in particular, the Panthers' free breakfast model put pressure on the Ronald Reagan administration to adopt a free, state-funded breakfast program in 1975 (Heynen 2009).

The establishment and expansion of federally funded school food programs can be considered a momentous victory in the campaign against hunger and a testament to the power of grassroots organizing. At the same time, government-sanctioned food programs also functioned to usurp and co-opt the Panther food programs as part of COINTELPRO's broader campaign to delegitimize, disrupt, discredit, and destroy the Black Panther Party (Heynen 2009; Churchill 2014). Former Black Panther Party chairwoman Elaine Brown (2018) argues that COINTELPRO's real concern was never the Panthers' armed militancy but that they were actively building an educated and organized Black proletariat. The Panthers were successfully convincing oppressed people of their rights to free food, health care, housing, and employment, and providing these resources where the state failed to do so. The Panthers' free breakfasts (and the political education that accompanied the meals) not only addressed hunger but also undermined and circumvented the logic of capitalist food system processes. Just as hungry children cannot concentrate in school, hungry communities cannot effectively organize. Once fed, however, oppressed people can begin to envision and build more just societies and institutions.

By providing free meals and groceries to people whose wage-based labor was not sufficient to keep food on the table, and offering health services to the sick and uninsured, the Black Panther Party reframed food and wellness as rights instead of commodities. Notably, the Panthers were clear that the food handouts were not, in themselves, the revolution. Rather, meeting the basic human needs of oppressed people was a precursor to the organizing and structured action that revolution required (Newton 1972). The survival programs were designed to fortify Black people at the level of the individual body first, and then scale outward to transform the wider community. JoNina Abron explains, "In order to fully develop the human capital of a community, the day-to-day needs of the people must be addressed. Party members understood that in order to maximize one's potential, personal safety, nourishment, and adequate health care was paramount" (1998, 179). Nourishing hungry people became a revolutionary preparatory act because, as Newton has said, "if the people are not here revolution cannot be achieved, for the people and only the people make revolutions" (quoted in Hilliard and Weise 2011, 161).

From Free Food to Food Justice

In just a few short years, the Black Panther Party was able to significantly improve the lives of poor Black people in urban spaces, and it provided a lasting template for social change "without a penny from the government or organized philanthropy" (Patel 2012, 2). By the early 1980s, however, the repressive efforts of COINTELPRO, the crack cocaine epidemic, and the rise of the prison industrial complex had effectively dismantled the formal structure of the organization. Fortunately, the Panthers had implemented long-term solutions that went beyond temporarily filling empty bellies, so their commitment to serving and nourishing the people lived on in important ways. In 1977 the Southern California Chapter founded Community Services Unlimited (CSU), a 501(c)(3) nonprofit organization (Broad 2016). In the forty-three years since its inception, CSU has developed into one of South L.A.'s most influential food justice organizations, offering fresh, affordable, culturally appropriate food through neighborhood produce stands, a produce bag subscription program, and by sourcing wholesale produce to local stores and restaurants. CSU also promotes health and sustainability in South L.A. through urban farming, nutrition education, and youth leadership training.

I was first introduced to CSU in 2010 as a volunteer and became a board member in 2012. As the current board president, I help provide foresight, oversight, and insight to support the organization's event planning, fundraising, and youth and community programming. Additionally, each semester I send new cohorts of my own service-learning students to CSU's mini-urban farms for a reciprocal work and learning experience. For the last decade, I have witnessed the creative and continual expansion of the Black Panther Party's food-based work. In 2018 I was especially proud to be part of the development and launch of the Paul Robeson Community Wellness Center, a five-thousand-square-foot wellness hub that offers health and wellness programming and houses the Village Market Place Social Enterprise—a full-scale organic market that serves plant-based foods, herbal teas, and medicinal salves to

Figure 3.1. Village Market Place, 2019. Community Services Unlimited, Sankofa Archive, Los Angeles.

address the high rates of diet-related illness and poor health plaguing South Los Angeles.[9]

Despite its 501(c)(3) nonprofit status, CSU has remarkably managed to stay rooted in community by fundraising among community partners and local residents who support their healthy food vision. Regrettably, many well-intended organizations are caught in the "nonprofit industrial complex": a never-ending cycle of applying for short-term funding to keep them afloat (Incite! Women of Color Against Violence 2007). Inviting the people to support and participate directly in its work has allowed CSU to become largely community sustained and reduce its dependency on government grants and foundation funds. As this volume demonstrates, an increasing number of companies and nonprofits are now centering food justice as part of their organizational mission. Although food justice is a relatively new framework, the Black Panthers' survival programs were an undeniable antecedent (Patel 2012; Sbicca 2018). The connection is not always obvious since the cuisine that characterizes our national memory of the civil rights and Black Power movements is a far cry from the gluten-free, dairy-free, cage-free victuals that distinguish twenty-first-century alternative food and health movements. The Panthers' grits, bacon, and pork sausage would be socially unacceptable in today's health-obsessed society, where culturally specific food practices are intrinsically linked to illness and death (Opie 2010; Hurt 2012; Garth's chapter in this volume).[10] Still, while the nature of food and its sociopolitical meanings may have changed, the simple act of feeding hungry people remains revolutionary. Raj Patel explains,

> The Black Panther Party's vision of a world where all children are fed, where food, healthcare, education, access to land, and housing and clothes are rights and not privileges is a vision that can and should spark the food movement today. Inspired by their example, and learning the lessons from their experience, we can dream beyond the limitations imposed by capitalism, of a world in which hunger is, for the first time, a specter of the past. (2012, 3)

Contemporary U.S.-based alternative food movements have per-
suasively identified the atrocities of the corporate food regime,
and the unveiling of hidden food system processes has captivated
mainstream audiences through popular books and documentaries
that explain the impact of a "profits over people" motive on our
bodies and lived experiences (Pollan 2006; Patel 2010; McMillan
2012; Schlosser 2012; Nestle 2013). Numerous groups are working to empower people to feed themselves in healthy ways and
stave off the symptoms of a modern industrial diet. However, fewer
are centering Black or other oppressed people in their analysis or
working to deconstruct the racialized processes responsible for
food apartheid and other forms of structural racism in the food
system (Guthman 2008a).[11] Barriers such as price, transportation
access, and limited leisure time prohibit many people from making healthier choices (Freeman 2007; Guthman 2008b). Encour-
aging consumers to "vote with our forks" and buy food solely from
local, organic farmers ultimately does little to dismantle poverty
and racial capitalism. Eric Holt-Giménez and Yi Wang argue that,
more than fifty years later, the Black Panther model remains an
important template.

> The Black Panthers sought to dismantle the capitalist structures
> of racism. They rooted out racism in the food system by bringing
> it under local, autonomous Black control. The call among many
> of today's [food justice] activists for local control over food and
> dismantling racism in the food system echoes some of the libera-
> tion politics of the Black Panthers. Less common today are the
> structural critiques of capitalism and racism that were integral to
> the Party's political work. (2011, 89)[12]

The production, distribution, and consumption of food are all
racialized economic processes: immigrant labor produces the majority of food grown in this country, and healthy food is often unavailable and vastly more expensive in low-income communities and
neighborhoods of color (Chung and Meyers 1999). The current
crusade against hunger and food inequality is further compounded

by new health challenges that were not on the public radar in the 1960s and 1970s. Substances like genetically modified organisms (GMOs), high-fructose corn syrup, and trans fats are present in the majority of commercially processed foods, and while there is a growing awareness about where and how our food is grown and produced, it is nearly impossible to avoid these additives when one is poor. Consequently, the prevalence of food-related illnesses like childhood obesity and diabetes has increased multifold in the decades since the Black Panther Party's decline, particularly in low-income urban neighborhoods that are inundated with fast food, processed junk food, liquor, and conventionally grown fruits and vegetables drenched in pesticides (Lee 1998; Kulkarni 2004; Belluck 2005). Using food as a lens to expose racism and inequality was a powerful part of the Panthers' strategy that could help contemporary food movements become far more accessible and impactful for the people most in need of better access to healthy food.

Sankofa: Learning from the Past to Build toward the Future

In 2015 Community Services Unlimited launched its "Sankofa Project," a community-based history and accessible photo/print archive that documents the Black Panthers survival programs in Los Angeles, and the radical principles and ancestry that have shaped South L.A.'s food and health justice scene. "Sankofa" is a Ghanaian word that means "to go back and get it," or "learning from the past to build toward the future." The goal of this collection is to illuminate the historical, present, and future role of food in processes of placemaking and social justice movement building in the United States and beyond. In keeping with Newton's (1972, 32) notion of "revolutionary intercommunalism" and solidarity, the Sankofa Project identifies other organizations that also use the Black Panthers model of food justice and health equity to transform Black and poor communities.[13] By building relationships and alliances along a national pipeline, CSU aims to develop a network of groups that are politically and methodologically aligned, with a shared objective of food systems change, community ownership, and long-term sustainability.

The Sankofa Project also seeks to create a working definition of food justice that is delinked from food security. In short, CSU posits that although food security projects (like food banks and pantries) do improve food access, they generally do little to critique or remedy corporate food regimes. Food security projects can also inadvertently contribute to poor health by distributing canned goods that are high in sodium and preservatives. Conversely, food justice provides fresh, local, and affordable alternatives and attempts to address and heal the root causes of food insecurity, such as racism and poverty. When done effectively, food justice is less synonymous with food security rhetoric and more closely related to the idea of food sovereignty—a transformative framework that seeks to produce a self-sufficient and generative food system that puts the means of production (and thus the means of reproduction) in the hands of people, not private companies. Teresa Mares and Devon Peña explain:

> The food justice movement should adopt an organizing frame of food sovereignty [that] . . . would allow activists, scholars, and cultivators to depart from focusing on issues of access (as dictated by a food security approach), to a more comprehensive focus on entitlements to land, decision making, and control over natural assets, structural conditions that would allow for the process of developing autotopographies that tie individual and collective identities to deep senses of place and healthy, culturally appropriate food practices. (2011, 202)

It has become clear that a solely access-based approach is not enough to achieve real justice in the food system (Alkon and Agyeman 2011; Sbicca 2018; Reese 2019). To be truly transformative, food justice movements must become much more expansive, inclusive, and intersectional. As the Panthers made plain half a century ago, providing food is not the revolution but a vehicle through which revolution is made possible. For Black Americans in particular, the promises of industrialization and modernity have gone largely unfulfilled, especially in the urban core. We have quantifiably more money, but it has less value, and the cost of living has skyrocketed—particularly in rapidly gentrifying neighborhoods (see chapter 6 of this volume). We have more access to information but less privacy, and smarter phones but poorer schools. We also have more food but less nutritional value, so we are at once obese and malnourished in the richest nation in the world (Dolnick 2010; Gallup 2013). Christina Sharpe (2016) argues that the violent, genocidal conditions of anti-Blackness still saturate the Black experience, centuries after the horrors of the transatlantic slave trade and decades since Jim Crow segregation. To be sure, race and racism continue to dictate the terms and conditions of our material reality and lived experiences. Food is still used as a tool of oppression, as demonstrated by the lack of healthy food outlets compared to the scores of liquor stores, convenience markets, and fast food restaurants in poor communities of color (Community Services Unlimited 2004).[14]

Today's grassroots efforts to dismantle and circumvent racism in the food system remind us that there is a radical possibility that arises from necessity in the most marginalized spaces (Du Bois 1935; Costa Vargas 2010; Lipsitz 2011). As increasing numbers of Americans (Black and otherwise) find themselves lacking health care, education, and access to healthy food, the Panthers' survival programs remain as relevant as ever. The Black Panthers implemented immediate and tangible solutions to social ills with a swiftness and intention that both shamed the state and held it accountable for its failures. Perhaps more profoundly, they envisioned long-term social change with Black and other oppressed communities at the forefront. The survival programs were a true model of how to care for the people and live (rather than die) for the cause because martyrs do not get to see the revolution (Brown 2018). As June Jordan would say, "we are the ones we have been waiting for" (1980, 42), and food is a powerful medium to shape the world that we want in place of the one we are critiquing. If we can excavate the radical principles of the Black Panther Party's survival programs and center them in our own contemporary work of creating a more just and equitable food system for the people most in need, we may indeed see the revolution.

Notes

1. The name and symbol of the Black Panthers were adopted directly from the LCFO, an independent political organization SNCC helped organize in Alabama.

2. In chapter 7 of this volume, Kimberly Kasper decodes the historicity of barbecue cuisine within the African American experience.

3. While this is true, Leah Penniman (2018) points out that the conditions of slavery and colonization often left little to no time for subsistence farming or gardening.

4. The impact of industry on Black relationships to food production is symbolized in Charles Burnett's (1978) film *Killer of Sheep*, in which the main character, Stan, works long hours for low pay at a slaughterhouse in Watts, California, surrounded by endless, monotonous carnage.

5. The Panthers had strong alliances with U.S.-based groups like the Brown Berets, the Red Guard, the Young Lords, the Young Patriots, and the Gray Panthers, to name a few. Internationally, they forged relationships with freedom fighters throughout Africa, Asia, Europe, Cuba, and Central and South America (Newton 1972).

6. At 5:30 a.m. on December 8, 1969, there was a massive attack by the Los Angeles Police Department's newly formed SWAT units on several Black Panther offices, the worst of which occurred at the Central Office at 4115 South Central Avenue (Churchill and Vander Wall 2002). A five-hour shootout between Panthers and police ensued, with hundreds of spectators watching.

7. A particularly devastating feud was the one instigated between the BPP and Maulana Karenga's US Organization, which led to the assassination of John Huggins and Bunchy Carter at UCLA in 1969.

8. The Women, Infants, and Children (WIC) Program was added to the Child Nutrition Act in 1972 as an amendment.

9. CSU's Village Market Place helps customers sign up for CalFresh and Electronic Benefits Transfer (EBT, formerly known as food stamps) and also gives discounts to shoppers using these benefits.

10. Even in the 1960s and 1970s, while the Panthers were serving soul food to hungry children, cultural nationalists like Amiri Baraka (LeRoi

Jones) and Maulana Karenga were advocating for vegetarian diets to offset health-related illness and develop a separate Black identity in the United States (see Wallach 2014).

11. *Food apartheid* has become a popular term to theorize differential racialized food access in communities of color (Bediako 2015; Penniman 2018). Sociologist Antwi Akom (2011) also offers the term *eco-apartheid* as a framework for understanding the relationship between the unequal distribution of institutional resources and environmental toxins, and the production of racialized space.

12. There are certainly several organizations (in addition to Community Services Unlimited) that *do* seek to rectify racism and economic exploitation in the food system while simultaneously using food to dismantle other oppressive systems like the prison industrial complex and discriminatory housing market practices. Planting Justice and Mandela Partners in Oakland, California; Soul Fire Farm in Petersburg, New York; and the Detroit Black Community Food Security Network are but a few of many.

13. See chapters 1 and 4 of this volume for more exploration of Black interventions into the burgeoning food justice movement.

14. Ashanté Reese (2019) demonstrates that despite uneven development and limited access to grocery outlets, Black residents are indeed feeding themselves, both within and outside formal food economies.

Bibliography

Abron, JoNina. 1998. "'Serving the People': The Survival Programs of the Black Panther Party." In *The Black Panther Party: Reconsidered,* edited by Charles E. Jones, 177–92. Baltimore, Md.: Black Classic Press.

Akom, Antwi. 2011. "Eco-Apartheid: Linking Environmental Health to Educational Outcomes." *Teachers College Record* 113 (4): 831–59.

Alkebulan, Paul. 2007. *Survival Pending Revolution: The History of the Black Panther Party.* Tuscaloosa: University of Alabama Press.

Alkon, Alison Hope, and Julian Agyeman. 2011. *Cultivating Food Justice: Race, Class, and Sustainability.* Cambridge, Mass.: MIT Press.

Allen, Will. 2012. *The Good Food Revolution: Growing Healthy Food, People, and Communities.* New York: Gotham Books.

Araiza, Lauren. 2009. "'In Common Struggle against a Common Oppression': The United Farm Workers and the Black Panther Party, 1968–1973." *Journal of African American History* 94 (2): 200–223.

Bediako, Jaqueline. 2015. "Food Apartheid: The Silent Killer in the Black Community." *Atlanta Black Star,* June 16. http://www.atlantablack star.com.

Belluck, Pam. 2005. "Children's Life Expectancy Being Cut Short by Obesity." *New York Times,* March 17.

Broad, Garrett. 2016. *More than Just Food: Food Justice and Community Change.* Berkeley: University of California Press.

Brown, Elaine. 2018. "The Importance of Black Student Organizations." *Kaltura,* February 8, https://www.kaltura.com.

Bullard, Robert D. 1994. "Environmental Justice for All: It's the Right Thing to Do." *Journal of Environmental Law and Litigation* 9: 281–308.

Burnett, Charles, dir. 1978. *Killer of Sheep.* London: BFi. Film.

Chung, Chanjin, and Samuel L. Myers Jr. 1999. "Do the Poor Pay More for Food? An Analysis of Grocery Store Availability and Food Price Disparities." *Journal of Consumer Affairs* 33 (2): 276–96.

Churchill, Ward. 2014. "'To Disrupt, Discredit, and Destroy': The FBI's Secret War against the Black Panther Party." In *Liberation, Imagination and the Black Panther Party: A New Look at the Panthers and Their Legacy,* edited by Katherine Cleaver and George Katsiaficas, 78–117. New York: Routledge.

Churchill, Ward, and Jim Vander Wall. 2002. *Agents of Repression: The FBI's Secret Wars against the Black Panther Party and the American Indian Movement.* Boston: South End Press.

Cleaver, Kathleen Neal. 1998. "Back to Africa: The Evolution of the International Section of the Black Panther Party (1969–1972)." In *The Black Panther Party: Reconsidered,* edited by Charles E. Jones, 211–54. Baltimore, Md.: Black Classic Press.

Community Services Unlimited. 2004. *ACTION Food Assessment Report: Active Community to Improve Our Nutrition.* http://csuinc.org.

Community Services Unlimited. 2019. "Village Market Place, 2019." Photograph. CSU Sankofa Archive, Los Angeles.

Conway, Marshall "Eddie." 2009. *The Greatest Threat: COINTELPRO and the Black Panther Party.* Baltimore, Md.: iAMWE Publications.

Cooley, Angela Jill. 2015. *To Live and Dine in Dixie: The Evolution of Urban Food Culture in the Jim Crow South.* Athens: University of Georgia Press.

Costa Vargas, João H. 2006. *Catching Hell in the City of Angels: Life and Meanings of Blackness in South Central Los Angeles.* Minneapolis: University of Minnesota Press.

Costa Vargas, João H. 2010. *Never Meant to Survive: Genocide and Utopias in Black Diaspora Communities*. Lanham, Md.: Rowman & Littlefield.

Covey, Herbert C., and Dwight Eisnach. 2009. *What the Slaves Ate: Recollections of African American Foods and Foodways from the Slave Narratives*. Santa Barbara, Calif.: ABC-CLIO.

Davis, Brenda, and Vesanto Melina. 2000. *Becoming Vegan: The Complete Guide to Adopting a Plant-Based Diet*. Summertown, Tenn.: Book Publishing Company.

Dodson, Howard, and Sylviane Anna Diouf. 2004. *In Motion: The African-American Migration Experience*. Washington, D.C.: National Geographic Society.

Dolnick, Sam. 2010. "The Obesity-Hunger Paradox." *New York Times*, March 12.

Douglass, Frederick. 1851. *Narrative of the Life of Frederick Douglass, an American Slave*. Oxford: Oxford University Press.

Du Bois, W. E. B. 1935. *Black Reconstruction in America, 1860–1880*. New York: Simon & Schuster.

Dunn-Emke, Stacey, Gerdi Weidner, and Dean Ornish. 2001. "Benefits of a Low-Fat Plant-Based Diet." *Obesity Research* 9 (11): 731.

Finney, Carolyn. 2014. *Black Faces, White Spaces: Reimagining the Relationship of African Americans to the Great Outdoors*. Chapel Hill: University of North Carolina Press.

Flamming, Douglas. 2005. *Bound for Freedom: Black Los Angeles in Jim Crow America*. Berkeley: University of California Press.

Freeman, Andrea. 2007. "Fast Food: Oppression through Poor Nutrition." *California Law Review* 95 (6): 2221–59.

Gallup. 2013. "Income, Not 'Food Deserts,' More to Blame for U.S. Obesity." Gallup, September 20. http://www.gallup.com.

Green, John J., Eleanor M. Green, and Anna M. Kleiner. 2011. "From the Past to the Present: Agricultural Development and Black Farmers in the American South." In *Cultivating Food Justice: Race, Class, and Sustainability*, edited by Alison Hope Alkon and Julian Agyeman, 47–64. Cambridge, Mass.: MIT Press.

Guthman, Julie. 2008a. "Bringing Good Food to Others: Investigating the Subjects of Alternative Food Practice." *Cultural Geographies* 15 (4): 431–47.

Guthman, Julie. 2008b. "'If They Only Knew': Color Blindness and Universalism in California Alternative Food Institutions." *Professional Geographer* 60 (3): 387–97.

Harper, Breeze A. 2010. *Sistah Vegan: Black Female Vegans Speak on Food, Identity, Health, and Society.* Herndon, Va.: Lantern Books.

Heynen, Nik. 2009. "Bending the Bars of Empire from Every Ghetto for Survival: The Black Panther Party's Radical Antihunger Politics of Social Reproduction and Scale." *Annals of the Association of American Geographers* 99 (2): 406–22.

Hilliard, David. 2008. *The Black Panther.* New York: Simon & Schuster.

Hilliard, David, and Donald Weise, eds. 2011. *The Huey P. Newton Reader.* New York: Seven Stories.

Holder, Kit Kim. 1990. "The History of the Black Panther Party, 1966–1971: A Curriculum Tool for Afrikan-American Studies." EdD diss., University of Massachusetts Amherst.

Holt-Giménez, Eric, and Yi Wang. 2011. "Reform or Transformation? The Pivotal Role of Food Justice in the U.S. Food Movement." *Race/Ethnicity: Multidisciplinary Global Contexts* 5 (1): 83–102.

Hurt, Byron, dir. 2012. *Soul Food Junkies.* Fanwood, N.J.: God Bless the Child Productions. Documentary.

Incite! Women of Color Against Violence. 2007. *The Revolution Will Not Be Funded: Beyond the Non-Profit Industrial Complex.* Boston: South End.

Jones, Charles E., ed. 1998. *The Black Panther Party (Reconsidered).* Baltimore, Md.: Black Classic Press.

Joseph, Peniel E. 2006. *The Black Power Movement: Rethinking the Civil Rights–Black Power Era.* New York: Taylor & Francis.

Joseph, Peniel E. 2007. *Waiting 'Til the Midnight Hour: A Narrative History of Black Power in America.* New York: Macmillan.

Jordan, June. 1980. "Poem for South African Women." In *Passion: New Poems, 1977–1980,* 42. Boston: Beacon.

Keeling, Kara. 2007. *The Witch's Flight.* Durham, N.C.: Duke University Press.

KPFA Radio. 1970. "Revolution for Breakfast." Pacifica Radio Archives, August 14.

Kulkarni, Karmeen D. 2004. "Food, Culture, and Diabetes in the United States." *Clinical Diabetes* 22 (4): 190–92.

Lee, Mary. 1998. *Drowning in Alcohol: Retail Outlet Density, Economic Decline and Revitalization in South L.A.* Los Angeles: Autumn Press.

Levine, Susan. 2011. *School Lunch Politics: The Surprising History of America's Favorite Welfare Program.* Princeton, N.J.: Princeton University Press.

Lipsitz, George. 2011. *How Racism Takes Place*. Philadelphia: Temple University Press.

Litwack, Leon F. 2010. *Trouble in Mind: Black Southerners in the Age of Jim Crow*. New York: Knopf.

Mares, Teresa M., and Devon G. Peña. 2011. "Environmental and Food Justice: Toward Local, Slow, and Deep Food Systems." In *Cultivating Food Justice: Race, Class, and Sustainability*, edited by Alison Hope Alkon and Julian Agyeman, 197–220. Cambridge, Mass.: MIT Press.

McMillan, Tracie. 2012. *The American Way of Eating: Undercover at Walmart, Applebee's, Farm Fields and the Dinner Table*. New York: Simon & Schuster.

Murch, Donna. 2010. *Living for the City: Migration, Education, and the Rise of the Black Panther Party in Oakland, California*. Chapel Hill: University of North Carolina Press.

Nelson, Alondra. 2011. *Body and Soul: The Black Panther Party and the Fight against Medical Discrimination*. Minneapolis: University of Minnesota Press.

Nestle, Marion. 2013. *Food Politics: How the Food Industry Influences Nutrition and Health*. Berkeley: University of California Press.

Newton, Huey P. 1972. *To Die for the People: The Writings of Huey P. Newton*. New York: Random House.

Newton, Huey P. 1980. "War against the Panthers: A Study of Repression in America." PhD diss., University of California, Santa Cruz.

Opie, Frederick Douglass. 2010. *Hog and Hominy: Soul Food from Africa to America*. New York: Columbia University Press.

Patel, Raj. 2010. *Stuffed and Starved: The Hidden Battle for the World's Food System*. Toronto: HarperCollins Canada.

Patel, Raj. 2012. "Survival Pending Revolution: What the Black Panthers Can Teach the US Food Movement." *Food First: Institute for Food and Development Policy* 18 (2): 1–3.

Penniman, Leah. 2016. "After a Century in Decline, Black Farmers Are Back and on the Rise." *Yes!* magazine, May.

Penniman, Leah. 2018. *Farming while Black: Soul Fire Farm's Practical Guide to Liberation on the Land*. White River Junction, Vt.: Chelsea Green Publishing.

Poe, Tracy N. 2013. "The Origins of Soul Food in Black Urban Identity: Chicago, 1915–1947." In *Food in the USA: A Reader*, edited by Carole Counihan, 101–18. New York: Routledge.

Pollan, Michael. 2006. *The Omnivore's Dilemma: A Natural History of Four Meals*. New York: Penguin.

Potorti, Mary. 2017. "'Feeding the Revolution': The Black Panther Party, Hunger, and Community Survival." *Journal of African American Studies* 21 (1): 85–110.

Pulido, Laura. 1996. *Environmentalism and Economic Justice: Two Chicano Struggles in the Southwest.* Tucson: University of Arizona Press.

Reese, Ashanté M. 2019. *Black Food Geographies: Race, Self-Reliance, and Food Access in Washington, D.C.* Chapel Hill: University of North Carolina Press.

Robinson, Cedric J. 1983. *Black Marxism: The Making of the Black Radical Tradition.* Chapel Hill: University of North Carolina Press.

Sbicca, J. 2018. *Food Justice Now! Deepening the Roots of Social Struggle.* Minneapolis: University of Minnesota Press.

Schlosser, Eric. 2012. *Fast Food Nation: The Dark Side of the All-American Meal.* New York: Houghton Mifflin Harcourt.

Seale, Bobby. 1991. *Seize the Time: The Story of the Black Panther Party and Huey P. Newton.* Baltimore, Md.: Black Classic Press.

Seale, Bobby. 2018. "The Free Breakfast for Children Program." Facebook, April 15. https://www.facebook.com.

Self, Robert O. 2005. *American Babylon: Race and the Struggle for Postwar Oakland.* Princeton, N.J.: Princeton University Press.

Sharpe, Christina. 2016. *In the Wake: On Blackness and Being.* Durham, N.C.: Duke University Press.

Terry, Bryant. 2009. *Vegan Soul Kitchen: Fresh, Healthy, and Creative African-American Cuisine.* Cambridge, Mass.: Da Capo.

Terry, Bryant. 2014. *Afro-Vegan: Farm-Fresh African, Caribbean & Southern Flavors Remixed.* Berkeley: Ten Speed.

Wallach, Jennifer Jensen. 2014. "How to Eat to Live: Black Nationalism and the Post-1964 Culinary Turn." *Study the South,* July 2.

West, Cornel. 2010. *The Black Panther Party: Service to the People Programs.* Albuquerque: University of New Mexico Press.

Whit, William C. 2007. "Soul Food as Cultural Creation." In *African American Foodways: Exploration of History and Culture,* edited by Anne Bower, 45–58. Urbana: University of Illinois Press.

Widener, Daniel. 2009. *Black Arts West: Culture and Struggle in Postwar Los Angeles.* Durham, N.C.: Duke University Press.

Wilkerson, Isabel. 2011. *The Warmth of Other Suns: The Epic Story of America's Great Migration.* New York: Knopf Doubleday.

Williamson, Joy Ann. 2005. "Community Control with a Black Nationalist Twist: The Black Panther Party's Educational Programs." *Counterpoints* 237: 137–57.

Witt, Doris. 2004. *Black Hunger: Soul Food and America.* Minneapolis: University of Minnesota Press.

Yentsch, Anne. 2007. "Excavating the South's African American Food History." In *African American Foodways: Exploration of History and Culture,* edited by Anne Bower, 59–98. Urbana: University of Illinois Press.

4

BLACKNESS AND "JUSTICE" IN THE LOS ANGELES FOOD JUSTICE MOVEMENT

Hanna Garth

• • •

In the fall of 2010 I joined David and Cheryl to speak to a high school class in East Los Angeles.[1] I had been working with them as both a volunteer for their organization, Bettering Life, and an ethnographer studying Los Angeles–based organizations with the mission to increase access to "healthy" food among residents of South L.A. and East L.A., predominantly Black and Latinx, respectively. Their organization had the goal of improving access to "healthy" food in South and East L.A. by targeting high school students and engaging them in community development projects, such as corner store conversion projects that introduce fresh fruits and vegetables to existing corner stores and liquor stores in the area. We met near where we live and carpooled to the location together as a team. David identified as white, Cheryl as East Asian, and I identify as Black. On that particular day, we were visiting a local high school where Bettering Life had been invited to do a full school-year-long curriculum with biweekly workshops on healthy eating. Although "healthy" was not explicitly defined by this organization, the implication was that fresh fruits and vegetables were the kinds of healthy foods that people *should* be eating. As part of the program, the students would design and implement projects to improve food access in their local community.

To begin, David and Cheryl asked everyone to introduce themselves and tell the group what their favorite food was. I jotted down the student's answers—tamales, BBQ ribs, pozole, pizza, carne asada, tortillas and butter. When it came around to me, I stated my name and that my favorite food was macaroni and cheese. Cheryl introduced herself after me and spoke at length of her love for brussels sprouts, which I also love to eat when they are prepared well. At the end of the session, after we left the classroom, Cheryl pulled me aside and said:

> I wanted to talk to you about your favorite food. We are here to get the kids to change the way that they eat. To get them to stop eating things like tortillas or macaroni and cheese and eat things like brussels sprouts, kale, broccoli, you know, healthy food. So next time, say that you like kale, OK?

David overheard the conversation but did not add anything. I responded that based on their own responses, I was thinking about culturally valued foods that matter to me, that macaroni and cheese was a central part of Black food in the way that pozole or tamales might have been for some of the students. Cheryl looked at me, tilting her head down with her eyes on mine, and said that macaroni and cheese was not a central part of Black food culture and that it did not matter if people were connected to their foods because of their culture, because they needed to get them to stop eating foods that were pure fat and carbohydrates and eat more vegetables. She finished by reminding me that this was what their grant had funded them to do, after all.

This encounter was one among many in which I came to see the ways that these types of interventions done in the name of food justice can range from uncomfortably bumping up against culturally significant food practices to being overtly racist. Through food justice interventions, the push to "healthy eating" becomes a way in which organizations work to produce a particular kind of neoliberal subject, bringing communities of color into a mold of the middle-class American citizen (Biltekoff 2013). This is often done without regard for culturally specific food practices that are often very important to the communities that are being intervened on. In this context, "healthy eating" took on an aura of "punitive justice," and Blackness, by way of Black food culture, was posited as an obstacle to remove or overcome in order to achieve a successful intervention. Additionally, these interventions can reproduce the narrative that Black and Brown people are in need of education and assistance and perpetuate ongoing forms of anti-Blackness (Jones 2018; see also Reese's chapter in this volume). I wondered how the organization might be utilizing my Blackness to legitimize its work while at the same time policing the way in which I express my Blackness and engage with Black food culture. How was this engagement with me a lens into the larger way of perpetuating forms of anti-Blackness in the food justice work of Bettering Life? These interactions led me to ask a series of questions in my research: What form of justice does the nonprofit "food justice" intervention take? How does it account for and understand racial and economic justice? To begin to get at these questions, I have been conducting ethnographic research on the growth of the Los Angeles food justice movement. Since 2009 I have been tracing how Los Angeles–based community, nonprofit, and governmental entities have developed programming to improve access to "healthy" food among residents of lower-income areas, such as South L.A. and East L.A., predominantly Black and Latinx, respectively.

In this chapter, I analyze a tension in food justice movements with respect to the meaning of justice and understandings of how to create just practices in the movement. In particular, I focus on this tension as it relates to how culturally valued foods intersect with others' notions of "justice" and "healthy." I analyze three different approaches to food justice that are representative examples of the approaches I have found in the food justice movement. I use these scenarios to think through food justice and some of the less visible, more quotidian forms of anti-Blackness that permeate the food movement (see also Guthman 2008; Cox 2015; Wallach 2015; Allen and Jobson 2016).

Culturally Black Foods

To understand the role of Black food culture here and the ways in which these encounters can be interpreted as anti-Black, it is useful to parse out Cheryl's understanding that "macaroni and cheese was not a central part of Black food culture." Cheryl's chastising of my food choice implies that foods like macaroni and cheese are not linked to culture and identity in the same ways as pozole or tamales. Thus her position makes it appear as if foods that are culturally Latinx are thought to be historically and culturally meaningful and legitimized, but foods that are culturally Black are questioned, delegitimized, or conceptualized as merely an excuse to eat unhealthy food. Through her word choice, she perpetuates an invisible form of anti-Blackness through delegitimizing Black food. These seemingly subtle interactions delegitimize not only Black food culture but also Blackness and Black culture more generally. In my analysis of Cheryl's account, Black people do not have a legitimate food culture or, by extension, a legitimate culture. Black is rendered merely a race in this case. A refusal to acknowledge macaroni and cheese as a culturally Black food then renders the dish as merely an "unhealthy" dose of fat and carbohydrates. As Katherine McKittrick has argued, the systematic erasure of Black culture is part of the "objectification of subaltern subjectivities, stories, and lands" that facilitates the logics of "spatial colonization and domination" (2006, x). This erasure of Black food culture takes place despite an established and growing literature that documents the role of certain foods in Black culture and everyday life. For instance, the foundational work of Psyche Williams-Forson extensively documents the historical and contemporary constitution of chicken as central to Black food culture. In shaping "a story of feminist consciousness, community building, cultural work, and personal identity," Williams-Forson argues, "black women have shaped vital aspects of their lives with food" (2006, 2, 1; see also Nettles-Barcelón et al. 2015). Demonstrating the ways chicken served as a "tool of self-expression, self-actualization, resistance, even accommodation and power" (2006, 2; see also Rouse and Hoskins 2000), Williams-Forson moves far beyond the well-documented stereotypes of Black people and chicken and instead illuminates Black people's own narratives of the role of chicken and other foods in their lives. Yet, despite the cultural significance of Black foodways, "foods like chicken are imbued with class tensions as African Americans struggled for citizenship and acceptance in American society" (Williams-Forson 2006, 7).

In *The Cooking Gene,* Michael Twitty beautifully paints a picture of the centrality of Black foodways—in particular soul food, as one type of many kinds of Black food, and its southern roots—to Black life in America. While Twitty notes that Black foodways sit within a "contested landscape" where there are concerns about "health, sustainability, environment, social justice, and the push-pull between global and local economies" (2017, 6), Black foodways still remain an integral part of Black life, of Black soul in America. Cooking is about memory and remembered pasts; it is connected to stories passed down through the generations, which link the present and one's ancestors. Twitty ties Black foodways to Africa through okra, red rice, pepper pot, barbeque, peanut soup, and fried chicken; he blends in European, Asian, and Native ingredients to arrive at the soul food we eat today.[2] The forms of consumption described by Twitty and Williams-Forson are central to understand Black food culture and are as much about sustaining life today as they are about sustaining connections to a meaningful past. This is not to say that everything Black people eat is central to Black food culture, nor that these foods are not eaten by non-Black people all the time as well. Instead, the point here is that there are particular dishes, ingredients, ways of preparing foods, or ways of engaging with foods that are historically linked to Black communities across the diaspora, and these foods have ongoing cultural importance for many Black communities. The bounds of what constitutes Black food culture are not set in stone; like most culturally constituted phenomena, there is ebb and flow over time and space, and Black food is not fixed. This understanding of Black food culture encompasses both what we eat and the ways we eat it as individuals, families, communities, and members of a broader diaspora.

Given this understanding of Black food culture, how does the food justice movement uphold these desires or tear them down?

The food justice movement grew out of the environmental justice movement in the mid-1990s (Gottlieb and Fisher 1996). Food justice emerged from a growing desire for equality and justice within community food security efforts and emerged from collaborations between academics and activists interested in understanding "the global and local dimensions of food systems" and "issues of access, justice, and environmental and community well-being" (Gottlieb and Joshi 2010, xvii). Robert Gottlieb and Anupama Joshi trace the definition of food justice to a 2000 edition of the journal *Race, Poverty and the Environment,* where the concept of environmental justice was applied to food to think of food justice as "seeking to transform where, what, and how food is grown, produced, transported, accessed, and eaten" (Gottlieb and Joshi 2010, 4–5). For Gottlieb, food justice was about "bringing about community change and a different kind of food system," and, critical to this approach, justice was thought to mean "ensuring that the benefits and risks of where, what, and how food is grown and produced, transported and distributed, and accessed and eaten are shared fairly" (2010, 5, 6).

To date, much of the literature that has characterized food in contemporary Black communities has painted a bleak picture — one of crumbling infrastructure (i.e., no large supermarkets; only liquor and corner stores), dire poverty (hungry children), abandonment (abandoned markets never reoccupied), and violence (fear of leaving the house to shop for food) (Alwitt and Donley 1997; McClintock 2011). Christina Sharpe also notes this and critiques the ways in which "blackness is always the register of abandonment" (2016, 5). This scholarship often calls for the need to improve, reform, intervene, or change Black and Brown communities. The desire to change Black and Brown communities is often steeped in a logic of white supremacy and an implication that Black and Brown people should conform to white standards and ways of being (Sojoyner 2016). Black communities are a common target of food interventions, ranging from programs that bring fresh fruits and vegetables to corner stores (Gittelsohn et al. 2010; Dannefer et al. 2012) to urban community gardening (Poulsen et al. 2014). The alternative food movement, a movement that precedes the food justice movement and is based on an idealized "agrarian imaginary" (Guthman 2004, 174), largely embraces a vision of a more ecological, small, family farm–based food system with locally produced foods and consumers getting to know the growers who produce them. This movement has been critiqued for its myopic approach. Many alternative food movement spaces are coded as white; they are assumed to be dominated by white consumers and based around their food preferences (Hill 1998; Guthman 2008), with the rhetoric of diversifying that space based around "inviting others" to this white-centered metaphorical table (Guthman 2008, 388). Julie Guthman has critiqued the alternative food movement for being too color-blind and universalizing whiteness in its logic of spreading awareness about healthy, local, and organic foods. There is an underlying assumption that mainly white and upper/middle-class people know where quality food comes from and with that knowledge are able to avoid industrialized food, categorized as "unhealthy," and consume local organic food, thought of as "healthy." The logic assumes that if these white upper-middle-class Americans simply educated the populations of Black and Brown lower-class Americans, our food system would be saved (Guthman 2008). This desire to "educate" and "improve" communities of color includes an implicit effort to limit or eliminate Black cultural forms, such as foodways, which are interpreted as problematic behaviors or practices rather than historically situated cultural practices. As Analena Hope Hassberg's chapter in this volume wonderfully illustrates, not all forms of food justice are centered on bringing Black and Brown communities into a white middle-class subjectivity; indeed, the Black Panther Party's form of food justice was grounded in the need to support Black communities and Black culture through food programs. Building on Hassberg's chapter, here I show how Community Services Unlimited (CSU), the daughter organization of the Black Panther Party, continues to serve the mission to support Black people's minds, bodies, and souls. Organizations like the Black Panther Party and CSU operate as an alternative to both dominant food systems and (white) alternative food movements.

In this chapter, I move through three approaches to food justice interventions, each of which has the goal of improving access to "healthy" food for residents of South or East Los Angeles (and by extension for Black and Latinx people). I analyze how these organizations approach racial and economic justice as part of their food movement work. While I have conducted research on the organizations and their activities overall, I focus here on the visions and orientations of the leaders of the organizations, which I believe to be strongly linked with the overall orientation of the organizations. I identify three approaches to justice (following Gottlieb's overarching definition): radical grassroots justice, policy-oriented justice, and punitive justice. I note the ways in which white supremacy and anti-Blackness can permeate some of the logics of justice used in the food movement. Finally, I demonstrate the ways that various forms of justice can be layered within an organizational approach and that the various configurations of justice can have widely differing implications for racial and economic justice.

Radical Grassroots Justice

The first case, Community Services Unlimited (CSU), is a very important organization in the history of Los Angeles and the food justice movement. CSU was originally part of the Southern California Chapter of the Black Panther Party. CSU is directed by Neelam Sharma, who grew up in London and traces her ancestry to India. Sharma was one of the founders of a Black and Asian organization called Panther in England, where, she noted, Blackness has a more expansive definition and can include Black and Brown people, and even those of Asian descent like herself. As Sharma pointed out to me in an interview, "Black in England means people of color, so when I use the term *Black* in England, that's what it means." Through Sharma's work with Panther, she met the folks from the Southern California BPP Chapter (by then closed), organizing through the vehicle of CSU. Original party members had come together with newly radicalized youth after the L.A. rebellion and the New African American Vanguard Movement (NAAVM) was born. Sharma visited L.A. representing Panther at the request of Community in Support of the Gang Truce, of which CSU was the fiscal agent. As a result of this meeting, Panther and the NAAVM built a relationship and published a joint newspaper. Sharma moved to L.A. in 1995 and began to volunteer with CSU. Thus CSU employs a broad understanding of Blackness and attends to the multiplicity of Blackness and variation of Black experience (Pierre 2004; Sexton 2010; M'charek 2013). Sharma was inspired by the Black Panthers to come together against the struggle of people of color across the diaspora. They brought Bobby Seale, a member of the Black Panther Party in the United States, to do a speaking tour in England, organizing the largest ever political rally of people of color.

As Sharma tells the history, CSU wanted to draw upon the "good aspects" of the Panthers, such as their food and educational programs, and learn from some of their mistakes. CSU's mission includes the overarching goal to "foster the creation of communities actively working to address the inequalities and systematic barriers that make sustainable communities and self-reliant lifestyles unattainable" (Community Services Unlimited 2004, 38). Members "envision equitable, healthful and sustainable communities that are self-reliant, inter-relating and where every individual has the support and resources needed to develop their fullest capacity" (2004, 38). Within this broad mission and vision, CSU's programs as described on its website are part of a "Community Food Village project" based on a community food assessment it calls ACTION (Active Community to Improve Our Nutrition) completed in 2004 (Community Services Unlimited 2004). Based on this assessment, CSU has developed programming to create a local food system with the goal of growing and distributing food within the community. CSU cultivates food on a minifarm—located near the EXPO Center in South Los Angeles, in a predominately Black, low-income neighborhood—on which it grows food that it characterizes as "beyond organic" (the produce is grown organically, meaning naturally, without the use of artificial chemicals or fertilizers, but it is not certified organic). Sharma and her staff host training programs for hundreds of youth and adult community members. CSU developed a community-supported agriculture program, distributing bags of fresh fruits and vegetables to hundreds of community members, many of whom live in walking distance, others who live nearby but must drive to the site. Additionally, CSU established weekly produce stands to sell food directly to the community. CSU offers cooking demonstrations showing how to incorporate fresh fruits and vegetables into meals. Linking to Sharma's heritage, CSU sometimes serves curried rice dishes and fruit chutneys as a subtle way of linking healthy eating to cultural foodways and demonstrating the multiplicity of Blackness. In July 2015, largely through crowd funding and donations, CSU was able to purchase a building, the Paul Robeson Community Wellness Center, where it has established South L.A.'s first organic produce market and local food hub through its retail food program, the Village Market Place Social Enterprise. CSU's approach to food justice folds in what might appear to be similar narratives of healthy eating adopted by organizations like Bettering Life. However, CSU's holistic approach to food as a part of community empowerment, self-sufficiency, and Black and Brown diasporic solidarity casts "healthy" not as a proxy for the white middle-class American citizen but as a form of healing communities of color through food.

CSU is a relatively mature and established organization that has been working toward "food justice" in Los Angeles before the term was commonly used. It claims to be "the only grassroots food organization" still functioning in South Los Angeles. With the exception of the South L.A. farm project, at various points in time CSU has been the only grassroots organization in South Los Angeles, and it continues to be one of the few organizations that works to serve community needs from a holistic approach. CSU as an organization and its staff are attuned to the needs of South L.A. residents in deeply committed ways; for instance, most of its staff members live in South L.A., are from South L.A., and send their kids to South L.A. schools. This lived experience of daily life in the area informs their decisions about programming, which is designed around a diverse set of needs in that setting. As Garrett Broad's book about the organization is aptly titled, CSU is about "*more than just food*" (Broad 2015). That is to say, CSU uses food justice to address myriad issues related to racial and economic justice in South Los Angeles, from employment, to transportation, to environmental justice, to housing and gentrification issues.

This organization represents one view of food justice—a very grassroots-centered form of food justice that is deeply focused on the needs of the community within South Los Angeles as CSU defines it. I am labeling this form of food justice as radical grassroots food justice, inextricably tied to racial and economic justice (Alkon and Mares 2012). CSU has a radical political orientation in the sense that it believes that "institutional and conventional political practices [are] unable to deal with certain social problems [that they] proclaim to be fundamental" (Hage 2012, 290). Members are working to solve problems fundamental to the community through their own tactics and strategies. Their insistence on recognizing their connection to the Black Panther Party and the Panther mission to "serving the people, body and soul" is a testament to their radicalism, and CSU also reminds us of other dimensions of the Black Panther Party that have been erased from our history.[3] CSU's approach is based on a grassroots orientation because of the long history, deep connections, and in-group membership within the immediate community and its dynamic concerns (Bettencourt 1996).

Blackness and the multiple historical and cultural dimensions of Black culture are central to CSU's approach to food justice. South Los Angeles residents who participate in CSA programming not only learn about good food, gardening, composting, and healthy eating options but also important Black histories of South L.A., and the links between anti-Blackness, state violence, and the loss of good jobs and state programs that may have supported the community in certain ways in the past. Upholding the beauty of Blackness and the perils of white supremacy, this organization not only nourishes but also empowers the community. CSU's radical approach and its embrace of Blackness are deeply intertwined; there is a recognition (even an insistence) that highly oppressive forms of government have never been concerned about Black life, and a radical rejection of those forms of intervention is the way that CSU works to uphold what matters to Black communities (see also Sojoyner 2017).

Policy-Oriented Justice

If CSU is an example of radical grassroots food justice, in this second case I turn to the less radical, more liberal democratic policy-oriented approach of the Los Angeles Food Policy Council (LAFPC). In many ways, the LAFPC is the heart of the Los Angeles food justice movement. It serves as a node that connects more than three hundred organizations and thousands of leaders, participants, and volunteers to one another and the broader Los Angeles community. In addition to its role at the forefront of the movement, its central role—to facilitate policy creation that allows for a healthy, affordable, fair, and sustainable local food system—is absolutely essential to the work of anyone else with the goal of improving food systems in Los Angeles. I therefore characterize LAFPC as espousing a policy-oriented form of food justice. This approach to food justice works within the existing legal and policy frameworks to make incremental change, but it does not attempt a fundamental change of the institutional and legal systems that underlie the patterns of structural violence and institutionalized racism that may cause inequality in the first place. I therefore do not consider it to be a radical approach to food justice.

The central areas of focus of the LAFPC are characterized by its working groups: Urban Agriculture, Farmers Markets for All, Food Waste Prevention and Rescue, School Gardens, Street Food Vending, and Food as Medicine. Although the LAFPC is not radical or grassroots in its orientation, it provides a fundamental service to the food justice movement; namely, it works to change laws and policies like legalizing street food vending and growing food in parkways.

The LAFPC is directed by UCLA Luskin School of Public Affairs alumna Clare Fox. Fox grew up in the L.A. area, studied "urban planning and community economic development," and identifies as a white woman. In 2010 we sat down for our second recorded interview at a café in Koreatown, and Fox explained to me how she formulated her views on race and social justice.

Well, I would say from a young age I was always sensitive to issues of injustice . . . and I felt like not only was [it] something I was aware of but [I] felt a responsibility to do something about [it], and that was partly, you know, something I got from my mom, who was a feminist and brought home kind of radical literature when I was young, and so that shaped me.

Fox went on to outline learning about histories of white supremacy and racism in the United States and, as she put it, "what it means to be a white person in that context and what it means to be an ally in that context." Fox's vision of what it means to be an ally in the fight for racial and economic justice includes protesting the illegality of street food vending and defending the rights of street food vendors in L.A. Fox participated in a protest that resulted in her arrest in March 2018 (Smith 2018); she is willing to stand up for what she believes in and fight alongside the people she advocates for within the auspices of her formal employment as the director of the LAFPC.

So, with Fox as a radical antiracist activist at the helm, the Los Angeles Food Policy Council is a huge and growing organization that is the largest and most commonly accessed food justice group in Los Angeles. The LAFPC is the heart of what I am calling a movement, even though it is not as grassroots as CSU, nor is it holistic, as it narrowly focuses on food issues, specifically those that are more likely to be effected by policy. It is no coincidence that the growth of the food movement has also coincided with the growth of the LAFPC. Although the LAFPC is directed by a radical antiracist activist, the organization itself is far less radical and maintains a focus on working within institutional and government structures to change policies that impact food access. This includes working to legalize street vending (Yesko 2017; Smith 2018), passing an ordinance requiring all farmers markets to accept food stamps through the CalFresh/Electronic Benefits Transfer (EBT) program (Ferguson 2016), and establishing Urban Agriculture Incentive Zones within the City of Los Angeles (LAFPC 2010), among many other initiatives and coalitions.

Although the LAFPC had not made an official statement on the relationship between food justice and racial and economic justice at the time of this research, based on conversations with the leadership and my attendance at several events I could see that the organization was working toward developing racial justice as a priority. The LAFPC was making a slow and concerted effort to develop that statement while working closely with community partners. The LAFPC has developed a "Good Food for All Agenda" that seeks to develop a "Thriving Good Food Economy for Everyone" (LAFPC 2010, 50). The LAFPC envisions the following goals:

- The new regional food system will create and retain Good Food jobs with opportunities for training and upward mobility available to residents of all racial, ethnic and socio economic backgrounds.
- The health and well-being of all workers will be a fundamental component of a sustainable food system. Workers will be treated with respect, justice, and dignity.
- City and County policies will encourage and incentivize the development of healthy food retail and alternative food resources in underserved areas, including communities of color. (LAFPC 2010, 50)

In setting its vision to include justice, respect, and dignity for all of Los Angeles and explicitly mentioning communities of color, the LAFPC attempts to underscore its commitment to racial and economic justice as a part of its policy-oriented food justice work. Nevertheless, as well meaning as these efforts may be, due to the nature of the policy-oriented justice framework, the LAFPC is simultaneously upholding a mainstream, white-centered form of food justice, in which it attempts to fold in Black and Brown Angelenos through efforts such as the legalization of street vending and the acceptance of EBT at farmers markets. Unlike CSU, the LAFPC is not interested in remaking the entire food system; it is not carving out Black spaces but merely inserting Black people into white spaces in a way that is legible and "acceptable" (i.e., through laws and policies). The case of the LAFPC points to the limits of food justice work within mainstream political structures. Organizations like CSU operate just beyond those limits, picking up some of the slack that LAFPC is unable to address due to its positioning.

Punitive Justice

Standing in contrast to both the LAFPC and CSU, the third case is an interpretation of food justice coming from a Los Angeles–based politician. Randy Johnson, a white, middle-aged, wealthy Angeleno, is something of a local hero in Los Angeles. He is the executive director of a nonprofit, Greening Life, that has made sweeping changes across the entire city of Los Angeles, a huge feat for any nonprofit in such a large and complex city. Johnson, a self-made millionaire who volunteers his time with his nonprofit, like many in the food movement, sees food as connected to many issues. Although he comes at the work from the "desire to improve access to healthy food," he notes that he is willing to work on any issue that he sees as related to food. He has been particularly successful in working with a large, city-based, heavily bureaucratic organization that had a notorious reputation for being impossible to work with and even less possible to change. Through Greening Life's efforts, Johnson has demonstrated that with persistence even in the toughest bureaucracy, change can happen.

Like many food justice organizations, Greening Life is focused on improving nutrition among young children. Greening Life has programs across the City of Los Angeles, with sites in South Los Angeles (predominately Black), East Los Angeles (predominately Latinx), and predominantly white areas like West Los Angeles, Larchmont, Los Feliz, and Silverlake. Greening Life tries to do a one-for-one match; for every site it develops in an upper-middle-class or wealthy area, it develops one in a low-income area. Greening Life grew very quickly, "too quickly," as Johnson told me. Because of this rapid growth, many of its sites were established and then faltered as Greening Life was understaffed and under-resourced. These faltering sites were overwhelmingly located in low-income areas, while the thriving sites were in wealthy areas. Johnson chalked up this phenomenon to the fact that "people were just more involved and had time to volunteer in their communities" in the wealthier areas. Johnson noted that he could have left things that way because the grants that Greening Life had received only cared that he established the sites, not that he made them sustainable. However, he felt that slowing down and giving these sites the proper attention was "the right thing to do."

I sat down with Johnson in January 2014 in a restaurant near his home one evening. We talked about his organization and how hard he worked to change the city bureaucracy around food justice issues. I asked him why he started his organization, and he explained that it was about his frustrations "with listening to adults talk about how the world ought to be, but nobody getting their hands dirty." Delving deeper into his motivations, he talked about his own children and their future. He told me:

> Only a fool thinks that if he takes care of his only family, he will be fine, it's gonna come back to you. It happened in L.A. in the early 1990s. They [Black people] didn't riot because they're bad people; they did it because they were desperate. We [white people] have it all; they don't. Obviously I see that other kids don't have the same thing, all across the city, and I suppose it is mostly about the young kids. I see everyone's kids as technically being my own child, and I'm not just saying that because you can't just take care of your own, because if you don't take care of everybody, *eventually they are going to come and steal from you and resort to crime or whatever.* Just because they are desperate. If you don't take care of them, you don't give them a good shot at a future. Whether it be health or education, or opportunity, or whatever. It's really simple. You take care of everyone, [and] you have a harmonious neighborhood; *[if] you don't it's eventually going to come back and bite you.* (emphasis added)

Johnson argues here that among several reasons to do the food work that his organization does, one is to protect himself, his children, and his community, an "us" that he sharply distinguishes from "them." Notably, he brings this particular point up twice, emphasizing its importance. By referencing the Los Angeles uprising of 1992, Johnson indicates that he is referring to Black residents of Los Angeles as "them," and he is characterizing Black residents as a violent mob.[4] Johnson perpetuates the false stereotype of Black people as criminal, as a force to fear that threatens to disrupt the harmony of white areas nearby (Page 1997).

When I asked him about whether he felt there was a "food justice" movement in L.A., he responded:

> So I don't like the term, because it just makes it a little patronizing. . . . To be honest I don't think there is, I think it is being approached in all of the wrong ways. It is not a justice issue. It is a . . . this whole patronizing approach to it is a problem. You can't be patronizing to a Spanish mom, you can't go in there with an English accent and say, "Well, I know better than you, you should be eating this, this, and this." If someone came up to me with another accent, I'd say, "Who the hell do you think you are telling me how to eat?" It tends to be white middle- and upper-class activists who are in the movement and that's kind of stupid. So my wife and I recognize that we are so freakin' white, so we see that the very people who are going in to these South L.A. [places] need to be from there. So we are changing that [part of the program] this year, so we hire or figure out who is down there and have them do it, rather than us. I think it would be a lot better way to do it.

Johnson began to discuss details related to the difficulties of hiring, but eventually he summarized his view on justice as follows: "To frame it as justice makes it sound like you're punishing us, the white people, when we really didn't do anything wrong."

Johnson shifts between overtly racist tones and the pernicious color-blind racism described by Eduardo Bonilla-Silva (2017) that many other white liberals espouse. Johnson's use of the terms *us* and *them* is quite telling. Randy may be a well-intentioned person who is doing some useful work, but his logics of improving the lives of others to protect his family from the future criminal activities of those imagined others are rife with racist logics and the same forms of paternalism and patronizing that he goes on to critique. It is not that he actually disagrees with the patronizing view that middle-class white folks should tell lower-income communities of color how to eat; it is that he feels it is not effective. He therefore wants to hire someone who looks like a community member to spread his message there. Johnson's approach in this respect is very common among these types of organizations in Los Angeles. This pattern of hiring also has the effect of perpetuating and redrawing the divisions between Black and white and us and them. This maneuver keeps Johnson safely ensconced in his white world. In a similar fashion, other food justice organizations draw on volunteers or interns from local schools, both to maintain a staff that is from the community and to cut costs by not paying them. These logics are part and parcel of the economic logics of cutting health-care costs derived from obesity and disease that are so often used in food work.

Blackness and Justice

The logics of Randy Johnson, Cheryl and David, and other food movement activists are steeped in paternalistic, white supremacist, and anti-Black ideologies. They lead organizations with the underlying message that Black and Latinx communities, like South L.A. and East L.A., need to be helped by others (often white) who are presumed to know more about what people in these communities should be eating. These assumptions also necessarily assume that people living in Black and Latinx communities are incapable of helping themselves and making their own decisions. Like the interaction with Cheryl as detailed at the outset of the chapter, there is an assumption that people living in South and East L.A. are unconsciously choosing to eat "unhealthy foods" like tortillas and macaroni and cheese, and if these organizations could just convince them to stop eating those things and eat fresh fruits and vegetables, everyone would be happier and healthier and safer! However, these kinds of organizations overlook the vital dimensions that Black and Latinx cultural foods bring to the table, namely a connection to family and heritage and a broader sense of social and cultural belonging. Macaroni and cheese is not merely an unhealthy food; it is a central part of Black food culture, part of the identity and heritage that Michael Twitty so eloquently connects to Black ancestry and Psyche Williams-Forson connects to the struggles for economic justice wrapped up in the consumption of chicken for Black communities. The organizations that use "food justice" to shift Black and Latinx communities away from their culturally valued food practices without taking into account the elements of racial and economic justice that are relevant to these communities can problematically perpetuate ideas that these culturally valued food practices are somehow deficient or deviant.

Conclusion

Although it is often characterized as a unified movement to increase access to healthy food in low-income communities, usually of color, the food justice movement includes a wide variety of approaches to this goal. Some of these approaches are more radical and grassroots, while others are confined to the dominant government structures of mainstream society, and others still are undergirded by a deep-seated sense of anti-Blackness and logics of white supremacy. On the more policy-oriented side, Clare Fox and the Los Angeles Food Policy Council are clearly doing extensive work to bring together individuals and organizations from disparate corners of our sprawling city of more than four million people under one united vision of improving our food system. Although they are not picketing, or protesting (much), like many of us who envision the action of social movements, their steady work over the past decade has clearly drawn in a large public and maintains direct connections with policy and governance. On the other hand, folks like Neelam Sharma and CSU concentrate on a more grassroots approach to justice, focused within and for their local community in South Los Angeles. CSU's work is inextricably intertwined with a love of Blackness, a sense of supporting it that may even go beyond the bounds of racial justice. CSU and the LAFPC work in collaboration even though they have different visions of system change. The LAFPC has been slowly and cautiously developing its own stance of food equity and a definition of food justice—working to connect with local communities and grassroots organizations in creating this definition rather than creating it from its own experiences. A sense of racial and economic justice increasingly undergirds this process.

Intermingled with organizations like CSU and the LAFPC, groups like Greening Life and Bettering Life also claim to be working for food justice and the goal of increasing access to "healthy" food in low-income communities. These groups tend to employ the logics of "healthy eating" as a weapon against Black food culture, which, when stripped of its cultural legitimacy, is rendered as merely unhealthy food. Their understandings of justice often do not align with those originally espoused by the food justice movement. Randy Johnson actually eschews a justice framework, essentially calling it reverse racism. Johnson's approach, and that of many similar organizations, is undergirded by an abstract, liberal, moralized orientation to "helping the poor." Based on a soft otherizing, this last approach is merely a "formidable political tool for the maintenance of the racial order" (Bonilla-Silva 2017, 3). The ways in which food justice organization leaders imbue their messages with implicit and explicit deprecations of Black foodways and Black culture are critical for assessing the role of racial and economic justice in their work. These approaches to food justice can either spread racist and anti-Black logics in their work or uphold the multiplicity of Blackness by celebrating myriad forms of Black food culture.

Notes

I am grateful to many friends, family, and colleagues who have given comments or advice that have improved this chapter. I thank Ashanté Reese for co-conceiving this volume and collaborating on two American Anthropological Association (AAA) panels together. I thank Psyche Williams-Forson for comments at our AAA 2018 panel, as well as the audience at the 2017 and 2018 AAA meetings, and the 2018 Association for the Study of Food and Society (ASFS) meeting. In 2016 I gave a talk at UC Irvine on an earlier iteration of this work where audience feedback was essential in refining my thinking. I thank my sister, Sara Garth, for the transcription assistance and childcare that allowed me to work on this chapter. Comments from Lee Cabatingan and Mrinalini Tankha were invaluable to me in improving this piece.

1. These are pseudonyms, as is the name "Bettering Life." This project was approved by the Institutional Review Board (IRB) at UCLA with permission to allow some participants to be anonymous and some participants to be named. Participants whose real names and organizations are used here have a high public profile and are likely to be identifiable because of the nature of their work and their role. Those participants gave permission to use their real names and the names of their organizations.

2. In a somewhat similar fashion, Fernando Ortiz, a Cuban anthropologist who wrote about twentieth-century Cuban society, used the making of a stew—*ajiaco*—as a metaphor for Cuban culture as an ongoing process of hybrid identity production ([1947] 1995; see also Garth 2013). Ortiz details forms of colonial-era mestizaje, mixing elements of African, Spanish, Amerindian, Chinese, and others as the foundation of Cuban *postcolonial* identity and the basis of its cuisine.

3. Laurence Ralph's *Renegade Dreams* (2014) includes a discussion of the ways that older generations of gang members reminisce about the good old days of the gang when it had far more of a community-building, political role. Some members of CSU reflect on the height of the Black Panther Party as an important organization for community building and community pride in similar ways.

4. I use the word *uprising* to refer to what is commonly called the Los Angeles riots as a way of destabilizing the racialized narrative power of many media sources. Shana Redmond and Damien Sojoyner (2015) describe the importance of using antiracist language to describe Black protest.

Bibliography

Alkon, Alison, and Theresa Mares. 2012. "Food Sovereignty in US Food Movements: Radical Visions and Neoliberal Constraints." *Agriculture and Human Values* 29 (3): 347–59.

Allen, Jafari S., and Ryan C. Jobson. 2016. "The Decolonizing Generation: (Race and) Theory in Anthropology since the Eighties." *Current Anthropology* 57 (2): 129–48.

Alwitt, Linda F., and Thomas D. Donley. 1997. "Retail Stores in Poor Urban Neighborhoods." *Journal of Consumer Affairs* 31 (1): 139–64.

Bettencourt, B. Ann. 1996. "Grassroots Organizations: Recurrent Themes and Research Approaches." *Journal of Social Issues* 52 (1): 207–20.

Biltekoff, Charlotte. 2013. *Eating Right in America: The Cultural Politics of Food and Health*. Durham, N.C.: Duke University Press.

Bonilla-Silva, Eduardo. 2017. *Racism without Racists: Color-Blind Racism and the Persistence of Racial Inequality in America*. 5th ed. New York: Rowman & Littlefield.

Broad, Garrett. 2015. *More than Just Food: Food Justice and Community Change*. Berkeley: University of California Press.

Community Services Unlimited. 2004. *ACTION Food Assessment Report: Active Community to Improve Our Nutrition*. http://csuinc.org.

Cox, Aimee Meredith. 2015. *Shapeshifters: Black Girls and the Choreography of Citizenship*. Durham, N.C.: Duke University Press.

Dannefer, Rachel, Donya A. Williams, Sabrina Baronberg, and Lynn Silver. 2012. "Healthy Bodegas: Increasing and Promoting Healthy Foods at Corner Stores in New York City." *American Journal of Public Health* 102 (10): e27–31.

Ferguson, Gillian. 2016. "All Los Angeles Farmers Markets Will Now Accept Food Stamps." *Los Angeles Times,* May 19.

Garth, Hanna. 2013. "Cooking *Cubanidad*: Food Importation and Cuban Identity in Santiago de Cuba." In *Food and Identity in the Caribbean,* edited by Hanna Garth, 95–106. New York: Bloomsbury Academic.

Gittelsohn, Joel, Sonali Suratkar, Hee-Jung Song, Suzanne Sacher, Radha Rajan, Irit R. Rasooly, Erin Bednarek, Sangita Sharma, and Jean A. Anliker. 2010. "Process Evaluation of Baltimore Healthy Stores: A Pilot Health Intervention Program with Supermarkets and Corner Stores in Baltimore City." *Health Promotion Practice* 11 (5): 723–32.

Gottlieb, Robert, and Andrew Fisher. 1996. "Community Food Security and Environmental Justice: Searching for a Common Discourse." *Agriculture and Human Values* 13 (3): 23–32.

Gottlieb, Robert, and Anupama Joshi. 2010. *Food Justice*. Cambridge, Mass.: MIT Press.

Guthman, Julie. 2004. *Agrarian Dreams: The Paradox of Organic Farming in California*. Berkeley: University of California Press.

Guthman, Julie. 2008. "'If They Only Knew': Color Blindness and Universalism in California Alternative Food Institutions." *Professional Geographer* 60 (3): 387–97.

Hage, Ghassan. 2012. "Critical Anthropological Thought and the Radical Political Imaginary Today." *Critique of Anthropology* 32 (2): 285–308.

Hill, Jane 1998. "Language, Race, and White Public Space." *American Anthropologist* 100 (3): 680–89.

Jones, Naya. 2018. "'It Tastes Like Heaven': Critical and Embodied Food Pedagogy with Black Youth in the Anthropocene." *Policy Futures in Education* 17 (7): 905–23.

Los Angeles Food Policy Council (LAFPC). 2010. *The Good Food for All Agenda: Creating a New Regional Food System for Los Angeles.* https://goodfoodlosangeles.files.wordpress.com.

McClintock, Nathan. 2011. "From Industrial Garden to Food Desert: Demarcated Devaluation in the Flatlands of Oakland, California." In *Cultivating Food Justice: Race, Class, and Sustainability,* edited by Alison Hope Alkon and Julian Agyeman, 89–120. Cambridge, Mass.: MIT Press.

M'charek, Amade. 2013. "Beyond Fact or Fiction: On the Materiality of Race in Practice." *Cultural Anthropology* 28 (3): 420–42.

McKittrick, Katherine. 2006. *Demonic Grounds: Black Women and the Cartographies of Struggle.* Minneapolis: University of Minnesota Press.

Nettles-Barcelón, Kimberly D., Gillian Clark, Courtney Thorsson, Jessica Kenyatta Walker, and Psyche Williams-Forson. 2015. "Black Women's Food Work as Critical Space." *Gastronomica* 15 (4): 34–49.

Ortiz, Fernando. (1947) 1995. *Cuban Counterpoint: Tobacco and Sugar.* Translated by Harriet de Onis. Durham, N.C.: Duke University Press.

Page, Helán E. 1997. "'Black Male' Imagery and Media Containment of African American Men." *American Anthropologist,* n.s. 99 (1): 99–111. doi:10.1525/aa.1997.99.1.99.

Pierre, Jemima. 2004. "Black Immigrants in the United States and the 'Cultural Narratives' of Ethnicity." *Identities* 11 (2): 141–70.

Poulsen, Melissa N., Kristyna R. S. Hulland, Carolyn A. Gulas, Hieu Pham, Sarah L. Dalglish, Rebecca K. Wilkinson, and Peter J. Winch. 2014. "Growing an Urban Oasis: A Qualitative Study of the Perceived Benefits of Community Gardening in Baltimore, Maryland." *Culture, Agriculture, Food and Environment* 36 (2): 69–82.

Ralph, Laurence. 2014. *Renegade Dreams: Living through Injury in Gangland Chicago.* Chicago: University of Chicago Press.

Redmond, Shana L., and Damien Sojoyner. 2015. "Keywords in Black Protest: A(n Anti-) Vocabulary." Truth Out, May 29. http://www.truth out.org.

Rouse, Carolyn, and Janet Hoskins. 2000. "Purity, Soul Food, and Sunni Islam: Explorations at the Intersection of Consumption and Resistance." *Cultural Anthropology* 19 (2): 226–49.

Sexton, Jared. 2010. "People-of-Color-Blindness: Notes on the Afterlife of Slavery." *Social Text* 28 (2 (103)): 31–56.

Sharpe, Christina. 2016. *In the Wake: On Blackness and Being.* Durham, N.C.: Duke University Press.

Smith, Dakota. 2018. "Street Vending Advocates Protest in Downtown L.A." *Los Angeles Times,* March 9.

Sojoyner, Damien. 2016. *First Strike: Educational Enclosures in Black Los Angeles.* Minneapolis: University of Minnesota Press.

Sojoyner, Damien. 2017. "Another Life Is Possible: Black Fugitivity and Enclosed Places." *Cultural Anthropology* 32 (4): 514–36.

Twitty, Michael W. 2017. *The Cooking Gene: A Journey through African American Culinary History in the Old South.* New York: Amistad/ HarperCollins.

Wallach, Jennifer Jensen. 2015. *Dethroning the Deceitful Pork Chop: Rethinking African American Foodways from Slavery to Obama.* Fayetteville: University of Alabama Press.

Williams-Forson, Psyche. 2006. *Building Houses out of Chicken Legs: Black Women, Food, & Power.* Chapel Hill: University of North Carolina Press.

Yesko, Parker. 2017. "Los Angeles Moves Closer to Legalizing Sidewalk Food Vendors." NPR, Morning Edition, June 26. https://www.npr .org.

5

GOOD FOOD IN A RACIST SYSTEM

Competing Moral Economies in Detroit

Andrew Newman and Yuson Jung

• • •

In recent years, Detroit has become well known as a place where postindustrial urban changes, racist patterns of urbanism, and a long tradition of Black politics have combined to give rise to well-developed movements centered around food justice and food sovereignty. This movement, and the role played by its Black activist founders and leaders, has been well documented (e.g. Pothukuchi 2011; White 2011; White's chapter in this volume).

Starting in the 1990s and continuing into the following decade, a Black-led alliance of growers and food justice activists fostered a food justice movement that addressed Detroit's specific urban predicament: high rates of vacant land and disinvestment and a general lack of commerce options for residents. The food landscape was then—and largely continues to be—centered around grocery stores that are operated by either regional chains or independent owners, as well as convenience stores, fast food restaurants, and emergency food providers such as pantries and soup kitchens. Though the city is sometimes labeled a "food desert," the Detroiters we spoke with did not lament a lack of food options and availability.[1] Instead of "lack" and "scarcity," the comments focused on the highly uneven quality of stores and of food in those stores as well as a lack of mobility in the sprawling car-centered city, where public transit is sparse and unreliable. Gradually from the 2010s, there was an onset of gentrification and major investment in the urban core, with a flood of upscale restaurants as well as the arrival of Whole Foods Market, which became the first national chain grocery store to open in Detroit in 2013, after nearly a decade of capital flight, followed by two Meijers (a large midwestern super-store chain that competes with Walmart) in outlying parts of the city (Skid 2011; Woods 2013). As such, Detroit's overall food land-scape reflects the broader patterns of economic polarization asso-ciated with gentrifying cities.

In this chapter, we focus on the moral meanings that activ-ists and Detroiters assign to the buying and selling of food in this environment. Scholars (e.g., Kneasfy et al. 2008; Holt-Giménez 2009; Gottlieb and Joshi 2010; Alkon and Agyeman 2011; Guth-man 2011) have rightly pointed out that movements organized around food justice are important not only because of their efforts at survival, resistance, and reimagining the food system but because of the larger structural and systematic issues they reveal. We look beyond the food justice movement as it is typically formulated and examine how individuals within these movements are con-testing and reworking the moral meaning of economic exchange itself, especially within Black communities. Just as importantly, we also look at the moral and political meanings of food provision-ing among individual shoppers who have no affiliation with food justice organizations in Detroit. Therefore, we look at the compet-ing, and at times contradictory, ways that the "transactional poli-tics" of food emerge in the everyday life experiences of shoppers while paying attention to the critiques within the food justice move-ment itself. The ethnographic data used in this chapter is from our fieldwork in Detroit from 2012 to 2016 regarding food politics in the city, especially in light of the critical events of major chain grocery stores (Whole Foods Market, Meijer) returning to the city.[2]

Our use of the term *transactional politics* is meant to highlight an aspect of E. P. Thompson's (1971) moral economy concept that is particularly salient for the literature on race and food security in the United States. This literature tends to link social inequality and structural racism in the food system with lack of access to healthy and fresh foods (e.g., Markowitz 2010; Walker, Keane, and Burke 2010; for a more critical view, see Guthman 2008). After considering the experiences of our ethnographic interlocutors in light of Thompson's writings, we realized the often-deployed framework of "access" seemed off-kilter with the way many people who supposedly lack access perceive their own experiences. To boil politics down to raw access to things (often broadly labeled as "healthy food") is to ignore many of the other meaning-laden aspects of food provisioning in daily life, including the appearance of stores, the appearance of the food itself, the prices at which it is sold relative to appearance, and other attributes that make shopping a profoundly political and moral experience.

The moral economy concept has been embraced by many anthropologists who typically utilize the metaphor literally: in other words, the *circulation* and *exchange* of moral meanings throughout a community, and one in which moral legitimacy can be accumulated, lost, and is unevenly distributed (e.g., Lock 2002; Quintero 2002; Edelman 2005, 2012; Trentmann 2008; Griffith 2009; Hickel 2014; Palomera and Vetta 2016). This, however, is not the usage intended by the originator of the concept, E. P. Thompson (1971). For Thompson, the moral economy had a very focused and nonmetaphorical meaning. It emerged specifically in a context where artificial food shortages led to violent protest among eighteenth-century English rural denizens and townspeople who were collectively scandalized when farmers of the time chose to export, speculate upon, and hoard crops instead of adhering to the custom of bringing goods to the market each season.

For Thompson, the moral economy was fundamentally about food, and it pertained to appeals to a generalized sense of human decency that was rooted in specific customs when issues of community survival were at stake. The key ideas here are his focus on "community survival" and the shared sense of "human decency" rather than the moral (or ethical) dimension of individual choices. This is an important focus to remember because much of the debate on food access, especially in economically depressed urban areas, reveals the tension between "individual agency" and "structural racism" in proposing an alternative. The moral economy framework works particularly well in this context for two reasons. First, it exposes the inherent racism in the supposedly neutral economy. Second, in proposing an alternative to the existing system, the moral economy framework places the ties to a community and a shared sense of human decency in place of the purely market-based rationalities that are commonly evoked.

In Thompson's usage, the moral economy referred to shared norms and customs dictating how much food *ought to* cost, how it *ought to* be sold, and how those whose livelihoods depended on the production and sale of food *ought to* behave, given the unique importance of their trade to collective survival. In other words, the moral economy customarily defined a "base" value of food that transcended market fluctuations. Adherence to this moral economy was tantamount. When those rules were violated, often by farmers, bakers, or merchants, for instance, the affront was of a moral nature against the community at large, and such a situation demanded a collective response in which protest and direct action against the violator(s) were justified. Thompson developed this concept as a corrective to the work of dominant historians whose "spasmodic view" of the political agency of the common people recast rebellion as "riot," a term that Thompson famously labeled as a "four-letter word" for social historians (1971, 76).

Thompson's concept has a special purchase to understand the varieties of politics related to food in Detroit, which include—and go beyond—food justice as it is commonly discussed (e.g., Gottlieb and Joshi 2010; Alkon and Agyeman 2011). Detroit is an 80 percent African American city, with a social landscape that has been shaped as much by Black politics and African American affluence as it has been by deindustrialization and disinvestment. As in other American cities shaped first by de facto racial segregation within the city and later by apartheid between city and suburb generated by the white flight, a profound awareness of Detroit's Black community as a self-contained economic unit emerged.[3] This awareness resembles Thompson's moral economy in the way many of our informants talk about food and economic relationships: a layer of moral reasoning underlying food procurement that explicitly transcends a market logic—a logic that is understood as not just brutally indifferent but racist.

As we will illustrate, people talk about moral obligation differently, be it to community, family, one's self, one's body, or even the city. The majority of our interlocuters, however, frame eating well in opposition to buying and eating "junk" and participating in an immoral economy of "junk."[4] Racism frequently enters the analysis as a structural force that prevents access to a "higher quality" food. The immoral racist economy is linked to a combination of exploitation by predatory corporations such as the fast food industry, including restaurants and convenience stores, as well as the strategic economic withdrawal of major chain (full-service) grocery stores, which can be both punitive and a strategy of underdevelopment, thus acting as instruments of power and exclusion.

These understandings of racism in the food system are frequently framed against Detroit's tumultuous history of racial politics and, in particular, the '67 uprising.[5] In this narrative, the flight of capital from the city to the suburbs in the wake of Detroit's '67 uprising is viewed as an intentional act of economic retribution for the rebellion, resulting in the closure of grocery stores, among other forms of disinvestment. The racist food system is understood as an inherently immoral economy, which proffers "junk" while denying access to consumption and "high quality" and "healthy" food. Among many people we spoke with, the emergence of this immoral economy is couched in the history of explicitly racialized antagonism between the predominantly African American city and its majority-white, affluent suburbs that defines the identity of metropolitan Detroit today.

"Stop Confusing Social Enterprise with Social Justice!"

At times, the notion of the food system as a moral economy is invoked in a way that can verge on the nostalgic, to describe both what has been lost or is threatened by neoliberal onslaught and a potential strategy for surviving it.[6] Karen, an African American woman in her sixties, who has been working as an activist and community organizer on health and food issues in Detroit since the 1970s, uses a concept familiar to many on the left, namely the commons, to describe this condition. However, her way of framing is also rooted in the histories of survival in African American communities, and it looks to this history as a way to find solutions to the problems of the present. Karen explained:

> They are the folks who are losing wealth in many ways beyond just materials; they are losing the wealth of the commons, so that they won't benefit in ways that I did as a poor kid growing up in [a segregated southern city]. . . . The commons was the wealth. . . . I think the emergency manager [during Detroit's bankruptcy era in 2013] in many ways represents that disinvestment in the commons . . . right? . . . That's drawn down the resources around neighborhoods and families.

She continued to connect her thoughts of the commons to food.

> When I grew up . . . we always had a relationship with the grocer. . . . My father for example would say: "Go down there and tell him I say . . . 'Give me half a pound of bologna and a loaf of bread and five apples . . . put it on the book'" [laughs]. That was a charge card, you know, they put it on the book [and] when my dad got paid on Friday, he'd stop by and pay it, you know. Living in a poor segregated community . . . you know we had credit at the store, charge . . . we just said "put it on the books," and hell, they'll deliver that shit to your house! They knew my dad was gonna turn that corner on Friday and walk past them to get home—there's no escape or no hiding, there's a bus stop right over there, you know.

In some respects, Karen's invocation of the commons that emerges in the space of a segregation is reminiscent of Stefano Harney and Fred Moten's concept of the undercommons: "life stolen by the enlightenment and then stolen back, where the commons can be a refuge, and the refuge gives commons" (2013, 28). Karen's undercommons can be interpreted as a kind of moral economy in the sense that relates quite directly to Thompson's usage. It represents a shared set of social (and moral) obligations deriving from a close-knit relationship between—in this case—grocery stores and communities. Informal systems of credit with the grocery stores within

African American communities embody this moral economy: there was a collective expectation that grocers *ought to* give food to a family that is short in cash; indeed, the grocers are arguably part of a kinship network: *"They knew my dad was gonna turn that corner on Friday"* (emphasis added). The moral economy arises out of an intimate familiarity between residents and the grocers and is linked itself to the shared economic and social stability (collective survival) of seeing a "dad" always turn the corner on "Friday." It is in this context that Detroit's state-imposed, austerity-oriented "emergency manager" becomes a metonym for decades of immoral economy governed by a raw market logic and corruption. From plant closures to municipal bankruptcy, the deindustrialization and disinvestment in Detroit are viewed as disrupting the stability underlying a dad's ability to "turn that corner on Friday" and the store's ability to provide credit. The neoliberal economic logic violates a shared sense of human decency that lies at the core of this moral economy.

Our discussion with Karen was additionally interesting because she took the often-vaunted members of Detroit's current urban agriculture movement to task, juxtaposing their values with those of the neighborhood where she grew up. In the contemporary moment, she refers to the visible tensions between emergency food providers (e.g., soup kitchens, food banks) and urban agriculture boosters. The existence of these tensions should not be surprising. In the early 2010s, urban farmers basked in the media spotlight with utopian narratives stressing the reinvention of Detroit, while emergency food providers saw themselves as laboring largely in the shadows to alleviate hunger, without benefiting from the media attention and the outpouring of philanthropic support that seemed to accompany it. One such tension includes moral expectations around cost. Here, for example, are the thoughts of Karen, who critiqued urban agriculture, stating that, while economic, it is not specifically tuned to the experience of low-income African American Detroiters.

> I can remember my fight this spring with growers . . . and when I say fight, I just mean direct conversation, OK? We have some

money in our [soup kitchen's] budget. . . . We want to buy healthy produce for our families which is organic, right? What can we buy? We can't pay five dollars for spinach! Five dollars a pound or three dollars a pound! We can't do that! And when you see what a pound of spinach looks like when you cook it, it's like the palm of my hand. Yeah? So what the fuck is this? What are you doing?! Three dollars a pound?! Who's buying this?? Who are you growing for? Even though we had a few dollars, we couldn't take advantage of it [urban agriculture] because we couldn't afford it, so our families have to wait for the GMO-modified shit to come from [an emergency food supplier]. It feels like people default to the economic argument . . . "Well, we gotta make money" . . . and I'm not saying they [urban agriculture] don't, I'm just saying, what is there to say about what your model is, your business model is . . . you know . . . so if it's straight up economic, neoliberal capitalist. . . . And that's what it is! Stop running around trying to claim like this isn't even what you're doing. . . . Stop confusing social enterprise with social justice; they're not the same thing [*bangs the table*]. . . . So we still don't get no spinach. And we argue with people: can somebody grow some collard greens, please? "Well, I can't make any money on collards, not organic collards anyway."

Karen takes "growers" to task for embracing "social entrepreneurship" over "social justice" and, in so doing, allying themselves with the market logic rather than a moral one. She bemoans the "model" that people now "default." For all the good intentions of "social entrepreneurs," Karen's argument boils down to the fact that if you are charging "three dollars a pound" for spinach or not growing "organic collards," then "Who's buying this? Who you're growing for?" These questions are followed by an outrage ["What the fuck is this?!"] at those who claim to participate in a moral economy that has long sustained African American communities while still adhering to a pure market logic. Karen's remark about collards, in particular, points to how foodstuffs typically associated with Black foodways are not attractive for the urban growers who adhere to a capitalist logic and target a particular group of consumers.

Last but not least, it should also be noted that Karen does not point out whether the growers she criticizes here are African American or white. There could be some strategic significance to this lack of specificity. Mainstream media representations of urban agriculture in Detroit have disproportionately focused on white newcomers, who have been criticized for not engaging with the Black communities where they grow.[7] At the same time, Karen's own network is primarily made up of African American growers. Her lack of specificity regarding this fault line can be read as a warning that all growers in Detroit, including African Americans with roots in the city, need to be wary of neoliberal ideologies that can allow growers to present commercial enterprise as a form of activism. In other words, given the number of entrepreneurs who seek to capitalize on their local roots, being a longtime Detroiter in itself is not enough: one must actively participate in the moral economy anchored in a shared goal of community survival and a shared sense of human decency in order to be part of the community.

Beyond Access: The Racial Politics of "Quality" Food

Karen's discussion of food access turned social justice critiques of the overall food system inward in Detroit, to take the world of small-scale urban agriculture to task for embracing the ideologies it was supposed to rebel against. Karen's use of access as a framework places her in the discursive domain of scholars, policy advocates, and activists concerned with food security and food justice. Scholars and food justice advocates frequently use the language of "access" to describe the unequal distribution of healthy eating options in society: namely, not all people have the same access to "healthy food."

When we spoke with a broad array of supermarket shoppers in Detroit who do not usually use the class-inflected language of specialists and policy makers, we found a different framework in use. In these discussions, which stressed the meaning of "good food" over access, we repeatedly came across comments that suggested "access" might imply too dichotomous a frame. Over-whelmingly, even when our interlocutors have to travel a long distance to a grocery store, they often perceive themselves as hav-ing "access" to food. But the cause of popular discontent often focuses on the theme of *quality*. Frequently, the idea that merchants would stoop to sell "low quality" food was viewed as an insult and tied to a racist immoral economy. Ironically, the concepts of negativity and "lack" that are most strongly conveyed in "food desert" literature (e.g., Gallagher 2007; Walker, Keane, and Burke 2010) were largely absent in the contexts where we worked.

This perception was particularly visible on a sunny late spring day in 2015 when our research team visited a community center on the east side of the city. We knew the leader, Mr. B., of this group consisting of senior citizens who socialized in the community cen-ter, sometimes taking hobby classes (e.g., knitting, beadworks) together or just hanging out. The group he led also participated in the "senior grocery shopping day" organized by a local grassroots organization, which offers regular bus services to Eastern Market (Detroit's farmers market) and a supermarket in the city for senior citizens without cars. We visited the group for a discussion about food access and their grocery shopping experiences in the city. The group of approximately twelve consisted mostly of African Amer-ican women and included four men, one of whom was white.[8]

When we discussed issues of food quality, the topic of the "manager's special," a sticker one can often see in the local inde-pendently owned supermarkets' meat section, came up. It appeared to be well-known common sense (given the affirmative nodding and knowing smiles that were exchanged in the group) not to buy such specials because of the "obvious practice" of the stores putting such stickers on either expired or near-to-expired food. One woman said, "You know, I even know some stores . . . they soak the meat in vinegar to make it look good, and then pack it for sale." Some people in the group appeared visibly unsettled by that comment and cringed. Two other people added that some stores would disguise the color of the (bad) meat by covering it in paprika. One man interrupted and made everyone quiet by raising his voice: "When you live in an area . . ." He paused for a while and then continued: "I am not trying to be racist, but when you live in a Black neighborhood, this is what you have to look out for. You know, this is what we deal with," he said in a firm tone, adding he could say this from his experience as a meat cutter. There was a brief silence after his comment, but the group continued to talk about their experiences with "bad quality" foodstuffs. At one point, Mr. B. said, with an animated voice, "I once bought a package of beef that said 'miscellaneous beef' because I thought it was funny. I still don't know what it is because it is still in my freezer! . . . No, it is not ground beef . . . but come on . . . how can you even think of putting such a label?" A woman shrugged her shoulders and said she knew all the stores in "this area" were like that. The conversation moved over to the safety of grocery stores in that neighborhood.

In our fieldwork, "quality" was often articulated as a broad moral attribute that connected food and the physical environment of a store. As this group of Detroit seniors emphasized, the frequent practices of the grocers in the independently owned stores in the city fundamentally violated a moral economy in the community. At a pop-up farmers market in a low-income housing development on Detroit's west side in the late summer of 2014, one of us (Andrew) had a conversation with a retired woman, Ms. Lila, who was eager to share her criteria for "quality." She said she was not particularly enamored of US Quality Foods, a grocery store that is very close, and said that quality was extremely important to her with grocery stores. She prefers to go to Kroger, Walmart, or Greenfield Market, each of which are significantly farther away. When Andrew asked her what she meant by "quality," she mentioned two factors: the "look of the store" and specifically "meat." For canned goods, she was not so picky for stores, though with vegetables she was sometimes worried about freshness. Meat, however, was a significant issue and she found the steaks to be tough at the nearby stores (such as US Quality Foods): for her, the condition of meat in a grocery store appeared to be a broader way of evaluating the quality of the store. For this need, she traveled to Greenfield Market or Piquette Meat, or as far as Kroger or Walmart in the suburbs.

Here, as with the example with the group of seniors, the condition of meat was viewed as a basis for broader quality judgment about a store.[9] That judgment—and Ms. Lila's self-identification as a person who knows and cares about quality—was the justification for her traveling quite far out of her way to buy groceries. Ms. Lila's explicit concern with the "look" of the store is interesting too when we consider that her preferred places to shop (Kroger, Walmart) are national chains that have eschewed Detroit itself.[10] In contrast, US Quality Foods, despite its explicit attention to the term, is the store she avoids and is part of a category of independently owned stores and regional chains that are commonly associated with Detroit. These stores vary widely in appearance and do not have the professionally branded emphasis on "immersive experience" and "retail curation" (Garth and Powell 2017) possessed by their larger corporate competitors. For Ms. Lila, the emphasis on manicured feel, along with a tender steak, was an important marker of quality, though in her view, one often had to travel beyond the city limits to find it.

In other cases, concerns surrounding the quality of stores were related to more fundamental needs, such as safety. For example, some of the senior citizens with whom we spoke at the east side community center had experienced being threatened with a weapon and robbed of their groceries. However, the security measures taken to prevent crime could communicate symbolic violence as well, and thus reflect on the quality of a store and, by extension, the food it carries. Two people in the same group found it offensive, for example, that supermarkets in the area were securitized "like prisons" with metal fences. Despite the potential for crime as experienced by friends, the physical appearance of gates and fences seemed to reflect a broader tendency toward violence experienced by Black communities. As with "manager's specials" and spoiled meat being repackaged to appear fresh, being subjected to gates and fences constituted an insult to residents, violating the rules of a moral economy in which merchants treat customers with honor, thereby preserving a shared sense of human decency. Indeed, the discussion of fences and security features, more than the actual threat of crime itself, led the retired meat cutter we quoted earlier to exclaim: "I'm sixty-seven years old and have seen no change! People will just buy what is near them and buy what they can because of hopelessness. It's pitiful." Here, a discussion around "quality stores" went far beyond the issue of food itself; his observation about the "pitiful" state of affairs raises the issue of collective dignity vis-à-vis an immoral food system.

Whether the topic was food itself or the physical environment and aesthetics of grocery stores, our discussions of quality revealed that people's perceptions of food procurement were far more complex than whether one has or does not have "access" to "healthy food" in their neighborhood. The everyday process of procuring food is an extraordinarily meaning-laden and politically loaded endeavor in which the Detroiters with whom we spoke connect everyday evaluations of food quality (i.e., how fresh is this meat?) with broader critiques of structural racism and economic inequality. For these Detroiters, these evaluations are beyond matters of *individual choices* for daily food provisioning. Whether these grocery stores really cleaned their close-to-expired meat in vinegar or covered it in paprika to make it look "fresh," or rather, whether Kroger really has higher quality food than US Quality Foods, is beside the point. The anxieties expressed by our interlocutors reveal the morally "suspect" nature of the food system as it was perceived by residents who believed their interests as distant from those who control the supply and production of food.[11] Through the idiom of "quality," our interlocutors in Detroit expressed how food access issues were not simply about the ability to obtain "healthy food." Rather, they raised the need to restore a moral economy where a shared sense of human decency as well as collective survival was practiced.

Eating Clean

As with "quality," we found that "eating healthy" can carry more complex and political meanings than what is often assumed. Healthy eating is linked to the care of the self, the body, and the overlapping bonds of obligation that structure communities and families. There are instances, however, when the care of the self can be linked directly to the care of the community, particularly when racially marked bodies become a target of political discourse around responsible ("right") or irresponsible ("wrong") eating (e.g., Biltekoff 2013; Guthman 2014; Jung, Klein, and Caldwell 2014). We saw this with Eva, who quickly made a point of talking about how she and her neighbors went to great lengths to eat healthy in a racist system. The fact that so many of our interlocutors were women who articulated healthy eating around care suggests that the links can logically be made between the care of self, the care of children and family, and the care of the broader community, by extension.

Eva worked at a residence center for senior citizens on Detroit's east side. We met her because she helped coordinate bus trips to grocery stores for the residents, and she herself did not have a car. Eva is a self-described gardening enthusiast and a former member of the Nation of Islam (NOI) but did not speak in the idiom favored by Karen and most other food justice activists in Detroit. Although she regularly attended the Black Farmers and Urban Gardeners Conference, she was less trustful of institutions and organizations and in fact declined being recorded for her interview with us. For her, the link between self-care and moral economy was gendered. "Women are interested in collective health and [they are] more inclined to nurture," she argued. As a result, Eva grew her own food out of a spirit of "collective conscience" and linked gardening to a broader social mission tied to "weeding out violence" and "negativity." In her work with seniors, she reached far beyond a typical gardener in Michigan when defining "healthy food."

Eva was particularly interested in foods that cleansed and purified, and "citrus" was her favorite food, but she also favored grapefruit, lemons, carrots, spinach, beet greens, vegetables, and beans. For example, she drank lemon tea every morning as well as a liver cleanser juice she made for herself. She also encouraged the seniors she worked with to eat less meat, and less pork in particular. For Eva, healthy eating was tied to a careful cleansing of the self, which was not just a matter of personal responsibility but part of a collective practice to adhere to living and supporting a healthy community, as her comment on "weeding out violence and negativity" implied. For Eva, a clean self and body were critical for a moral economy. While Eva did not specify the extent to which her approach was influenced by her past involvement with the NOI, these connections between food, self-care, and self-sufficiency have a deep connection with a broader Black nationalist politics (see McCutcheon 2011).

This idea was somewhat echoed by Amina, who described her work as an "interim manager" in a Detroit company. For Amina, "eating clean," as she described it, was avoiding "party stores," a Michigan slang for convenience stores that double as liquor stores. Unless it was "just to pick up a few items," she would not buy the meat or anything like that in those stores. For health reasons, she stated, "we don't really eat pork," and "my kids don't eat red meat" but instead eat "real fish" (i.e., nonfrozen, non-processed; there is a long tradition of fishing along the Detroit River among African American residents who consider fish as heritage food). In opposition to Karen, however, she linked the quality of food to price, arguing, "You get what you pay for." Amina mentioned that the opening of a Whole Foods Market (WFM) in Detroit corresponded to these goals, though she also automatically linked the grocery store with "the people that are moving down here" as opposed to "people in the housing projects down here," drawing a distinction between newcomers and long-time Detroiters in terms of the primary clientele for WFM. She pointed to WFM as an example for where one could buy "clean food." Urban farms could be an option as well, but she insisted there was no guarantee that these urban farms produced "clean food" because "you have to ask," she said, "what's in that land, you know? Pollution?"

Regardless of the source, Amina was unique among our inter-locutors for the degree to which she linked the importance of the moral economy not only to consumption but to her own labor and finesse: skills were required to "eat clean." She maintained: "I've seen people eating vegetables, but it's mush. . . . You just cooked all the nutritional value out. . . . It's totally a different color." Instead, she said "less is more" and advocated a kind of minimalism when it came to eating clean. Even if one bought "quality" ingredients, if one just adhered to the habitual way of cooking vegetables, for instance, to the point that all nutritional values were depleted, one could not really fulfill the moral obligation to one's body. Hence for Amina, there is a different moral economy, based not on relationships between grocers and neighbors/community but on the labor of discerning quality food ("clean food") and preparing it adequately for one's self/body and by extension for one's family. In other words, the moral obligation was to use her skills, both as a discerning shopper and as a knowledgeable cook, to feed herself and her family. Her critique against the habitual way of cooking vegetables until "it's mush" is linked with her ideas of care for her community and collective survival by eating "properly" and using one's skills. Amina's ideas regarding the importance of not only "what" one consumes but "how" one consumes also reveal the more nuanced and complex ways to think about "access" and the moral and political meanings of food.

The Moral Economy of Whole Foods Market in Detroit

Around the same time we interviewed Amina in 2015, we had a chance to sit in on a meeting with an executive of Whole Foods Market, who explained to us that some items, like meat, were indeed more expensive at WFM compared to other supermarkets. But considering the high quality of the product, including the ethical treatment of animals and sustainable farming practices employed (no added hormones, antibiotics, grass-fed, and so on), there simply was no other way—economically speaking—that prices could be lower. According to this executive, however, the provisioning of high-quality meat and, by extension, high-quality food in general, priced as cheap as they could possibly make it for its quality, was not just a business strategy but a moral mission. According to him, the very idea of opening a store in Detroit stemmed from a conversation with the then U.S. secretary of agriculture, Tom Vilsack, about the contrasting rates of morbidity north and south of 8 Mile, the northern border separating the city from its suburbs. He learned that Detroiters had twelve years less of life expectancies compared to the suburbanites. In the executive's telling, Vilsack said, *"There should be a Whole Foods in Detroit"* (emphasis added). It was this missionary approach that subsequently animated the corporate strategy, which WFM later described itself as "going after elitism, racism" in Detroit (Woods 2013). The store in Detroit was branded carefully to align with Detroit along these lines. Not only did the store embrace imagery relating to the city itself, but it sought to embrace food activists in Detroit. It also rolled out a successful outreach program in Detroit churches, coordinated by a nutritionist with a background in community organizing, that led to WFM's offering of well-attended cooking and nutrition education classes. Nicknamed "Learning Kitchen," these classes have been running continuously since 2013 and are attended consistently by Detroiters, including Amina.

Food justice activists, who are not a homogeneous group, however, have had split reactions to the opening of WFM in Detroit. Some have allied themselves with the company's efforts and mission, appearing at public events and participating in the Learning Kitchen as instructors and guest speakers. Others, such as Vincent, an activist who works in urban farming as well as at a soup kitchen, were particularly rankled by the moralism surrounding the company's mission. "If the community itself is not defining what is ethical, then you can talk that smack all day long. . . . You are just imposing your viewpoint on people," he said of WFM's engagement with Detroit, and he critiqued the corporate chain in moral terms for being accountable only to its "investors." Karen, for her part, had in fact negotiated with the company for community benefits such as hiring more Detroiters and providing lower-priced options when the store was being opened. She was thanked by name by then-CEO Walter Robb during his grand opening speech for the store in 2013, though she was conspicuously absent from that particular event and in hindsight felt there had never been the negotiating room the activists and residents had been led to believe. She spoke to one of us (Andrew) about how differently the store felt inside from other grocery stores in Detroit.

> When you go, and it's almost like they [Whole Foods] created this community, and you very much wanna be a part of this

community . . . it's like a social experience. I don't think these mom-and-pop stores or the Spartan [a regional chain with stores in Detroit], they can't compete with that, you know. It's a mind thing, they are masters in making you feel like you are part of it, that somehow you transcended what's right around you and become a part of this bigger, better thing. People want that, they wanna be a part of that . . . "I should go to Whole Foods, I see people prancing around in there."

Ironically, it is quite common to hear the claim that there were grocery stores in Detroit prior to Whole Foods Market opening in 2013. In fact, there were more than seventy full-service grocery stores in Detroit (Hill 2016), although none of them were national-chain grocery stores, which did not exist between 2007, when Farmer Jack's (acquired later by Kroger) closed its last Detroit store, and 2013, when WFM opened. During this time period, many Detroiters who had cars ended up driving to nearby suburbs to shop in national-chain supermarkets, and Walmart buses would come to the city to shuttle people to and from the suburban Walmart stores. In any case, for Karen, few, if any, were so skilled at creating the "aura" of middle-classness as WFM had, through a combination of factors ranging from product selection and customer service on the store floor to lighting and overall aesthetics inside the store. In fact, some of our interlocutors explicitly mentioned how WFM "was a different experience" of grocery shopping, and how they were treated differently there (i.e., they could ask questions about products and receive friendly responses and assistance).[12] This, combined with the fact that the place was always crowded with salaried professionals employed by the nearby hospitals, university, and downtown companies "prancing" in the store, gave the feeling of "community" that Karen described. To some residents, WFM's presence in the city also offered a sense of belonging to the rest of the country and of not being treated as "lesser (second-grade)" citizens compared to other cities and their suburbs.

This missionary approach is disparaged by many, but not all, food justice activists. A chef and food activist who has been a core member of Detroit's Food Policy Council, Mr. J., for example, is a native Detroiter who considers it important to work together with a variety of community partners, including WFM, because sharing "good food" and knowledge about food and cooking is ultimately connected to a collective survival. He bemoans that African foods and foodways are not appreciated and celebrated enough, and he actively participates in community events across the city, including Eastern Market and Wayne State University's farmers market, as well as WFM's Learning Kitchen, to share stories, recipes, and more "healthful" cooking methods of Black foods and foodways.

Similarly, many of the Detroiters who attended the Learning Kitchen classes offered free by WFM did not always dismiss the missionary approach, even though they were far from being uncritical of WFM and its market logic. They often referred to the store by the well-known nickname of "whole paycheck," and there were many who methodically bypassed all the high-priced and branded items in the store, only to buy a handful of bulk items or WFM's generic label items (365 brands), and special items such as almond milk.[13] In many respects, when one looks at the branding of the store, it is as if one is participating in a particular definition of the revitalization of Detroit. In a way, WFM sells its version of a moral economy in Detroit: the opportunity to consume one's way into the revitalization of Detroit while procuring healthy — and higher-quality—food for one's self and family.

Another aspect of the moral economy advocated by Whole Foods is disseminating an authoritative knowledge about "good food." Similar to what Eva and Amina referred to as "clean food," Whole Foods in Detroit took it as a moral mission to show and teach Detroiters what "good food" is, or what good food *ought to* be, and how good food is prepared and cooked, or how good food *ought to* be prepared and cooked. Many participants in these Learning Kitchen classes expressed how having access to this kind of knowledge on "good food" and "healthy eating" is important for the care of their body, family, and community. Often comparing it to the information they got from the TV show *Dr. Oz,* several participants expressed how the information from these classes seemed more credible. This idea was reinforced through community events such as a voluntary diet and cleansing program (like a four-week detox program), or feedback events where food was prepared by WFM to be shared with the participants. After such events, participants shared their experiences with "good food" and "healthy eating" with other participants, which reinforced their skills and knowledge gained from the Learning Kitchen classes. In a way, the Learning Kitchen class participants partake in acquiring a particular cultural capital (Bourdieu 1984) regarding "good food" and healthy eating and learning how to use it within the confines of their economic capital. Furthermore, they are taught that is the "right" thing to do to one's body and family. Needless to say, WFM's marketing of high-quality food also resonates deeply with individual shoppers in Detroit, given their experiences with the independently owned grocery stores' "manager's special."

A grocery store, in this context, is addressing the immoral food provisioning and consumption conditions in Detroit by means of revitalizing the city through its presence. Hence, a "good" grocery store contrasts with party stores, junk food restaurants and stores, *Dr. Oz,* and so on, which relate to the supposedly higher morbidity rate in the city by twelve years compared to the suburbs. In addition, a grocery store contributes in disseminating "legitimate" knowledge on good food and healthy eating beyond the "higher quality" commodities it sells. In this way, grocery stores such as Whole Foods are also competing with food justice activists over controlling the content of what constitutes legitimate and authoritative knowledge of "good food" and "healthy eating."

Conclusion

In considering these ethnographic snapshots, we have sought to expand the political and moral meanings of food provisioning in Detroit beyond the degree to which it is normally discussed. E. P. Thompson developed the concept of moral economy in order to understand how the emergence of capitalist logics of exchange changed the way people in eighteenth-century England thought about how food ought to be bought and sold. Thompson's concept is valuable for expanding our understanding of food politics in the changing economic and urban landscape of twenty-first-century

Detroit. The moral economy concept, however, must be combined with an understanding of race, specifically the "Black economies" and undercommons that develop in the space of the segregated American metropolis. This approach has several implications for the morality and importance of buying, selling, eating, and cooking "good food" in a Black urban context.

First, Karen's interview points to a tension within food movements between social enterprise and social justice. Fundamentally, this rift centers around disagreements over the moral meaning of economic exchange: Can one still participate in the moral economy that has sustained Black communities for generations while adhering to a pure market logic? Will adherence to these purely capitalist logics always reproduce racist forms of inequality? In following a social entrepreneurship line of thinking, is it possible to buy and sell one's way to the betterment of broader communities and not just for the enrichment of the individual bottom-line-minded entrepreneur? As the discourse of food movements creeps into food-related enterprises, and vice-versa, this tension will only become more pronounced and politically significant.

Second, many shoppers who were not affiliated with food justice movements in any formal way nevertheless discussed the meaning of food procurement in ways that resonated with activists' critiques of a racist food system, albeit in a different language. Many people often articulate the importance of "good food" by invoking their relationships with others, particularly when it is caring for children or loved ones. It was often common for our interlocutors to articulate the meanings of "good food" in ways that connect *individual choices* to broader obligations to family as well as the community. The collective stakes that lurk behind taking care of one's self through seeking out "good food" are yet another example of the continuing relevance of W. E. B. Du Bois's famous question: "How does it feel to be a problem?" The racial politics of food transforms food provisioning from something that is about the individual choices of shoppers and instead connects it with the deeply ideological politicization of the Black family and Black body in American media.[14]

Third, if academics, policy makers, and many activists speak the language of "access" regarding food inequality, Detroit residents with whom we spoke used a different language, centering around the more nuanced category of "quality." Quality is a very broad, morally inflected attribute that describes not only food itself but also the store, and in fact connects them. Thus, people often do not view their own predicament in the dichotomous fashion that is implied by the notion of "access," which one either has or does not have. Moreover, the people with whom we spoke did not consider themselves as surrounded by scarcity, namely living in a food desert. In contrast, people bemoaned the excess of "low-quality" food associated with a low-income urban retail environment. The moral meanings associated with exchange therefore centered on the exploitative racism of merchants who knowingly sold "low-quality" food. "High quality" was therefore related to participation in the moral economies that have long sustained Black communities, whereas "low quality" or "junk," often linked to global fast food chains as well as unscrupulous small merchants, was considered part of an assault upon the community.

From a marketing perspective, WFM plays this angle quite effectively. The store aims to present itself as a positive moral agent by providing consumers with "healthy choices" and "high-quality" food while supporting them with free classes on food, cooking, nutrition, and overall well-being. In many respects, the store's marketing strategy resonates with the moral economy of residents who are concerned about "quality" food in the city; it competes with the moral economy of food justice activists who are suspicious of the "pure" market logic. WFM promotes its morality through its "commitment" to bringing "quality" food to the city. In the early 2010s, it argued that even if the prices were higher than at other stores, it viewed itself as never compromising on quality, and thus sought to earn the trust of consumers. It also argued that when it came to basic foodstuffs, its prices were competitive with those at other stores, especially considering the quality of its products. Food justice activists had a range of reactions to this approach. Some allied themselves with this project because of the sentiment that WFM contributes to providing healthy food access and higher-quality food in Detroit. Others are suspicious of an economic agent that is linked to Wall Street and global finance rather than to the moral economy of the community. For its part, WFM, like its proudly libertarian founder and former CEO, John Mackey, seemed to claim that it is possible—and profitable—to do both, though by 2017, Wall Street seemed to think otherwise. After years of declining share prices and a shake-up by investors, the company was bought by Amazon, which has made slashing prices a newly visible priority (see Wingfield and Gelles 2017).

In our focus on the moral meanings of "good food," we have found that the analysis of everyday shoppers is no less political, and they frequently offer a more nuanced picture of how racism in the food system is understood and experienced, as well as the multiple ways that the politics of racial inequality and Black food matters, across the domains of community, city, self/body, and grocery stores. Detroit is a prime example of a setting where food justice activists and scholars have drawn vivid connections between structural racism, social inequality, and unequal access. The impact that the city's history of radical Black politics has had on food provisioning offers an opportunity to engage with E. P. Thompson's original concept of moral economy. For Thompson—as well as our interlocutors—simply trying to obtain food can lead one to demystify the supposedly natural and self-evident rationality underlying the operation of market capitalism. However, in their own ways, many Detroiters take this analysis farther than Thompson: the "invisible hand" is a ruse not merely for economic exploitation but of racial capitalism. In other words, food procurement becomes a site where everyday people analyze and navigate the racial logic of markets in order to survive and thrive. To find and cook "quality" food is about not only confronting racial capitalism but living the good life while trying to overturn it.

Notes

1. "Food desert" has become a popular label to refer to places with difficult food access, especially to fresh produce. While Detroit is sometimes referred to as an emblematic example of a food desert, compelling residents to rely on convenience stores and gas stations for food provisioning, independently owned (although not national-chain grocery stores such as Kroger and Walmart) full-service supermarkets have always existed

in the city. The quality and price of the groceries available in these independently owned stores, however, were a frequently contested topic in regard to food access. See Hill 2017.

2. Research was supported by the Wenner-Gren Foundation. Ethnographic fieldwork was conducted by the authors and two graduate research assistants, Erika Carrillo and Jaroslava Pallas. We did participant observation and semistructured in-depth interviews among food justice activists, Whole Foods Market-Detroit's educational outreach program participants, Whole Foods Market employees, and eastside residents, especially senior residents who participated in a grocery bus service program organized by a local NGO. To protect the privacy of the research participants, we use pseudonyms in this chapter.

3. For classic works on "Black economy" in segregated urban settings, see, for example, Du Bois (1899) 2010; Drake and Cayton 1946; Wilson 2000.

4. "Junk" here is not only confined to the conventional "junk food" such as soda and chips but can include things like unfresh meat/vegetables/fruits.

5. In naming the events of '67, *uprising* and *rebellion* are frequently used by Detroiters but not *riot*. Many people who identify themselves with Detroit would likely agree with E. P. Thompson's (1971) description of *riot* as a four-letter word. The use of terms such as *rebellion* and *uprising* in place of *riot* indexes local belonging in Detroit. In other words, one's sense of attachment to the city in the present is often claimed through narrating this popular historiography. See Redmond and Sojoyner 2015 on using the term *uprising* instead of *riots* when referring to L.A. in 1992.

6. For more on the politics of nostalgia and urban food systems, see Munoz 2017.

7. For descriptions of the tensions between white newcomers engaged in urban agriculture and longtime residents, see Kinder 2016; Campbell et al. 2020.

8. These observations are based on fieldnotes. Those who were present did not self-identify.

9. For more on the importance of meat as a boundary-marking food in Detroit grocery stores, see Alex Hill's survey (2016) of Detroit grocery stores.

10. Walmart has aroused controversy due to its decision to either close stores or not invest in other predominantly Black areas. See, for example, Hiltzick 2016.

11. Michigan's only Black-owned grocery store, which was located in Detroit, closed its doors in 2014.

12. Regarding store aesthetics as retail strategy and impact on shopping experience, see Garth and Powell 2017 for a similar observation.

13. Almond milk was one item that was frequently brought up by our interlocutors who consumed it due to lactose intolerance and health reasons; they could not often find it in the neighborhood stores.

14. We thank Pysche Williams-Forson, our panel discussant at the 2017 meeting of the American Anthropological Association, for providing this insight in her comments.

Bibliography

Alkon, Alison Hope, and Julian Agyeman, eds. 2011. *Cultivating Food Justice: Race, Class, and Sustainability.* Cambridge, Mass.: MIT Press.

Biltekoff, Charlotte. 2013. *Eating Right in America: The Cultural Politics of Food and Health.* Durham, N.C.: Duke University Press.

Bourdieu, Pierre. 1984. *Distinction: A Social Critique of the Judgement of Taste.* Cambridge, Mass.: Harvard University Press.

Campbell, Linda, Andrew Newman, Sara Safranksy, and Tim Stallmann, eds. 2020. *A People's Atlas of Detroit.* Detroit: Wayne State University Press.

Drake, St. Claire, and Horace R. Cayton. 1946. *Black Metropolis: A Study of Negro Life in a Northern City.* Chicago: University of Chicago Press.

Du Bois, W. E. B. (1899) 2010. *The Philadelphia Negro.* New York: Cosimo.

Edelman, Marc. 2005. "Bringing the Moral Economy Back in . . . to the Study of 21st-Century Transnational Peasant Movements." *American Anthropologist* 107 (3): 331–45.

Edelman, Marc. 2012. "E. P. Thompson and Moral Economies." In *A Companion to Moral Anthropology,* edited by Didier Fassin, 49–66. Malden, Mass.: Wiley-Blackwell.

Gallagher, Mari. 2007. *Examining the Impact of Food Deserts on Public Health in Detroit.* Chicago: Mari Gallagher Research & Consulting Group.

Garth, Hanna, and Michael G. Powell. 2017. "Rebranding a South Los Angeles Corner Store: The Unique Logic of Retail Brands." *Journal of Business Anthropology* 6 (2): 176–98.

Gottlieb, Robert, and Anupama Joshi. 2010. *Food Justice.* Cambridge, Mass.: MIT Press.

Griffith, David. 2009. "The Moral Economy of Tobacco." *American Anthropologist* 111 (4): 432–42.

Guthman, Julie. 2008. "Bringing Good Food to Others: Investigating the Subjects of Alternative Food Practices." *Cultural Geographies* 15 (4): 431–47.

Guthman, Julie. 2011. *Weighing In: Obesity, Food Justice, and the Limits of Capitalism.* Berkeley: University of California Press.

Guthman, Julie. 2014. "Introduction: A Special Issue on Dietary Advice and Its Discontents." *Gastronomica* 14 (3): 1–4.

Harney, Stefano, and Fred Moten. 2013. *The Undercommons: Fugitive Planning and Black Study.* New York: Autonomedia.

Hickel, Jason. 2014. "'Xenophobia' in South Africa: Order, Chaos, and the Moral Economy of Witchcraft." *Cultural Anthropology* 29 (1): 103–27.

Hill, Alex B. 2016. "Treat Everybody Right: Multidimensional Foodways in Detroit." Master's thesis, Wayne State University.

Hill, Alex B. 2017. "Critical Inquiry into Detroit's 'Food Desert' Metaphor." *Food and Foodways* 25 (3): 228–46.

Hiltzick, Michael. 2016. "How Walmart 'Absolutely Shafted' Washington, D.C. by Reneging on a Promise." *L.A. Times,* January 22.

Holt-Giménez, Eric. 2009. "From Food Crisis to Food Sovereignty: The Challenge of Social Movements." *Monthly Review* 61 (3): 142–56.

Jung, Yuson, Jakob Klein, and Melissa Caldwell, eds. 2014. *Ethical Eating in the Postsocialist and Socialist World.* Berkeley: University of California Press.

Kinder, Kimberley. 2016. *DIY Detroit: Making Do in a City without Services.* Minneapolis: University of Minnesota Press.

Kneafsy, Moya, et al. 2008. *Reconnecting Consumers, Producers and Food: Exploring Alternatives.* New York: Berg.

Lock, Margaret. 2002 *Twice Dead: Organ Transplants and the Reinvention of Death.* Berkeley: University of California Press

Markowitz, Lisa. 2010. "Expanding Access and Alternatives: Building Farmers' Markets in Low-Income Communities." *Food and Foodways* 18 (1): 66–80.

McCutcheon, Priscilla. 2011. "Community Food Security 'For Us, by Us': The Nation of Islam and the Pan African Orthodox Christian Church." In *Cultivating Food Justice: Race, Class, and Sustainability,* edited by Allison Hope Alkon and Julian Agyeman, 177–96. Cambridge, Mass.: MIT Press.

Munoz, Lorena. 2017. "Selling Nostalgia: The Emotional Labor of Immigrant Latina Food Vendors in Los Angeles." *Food and Foodways* 25 (4): 283–99.

Palomera, Jaime, and Theodora Vetta. 2016. "Moral Economy: Rethinking a Radical Concept." *Anthropological Theory* 16 (4): 413–32.

Pothukuchi, Kameshwari. 2011. "Building Sustainable, Just Food Systems in Detroit." *Sustainability: The Journal of Record* 4 (4): 193–98.

Quintero, Gilbert. 2002. "Nostalgia and Degeneration: The Moral Economy of Drinking in Navajo Society." *Medical Anthropology Quarterly* 16 (1): 3–21.

Redmond, Shana, and Damien Sojoyner. 2015. "Keywords in Black Protest: A(n Anti-) Vocabulary." *Truthout,* May 29. https://truthout.org.

Skid, Nathan. 2011. "Whole Foods Moving into Midtown." *Crain's Detroit Business,* July 27. http://www.crainsdetroit.com.

Thompson, E. P. 1971. "The Moral Economy of the English Crowd in the Eighteenth Century." *Past & Present,* no. 50: 76–136.

Trentmann, Frank. 2008. "Before Fair Trade: Empire, Free Trade and the Moral Economies of Food in the Modern World." In *Food and Globalization: Consumption, Markets and Politics in the Modern World,* edited by Alexander Nützenadel and Frank Trentmann, 253–76. New York: Berg.

Walker, Renee E., Christopher R. Keane, and Jessica G. Burke. 2010. "Disparities and Access to Healthy Food in the United States: A Review of Food Deserts Literature." *Health & Place* 16 (5): 876–84.

White, Monica M. 2011. "D-Town Farm: African American Resistance to Food Insecurity and the Transformation of Detroit." *Environmental Practice* 13 (4): 406–17.

Wilson, Bobby M. 2000. *America's Johannesburg: Industrialization and Racial Transformation in Birmingham.* New York: Rowman & Littlefield.

Wingfield, Nick, and David Gelles. 2017. "Amazon's Play to Rattle Whole Foods Rivals: Cheaper Kale and Avocado." *New York Times,* August 24.

Woods, A. 2013. "Walter Robb, Whole Foods CEO, on Opening Detroit Store: 'We're Going after Elitism, Racism.'" *Huffington Post,* April 30. http://www.huffingtonpost.com.

6

SOUL FOOD GENTRIFICATION

Food, Racial Heritage Tourism, and the Redevelopment of Black Space in Miami

Billy Hall

• • •

Eras of racist public policy and governmental neglect have long brought harm to Miami's historically Black Overtown community. Since its founding in 1896, Overtown has weathered Jim Crow segregation, slum clearance and urban renewal, destructive infrastructure projects, routine police violence, and sustained disinvestment. Today the community faces a new threat as it becomes absorbed into Miami's real estate and tourism-based growth machine. While still in the early phases of what we might call gentrification, Overtown is currently undergoing a capital-intensive cultural rebranding and material makeover. In an effort to lure investors, tourists, and gentrifiers to a neighborhood long stigmatized as poor and dangerous, elite public and private actors are remaking parts of Overtown into an entertainment district thematically based on a curated narrative of Black heritage, with an emphasis on food and dining.[1]

This chapter examines the role of Black-owned restaurants in an urban growth strategy to convert economically distressed sections of Overtown into gentrified spaces for tourism and leisure. I argue that these restaurants are targeted by a local "racial redevelopment machine" (Wilson 2018) as key sites for the marketing of Black heritage and the beginning of a wider aim to transform the function and use of Black residential space. I show how heritage is narrowly constructed around Overtown's so-called hey-days, when it was an entertainment and dining destination during Jim Crow. As part of the commodification of this specific notion of heritage, older restaurants that for decades functioned to nour-ish neighborhood residents and sustain ties between Miami's dis-persed Black community as well as new upscale restaurant concepts are being marketed to people with money as places to experience Overtown's historical and cultural authenticity. The flipside of this approach to constructing Black heritage spaces, however, is an erasure of more recent histories of struggle and the gradual destruction of places, practices, and ways of life that support long-time neighborhood residents and business owners.

The research presented here draws from eight months of field-work conducted between 2014 and 2016 as well as newspaper articles, radio interviews, public documents, and secondary sources. But perhaps more important than the observations and sources I draw upon is the fact that I come to this research as a cis, white, educated man. These labels do not wholly define me, but in a world fractured by the historical injustices of colonialism and racial cap-italism, they are undoubtedly meaningful and profoundly shaped the research process. After decades of community trauma and broken promises from white people representing white institu-tions, many folks in Overtown have a reasonable distrust of out-siders intervening in the "problems" of their community. I should be clear at the outset that this is not a work of ethnography. Developing the trust necessary to share in people's deeper experi-ences, worldviews, fears, and dreams takes time and consistent engagement, and I am admittedly still building toward that. Still, I am grateful to have begun this process with several residents and business owners and have tried to cultivate a shared praxis of responsibility with those who participated in this research. Part of this entails lots of listening and giving up enough control to allow participants to delve into topics more directly relevant to their lives. In this vein, I have taken seriously stories and experi-ences, especially about policing, that were initially outside the purview of my intended research. I am indebted to all the people who gave their time and patience to help me understand some of the more hidden connections between food, race, state power, and gentrification.

"Eating the Other" in Gentrified Black Heritage Tourism Spaces

Research on urban restructuring has increasingly focused on postindustrial growth strategies oriented around leisure and tourism (Chang et al. 1996; Judd and Fainstein 1999; Gotham 2005, 2011; Coakley 2007). As cities compete regionally and globally to attract mobile capital, they often partner with private investors and developers to create new aestheticized spaces for middle-class consumption (Hackworth and Smith 2001), or what Sharon Zukin calls the "24/7 entertainment zone" (2010, 4). Here cities redevelop and rebrand older neighborhoods, promoting their distinct cultural identity to tourists, potential gentrifiers, and new investors. Within this political economic landscape, particularly in the United States, there has been a rise in the transformation of historically Black residential communities into consumptive spaces for cultural heritage and tourism. David Wilson (2018) writes that commodifying the historical value of older Black communities has enabled a "racial redevelopment machine" (a metaphor used to describe the partnership of developers, investors, planners, and government officials) to incorporate neighborhoods formerly viewed as dangerous and economically distressed within a broader urban growth agenda. Examples of this include the redevelopment of Harlem in New York City, U Street and Shaw in D.C., Sweet Auburn in Atlanta, various wards in New Orleans, and blocks of Chicago's South Side (Jackson 2001; Hyra 2006; Boyd 2008; Inwood 2010; Gotham 2011; Wilson 2018).

In cities, cultural heritage tourism relies on not only significant political and economic support but also the curation of an "authentic" narrative of place that can be effectively commodified for tourists seeking experiences beyond suburbia and mainstream culture (Inwood 2010; Zukin 2010). This generally involves preserving and restoring historic buildings (Waitt 2000) and emphasizing symbolic elements, including art, music, entertainment, food, and other cultural forms (Ashworth 1994). However, as Zukin points out, this is generally done not to preserve a way of life for existing residents but to maintain just enough of a veneer of authenticity to simulate "the *experience* of origins" for outsiders (2010, 3). In her work in Chicago's Bronzeville neighborhood, Michelle Boyd makes an important distinction between history, "the remembered record of the past" (2000, 108), and Gregory Ashworth's definition of heritage as "a contemporary commodity purposefully created to satisfy contemporary consumption" (1994, 16). In other words, heritage is not so much an objectively identifiable thing as it is a "constructed discourse strategically deployed for political, economic, or ideological goals" (Di Giovine and Brulotte 2014, 1).

In line with this idea, Athinodoros Chronis (2012) suggests that the commodified reconstruction and representation of heritage is often a scheme to invite tourists to participate in a whitewashed fantasy of the past that elides uncomfortable histories of racism, dispossession, violence, and trauma. Much of the appeal of heritage tourism, and particularly racial heritage tourism, is that it provides a space of mitigated racial tension where tourists can enjoy what bell hooks calls "eating the Other" (hooks 1992). This appeal is provocative because it draws on what hooks identifies as mass culture's declaration and repetition of "the idea that there is pleasure to be found in the acknowledgment and enjoyment of racial difference" (1992, 366). In this way, heritage tourism taps into and satiates middle-class, and often white, desires to derive pleasure and power through the consumption of racial/ethnic culture, providing an intense experience that affirms the tourist as open-minded and adventurous in their pursuit of the exotic (Molz 2007).

Although hooks uses the phrase "eating the Other" to refer more broadly to the consumption of race and ethnicity, its literal usage is particularly relevant for thinking through the strategic use of food in creating zones for Black heritage tourism, especially given the contemporary foodie craze for traditional African American staples like fried chicken, bacon, collard greens, and macaroni and cheese. As Dallen Timothy and Amos Ron note, "Cuisine is, without a doubt, one of the most salient and defining markers of cultural heritage and tourism" (2013, 99). In recent decades, local and regional foodways have been used in identity claims of heritage (see Brulotte and Di Giovine 2014) and deliberatively woven into development strategies to promote tourism (Zukin 1991; Esperdy 2002; Bell 2007). Places are promoted as hospitable "destinations where tourists can buy 'ethnic' foods, buy 'ethnic' goods, and 'experience' ethnic cultures" (Alonso 2007, 165). These schemes are bolstered by neoliberal discourses of multiculturalism that rhetorically promote the celebration of racial and ethnic differences while actually obfuscating and reproducing racial hierarchies and inequality (Lentin and Titley 2011).

Neoliberal approaches to cultural heritage and tourism can harm host communities in a number of ways. As Zukin writes, "The tastes behind . . . new spaces of consumption are powerful because they move longtime residents outside their comfort zone, gradually shifting the places that support their way of life to life supports for a different cultural community" (2010, 4). By attracting more affluent consumers and gentrifiers, new spaces of consumption drive up property values and rents, pricing lower-income residents out of the market. Yet while research has brought important attention to the ways in which longtime residents can be culturally and economically marginalized by postindustrial redevelopment strategies, little has focused on the ways in which they are more forcibly pushed out through the state power of policing. As the neoliberal racial capitalist state seeks to attract whiter and wealthier people to racialized communities, it also works to remove people of color and the poor through processes of "racial banishment" (Roy 2018). Focusing simultaneously on the urban processes that create spaces of nourishment and excitement for white people while displacing Black people and destroying their life-sustaining networks can help us better theorize the racialized (or racist) "entertainment city" and resist gentrification strategies that appear to celebrate Black cultural heritage.

Making a Heritage Tourism Destination in Overtown

Overtown encompasses roughly three-quarters of a square mile just northwest of Miami's downtown district. Dating back to the founding of the City of Miami in 1896, Overtown was originally designated as a labor camp for many of the southern and Caribbean Blacks who built the city's early buildings and infrastructures and worked in its growing number of hotels, factories, and farms. In the ensuing decades and in the face of Jim Crow segregation and violence, Overtown (known then as Colored Town or the Central Negro District) grew into a mixed-income community of up to forty thousand residents and contained hundreds of Black-owned businesses as well as one of Miami's most thriving entertainment districts (Dunn 1997). Its many nightclubs, hotels, and restaurants on the "Little Broadway" strip hosted a constant stream of national celebrities and entertainers, including Billie Holiday, Ella Fitzgerald, Cab Calloway, Bessie Smith, Louie Armstrong, and Muhammad Ali. Despite the presence of this vibrant nightlife, much of Overtown was gripped by deep poverty as a result of public neglect and the exploitative practices of mostly white absentee slumlords (Connolly 2014).

In the postwar era, city officials and influential members of Miami's Black middle class pointed to overcrowded row housing conditions in Overtown as an embarrassing visual threat to the city's image as the "Magic City" and its growing tourism industry (Connolly 2014). By the late 1960s, a collective impulse among Miami's powerful elite to erase the physical vestiges of formal segregation and modernize white supremacy through slum clearance, urban renewal, and the construction of an expressway system had resulted in the displacement of hundreds of businesses and thousands of residents (Rose 1989; Mohl 1993; Dluhy, Revell, and Wong 2002; Connolly 2014).

After the passing of the Florida Community Redevelopment Act in 1969, community leaders worked with city officials to designate Overtown as a redevelopment district and plan its rebuilding. In 1982 a district was officially drawn, combining parts of Overtown with sections of neighboring Park West, and the city authorized the creation of a community redevelopment agency to access public funds and manage projects to address "slum a nd blight." At this time, just two years after the Mariel boatlift brought more than 125,000 Cubans to Miami, the city struggled financially amid rampant corruption, increased crime, and boiling racial and ethnic tensions. While Black communities were being torn apart by urban renewal and disinvestment, Cuban immigrants, especially those who came after Fidel Castro's rise to power, received unprecedented public resources and support. In its first two decades, the Southeast Overtown Park West Community Redevelopment Agency (SEOPW CRA) had minimal resources available for improvement projects in Overtown. Redevelopment was further stymied during the 1980s and early 1990s when the killing of Black residents by white and Latinx police officers—and the subsequent acquittal of these officers in the cases brought to trial—escalated frustrations of an already aggrieved Black community, triggering a series of riots that burned out substantial sections of Overtown and nearby Liberty City (Dunn and Stepick 1992). The heavy media coverage of these events combined with ongoing coverage of crime and drug use in Overtown led to a widespread stigmatizing of the neighborhood as violent, dangerous, and too risky for investment.

At the turn of the century, however, Overtown's economic trajectory began to change as global flows of investment capital spurred a condominium boom and the rapid gentrification of formerly working-class areas in and around downtown Miami. Paralleling changes in the built environment, Miami's tourism industry shifted away from promoting the region's "tropicalized" social and natural environment (Aparicio and Chávez-Silverman 1997) toward an emphasis on its modern, cosmopolitan features, including its expanding skyline, world-class shopping centers, art galleries and murals, museums, performing arts centers, and restored Art Deco architectures (Alonso 2007). As property values in the city skyrocketed, including those in Park West, the CRA's coffer increased, opening new possibilities for reinvesting in Overtown.

Much of the CRA's focus in Overtown concerns the Third Avenue business corridor and a handful of surrounding blocks. Fresh coats of paint, new building construction and rehabilitation, and teams of street cleaners have dramatically enhanced the physical appearance of this area, which stands in stark contrast to nearby blocks replete with older, ill-maintained concrete tenements. The

CRA has helped preserve and renovate several twentieth-century buildings into a cultural arts complex, a performing arts center, a boutique hotel, and museum and gallery spaces. Millions of dollars have been granted for the renovation and construction of soul food and barbecue restaurants, an upscale supper club, and a coffeehouse and wine bar. Some housing and commercial structures have been rehabilitated, parks and facilities revamped, and public services better provided. In addition, a handful of new mid-rise apartments and mixed-use developments have also been completed or are currently under construction. Together these efforts have set the stage for the development of what is tentatively called the Overtown Cultural and Entertainment District.

The vision for tourism in Overtown is outlined in the CRA's redevelopment plan. Among its nine main goals are to

> Preserve Historic Buildings and Cultural Heritage; by incorporating the Cultural Arts as a critical component of Economic Development through public private partnerships . . . [and] Promote and Market the Community as a Cultural and Entertainment Destination rich in history with a distinctive and strong sense of place that is attractive to families and individuals of all backgrounds making the SEOPW area a unique community. (E. L. Waters and Company 2018, 10)

The plan later elaborates on a specific place-marketing strategy.

> Develop a magnet area within the target community for the purposes of: (1) re-establishing a special identity for Culmer-Overtown by focusing on one era in its history, the "Little Broadway" jazz era; (2) to establish interest in the Afro-Caribbean heritage by encouraging tourism, trade and cultural exchanges. The development of the Cultural and Entertainment District will promote these themes to attract night clubs and restaurants; programming special cultural events, designing signs, street furniture and public plaza spaces; and creating promotional literature for tourism and local marketing. (E. L. Waters and Company 2018, 54)

As we can see, the SEOPW CRA redevelopment plan highlights the specific parameters of Overtown's history that should be marketed as heritage, in this case the "Little Broadway" era, which roughly occurred between the 1930s and the early 1960s. This has been a cornerstone of the plan and has remained largely unchanged since it was initially created in the early 1980s. What makes this notion of heritage complicated though is the lack of continuity between Overtown's present and past communities. The mass displacement caused by urban renewal and highway construction, the out-migration of more affluent residents, and the ongoing influx of poorer Latin American and Caribbean immigrants has dramatically reshaped the community's social ties. The vast majority of present-day Overtown residents did not experience Overtown's early history, and few have relatives who did. Thus, while former residents (typically among the Black middle and millionaire classes) have championed a vision to establish a heritage identity for Overtown based on its origins, this identity does not reflect the lived experiences and memories of existing residents. Still, this notion of heritage need not be inherently exclusionary if its attendant redevelopment processes protected and supported existing ways of life.

According to the SEOPW CRA redevelopment plan, branding Overtown's heritage is important for developing cultural themes and activities that can generate tourism. In recent years, the CRA has funded building restorations and programming for music performances and art exhibits as well as the preservation of key historic sites. Restaurant development has also been identified as crucial for attracting tourists. In public comments during a Miami-Dade Board of County Commissioners meeting in 2015, CRA chairman Keon Hardemon stated:

> We've invested $1 million in businesses . . . like . . . People's Bar-B-Que, Two Guys, and Groovin' Beans . . . to bring more jobs, to create more of an industry there. These are places that are going to attract people to our community, because you have to ask the question: What reason do *you* have to come to visit Overtown?

The idea here is that food is an untapped cultural resource, which when properly invested in and marketed will bring folks with money and prosperity to the area. At present, Overtown has only a small handful of restaurants, though some are regarded as neighborhood institutions after having served residents for sixty years or more. These restaurants perhaps most seamlessly uphold a sense of continuity between Overtown's present and past, having weathered multiple generations of community struggle while serving meals to both former and current residents. It is these restaurants that have received the largest sums of CRA funding, more than a million dollars in grants each, for business renovation and expansion.

Marketing Overtown's heritage is also intended to solicit new public–private partnerships, especially from restaurateurs. In 2016 the SEOPW CRA issued a press release declaring Overtown the "new foodies destination." The CRA announced that award-winning celebrity chef and restaurateur Marcus Samuelsson and his development group had won a proposal bid to receive a $1 million grant to develop a restaurant concept in the historic Clyde Killens Pool Hall. Clyde Killens was Overtown's chief entertainment promoter during the 1950s and 1960s, booking celebrities for the major hotels and nightclubs on the famous "Little Broadway" strip. Samuelsson, born in Ethiopia and raised in Sweden, is best known for his frequent appearances on food television shows like *Top Chef, Iron Chef,* and *Chopped* as well as his popular restaurants in New York's Harlem neighborhood, such as the famed Red Rooster. In addition, he and his development group have opened a number of restaurants in New York, Chicago, D.C., London, and Bermuda, and throughout Sweden, Norway, and Finland.

In a recent media interview, Samuelsson stated, "I want to do in Overtown what we do in Harlem. . . . I always try to look at projects that are part of an African-American narrative" (Balmaseda 2018). Samuelsson has cleverly carved a niche in the restaurant industry that taps into the promise of multiculturalism, rising interest in public history, and trending foodie-ism around traditional African American cuisine. Although Samuelsson is not African American, because American racial politics "flattens blackness to a single class and way of being" (Canham and Williams 2017, 38), he can more easily use his Black African heritage as a biological credential for innovating and capitalizing on Black American food culture and establishing his businesses in Black neighborhoods in the United States. Samuelsson also draws from local history (Red Rooster is named after a famous Harlem speakeasy) to brand his restaurants and food with cultural authenticity and then uses this legitimacy to market them to a middle-class, multiracial clientele. Samuelsson's invitation to develop a restaurant in the heart of Overtown's cultural district speaks to Zukin's idea that "in modern times, it may not be necessary for a group to *be* authentic; it may be enough to claim to see authenticity in order to control its advantages" (2010, xii). A celebrity chef creating an interpretation of Overtown culture is sufficient so long as it produces the intended results.

To promote this new "foodies destination," CRA publications, T-shirts, and street banners read: "Experience Overtown," followed by "Eat," "Live," "Create," and "Grow." The CRA also recently began to annually fund a $1 million neighborhood police force that coordinates with the Overtown Neighborhood Enhancement Team (NET), an arm of the city government, to handle crimes and nuisances. During a CRA board meeting, Hardemon stated:

> The presence of police officers . . . is important to invite business, to invite development. . . . In order for this community to move forward in a positive way, and for people to feel safe walking our community, and coming there in the evenings to enjoy themselves at fancy restaurants, . . . there has to be the perception of safety. And I think that our boys and women in blue give us that. (City of Miami 2015, 43)

Here Hardemon leans on prevailing social constructions of poverty as "scary and dangerous," a threat to the normative order of public space (Cresswell 1996). His phrasing makes clear that the intended beneficiaries of Overtown's ramped-up policing efforts are those he seeks to invite rather than the existing residents who it is implied must be policed. In the next section, I discuss some of the ways in which tourism in Overtown is beginning to impact business owners and residents.

Exclusion and Erasure

While some business owners have been generously subsidized to renovate and expand their enterprises, others have been excluded from accessing the millions of dollars in redevelopment grant funds doled out each year, or from the benefits of increased tourism. Several owners of grocery stores, the most common brick-and-mortar business in Overtown, expressed concern that, despite their long-standing embeddedness within the community, their future appears uncertain and unsupported by the CRA. "That's what I never got, a loan from the CRA," said Etta Thomas, a grocer and chef who runs one of the last Black-owned groceries in Overtown.[2] "You know what it take . . . to help me," she explained during an interview, "and instead of you helping me, you trying to destroy me."

Thomas moved to Overtown from Mississippi in 1971, shortly after the completion of the I-95/395 expressway system. That year she met her future husband, who worked for a small grocer, and shortly afterward the two decided to open their own store with "just a little cigar box" for a cash register. Despite the devastating impact urban renewal and the highways had on the neighborhood, Thomas describes the early years as the best years: "Overtown was happenin'. They had a lot of businesses owned Black. . . . I enjoyed it because I had a lot of clients . . . coming in, and a lot of people stopping by." But as Overtown spiraled into further economic decline and residents moved out, the Thomases struggled to keep their business in the black. After the opening of two national supermarket chains just outside Overtown's eastern and western boundaries, the Thomases decided to add a bakery and prepared foods section, hoping to increase revenues at a time of dwindling grocery sales. They also looked into opening a small restaurant inside the store but were told by City of Miami officials that the building next door was too close to where their smoke vent would need to be placed. When Etta Thomas asked them, "'Could I have my vent [facing] up?,' they told me if I carry it straight up my building, that it'd be on the expressway. The smoke would be goin' up on the expressway."

Luis Castillo, a Dominican man who has run a meat market and grocery for nearly twenty years, also worries about his long-term prospects in Overtown. When I asked Castillo how he has managed to stay in business over the years, he tells me that, in addition to supplying meat and produce for some of the neighborhood restaurants, he has learned to stock his store with goods specific to the needs and preferences of residents, including various kinds and cuts of meat like oxtail, neckbones, ham hocks, and chitterlings; fresh fruits and vegetables like yucca, lima beans, and collard greens; and other items like made-to-order sandwiches, work shirts, and hair products. Sometimes, Castillo tells me, if a customer is unable to afford a needed good, he will often give it to them, which has earned him the reputation of caring and providing for the Overtown community rather than simply profiting from it.

As we talk further, it becomes apparent that Castillo has also helped facilitate the intergenerational sustainability of cultural food practices by learning to prepare some of his customer's favorite dishes and passing the knowledge on to younger residents. He explained to me:

> In the past five to seven years, we have lost a lot of old people, so . . . we're getting the daughter, the grandkid coming and buying the same item[s] that the grandma usually comes [in to buy]. Some of them will ask me how they will cook some certain things . . . like "How you cook . . . the collard greens, lima beans, uh, the bones. . . . Also, what do they put when they cook oxtail? What do they cook when they cook neckbone?" . . . A lot of them, you know, they young people. They look at the mom or at the grandma, but they never pay attention to it, so now they have to do it. So lately I've been getting a little more involved in how to prepare certain things. . . . Like I said, it's a lot of young kids.

So . . . they haven't passed through them how to cook it. They
seen it, they be eating it for the rest of their life. They wanna
cook it. It's part of the tradition, so they wanna do it.

But while responding to the needs of longtime residents has been
crucial for staying in business, Castillo's future in Overtown grows
increasingly precarious in the midst of neighborhood change. For
one, he does not own the property where his grocery is located
and is at risk of increasing rents or the threat of building demoli-
tion. And like many other businesses in the area, although he has
been established in the community for decades, his store does not
evoke the narrative of heritage deployed to attract tourism and
thus falls outside the CRA's vision for investing in local economic
development. More pressingly, the CRA recently supported the
opening of a regional supermarket chain with a $200,000 grant,
a $400,000 loan, and space inside a newly renovated shopping
plaza located directly across the street from Castillo's market. The
CRA justified its investment in a supermarket on the basis that
it would solve the community's food desert problem, a popular
spatial narrative that often vilifies small groceries on the basis of
selling "junk" food while erasing their historical struggle to compete with corporate food retail.

The experiences of Etta Thomas and Luis Castillo, while not
identical, are similar to other food business owners who cater
specifically to a neighborhood clientele while offering very little
to visitors passing through for a meal or to see a show. Who can
participate in Overtown's redevelopment is a question of access
to the resources and opportunities that heritage tourism affords.
For now, those best positioned to capitalize on this redevelopment vision are those already endowed with property, political
ties, and wealth, such as those restaurant owners receiving the
largest grants or new investors and developers buying up relatively cheap property. Many business owners have anxieties that
monied interests will assume the reins of power in Overtown and
eventually push out lower-resourced small business owners and
residents. Observing the very beginnings of this process, one small
restaurant owner stated, "As far as I'm seeing, the rich folks just

will come and take over Overtown. . . . Very soon none of us won't be here" (Herring 2018).

In addition, many of Overtown's small food business owners are marginalized by a vision of heritage that celebrates Black cultural achievement during Jim Crow while ignoring, silencing, and erasing a more recent history of struggle in the wake of urban renewal, economic decline, and institutional neglect. Because most of the people working and living in Overtown were never alive or present to witness the so-called heydays inspiring local tourism and hospitality development, their histories, lived experiences, notions of community, and claims to place are "rendered ungeographic" (McKittrick 2006, x) by a redevelopment vision ironically predicated on local Black histories.

For some businesses, however, the uptick in tourism has been welcomed for producing higher revenues, and owners and employees are beginning to associate the presence of white people with this benefit. One restaurant's longtime chef explained in an interview with me:

> There was some tough times where it looked like we was gon' be shut down. But Overtown's changed tremendously, especially the people. We have more different groups of people here, like a lot of Spanish [Latinx], a lot of Caucasian people. Now the neighborhood is way better, and we got different ethnic groups that come in here now. 'Cause usually it only be people from our neighborhood, but now it's a lot of tourists. . . . I know people that come from Palm Beach, Boca [Raton], all the way up in Broward [County] that come down just to eat. They pass all them restaurants just to come here.

Similarly, while most restaurants still have a diverse clientele, as one new restaurant owner stated in a January 2018 interview on the *Redevelopment Radio Talk Show,* "most of our success and most of our customers and those who spend the bigger tickets are tourists, people who may have never had a reason to come through Overtown unless they're driving up Third Avenue to get to Wynwood from [Interstate] 95. It's funny, . . . our audience tends to get more Caucasian the later it gets and on the weekends."

As restaurants seek to create dining spaces that will attract tourists, some struggle to navigate conflicting classed and cultural norms. In this same radio interview with members of the CRA, one restaurant owner stated:

> You know, there were people who knew us and had eaten when we were running the park concession but they would not come into the restaurant because they thought, one, we were overpriced. They thought they had to be, you know, completely dressed up. They thought we were too fancy. You know, the rumors had spread that . . . "she don't want nobody wearing hair bonnets in there." And that's true. I said that. And you have to do it with love. But you have to be firm and you have to be courageous and brave because nothing will change if we allow it.

Despite the fact that the owner tries to hire locally, provides customer service and restaurant industry skills to people with few employment prospects, and allows local kids to order more affordable meals not included on the menu, the aesthetic rules of attire she enforces make some residents feel excluded.

Aggressive—and selective—policing and city regulation, particularly around Overtown's commercial strip, is also beginning to render some residents, businesses, and community spaces as out-of-place. Several residents informed me that prior to my fieldwork, the Overtown NET office had shut down a community fish fry that regularly brought more than one hundred residents together to eat. In September 2016, at the City of Miami's Nuisance Abatement Board meeting, the Overtown NET office reported multiple incidences of drug deals outside a Black-owned grocery that has been in operation since the late 1960s. Despite the owner's response that transactions only occur on the public sidewalk in front of her store, the board demanded she allow city police to install security cameras on the inside and outside of her building and provide them with a constant live feed of the store. Police officers also presented a list of people who are banned from the store and have since arrested people for trespassing.

In early 2015, police shot and killed a Black homeless man holding a metal pipe on a street corner of Third Avenue. According to a Middle Eastern grocer I spoke with who has operated his store for nearly thirty years, the incident

> shut down to the whole area, from the street here all the way down. Nobody walking, nobody out. . . . There is no business. And you do stuff like that? Forget it. Your rent is still the same, your electric the same, your employees the same, you don't make enough money, you have to pay your bills. I cannot pay my bills. I barely pay my employees. So, I'm done. Whatever I save is gone.

Said one resident who runs a small barber shop on the corner of Overtown's Third Avenue commercial strip,

> The police is just a gang . . . that's going against the community. That's all it is. . . . Like I even stand outside, smokin' a little Black and Mild or something. They done rolled by and told me to get off the corner not even knowin' that I own the business. [They] tell me, "You need to get off the corner." Most police around here, man, they'll just write you up a charge: trespass, loitering, resisting arrest without violence. They take you to jail. Then if you're like, "Whatever I did wrong, I'm sorry," they be like, "Oh, it ain't my problem. I'm going home and *you* going to jail."

The subjecting of Black bodies and spaces to new modes of discipline, violence, and erasure is reflective of the reinstantiation of the white gaze in a historically Black space (Yancy 2008). For George Yancy, the white gaze is a form of hegemonic power that "function[s] to objectify the Black body as an entity that is to be feared, disciplined, and relegated to those marginalized, imprisoned, and segregated spaces that restrict Black bodies from 'disturbing' the tranquility of white life, white comfort, white embodiment, and white being" (2008, xxx). The neoliberal approach to Black heritage tourism development leaves unchecked the status quo power of the racial state and the market, allowing Blackness to come under control of the white gaze. The power of the white gaze determines which forms of Blackness can be objectified, commodified, and made hypervisible and which must be rendered invisible. In policing Black bodies and spaces to function for white audiences and white lifestyles, they gradually cease the ability to support Black ways of life.

Conclusion

In this chapter, I have examined how Black food culture figures into the calculations of local development authorities aimed at gentrifying core blocks of Miami's poorest neighborhood. I showed how the SEOPW CRA envisions Overtown as a heritage tourist destination constructed as a revived heyday of Black business, entertainment, and dining. At a time of exploding foodie-ism oriented around white, middle-class desires for Black working-class food traditions, the commodification of food culture is at the crux of efforts to lure tourists and gentrifiers to a neighborhood long stigmatized as unsafe and impoverished. As the CRA's executive director put it in a recent interview with the *Miami Herald,* "I'll know we're heading in the right direction when you have very rich people from New York eating fried chicken in Overtown" (Herring 2018).

As part of this redevelopment plan, public resources are leveraged to spur private investment. To establish trust and credibility, the CRA proudly boasts its investments in select neighborhood and Black-owned businesses through various media and in public meetings. Yet even at this pre-gentrification stage, it is clear that these investments mask larger processes of cultural extraction and racial exclusion that are already starting to apportion redevelopment's winners and losers. While development authorities have recognized elements of Overtown's history and culture as an important mark of pride and a lucrative opportunity for Black business, this approach to redevelopment fails to meaningfully address the historical dispossession of land and resources and the deepening of racial and economic inequality that prompted the creation of a CRA in the first place. Not everyone has the ability to harness Overtown's history and culture as an asset for accumulation, particularly if they do not already possess significant capital, have close ties to political officials, or have a business that caters to affluent tourists and gentrifiers. Punishing these residents and entrepreneurs while subsidizing already successful local businesses and outside developers will likely only exacerbate existing social and economic inequalities (Barton and Leonard 2010). Moreover, these practices are working against, and in some cases eliminating, geographies of self-reliance (Reese 2019) that have long served the Overtown community, instead instantiating modes of accumulation predicated on satiating white middle-class desires to "eat the Other."

A more inclusive approach to community rebuilding might consider alternative forms of tourism development as well as alternatives *to* tourism. Regarding the former, as Alan Barton and Sarah Leonard note, "Tourism can serve as a vehicle for sustainable community development by contributing to equity and social justice" (2010, 298). For them, tourism can be used to educate outsiders about the histories of injustice that have beset host communities and to facilitate development projects aimed at reducing inequities. On the latter point, rather than mobilizing state resources to reconfigure Black residential space into an entertainment space whose theme is "Jim Crow nostalgia" (Boyd 2008), development authorities and local residents might co-construct new spatial imaginings for rebuilding focused on the cultural sustainability of existing lifeways. Such spatial imaginings would recognize a more complete account of local histories, experiences, and struggles rather than render them invisible and disconnected from dominant notions of heritage. Investing in and protecting the cultural sustainability of Overtown would also mean abolishing policing practices that reterritorialize space in the interest of developers and instead building and supporting community-led institutions and programs that focus on redressing histories of racism through urban land justice (Safransky 2018) and equitable access to quality housing, financial resources, and food.

Notes

1. I use the word *tourists* to broadly refer to visitors of Overtown whose primary business is consumption.

2. I use pseudonyms for those I interviewed personally.

Bibliography

Alonso, Gastón. 2007. "Selling Miami: Tourism Promotion and Immigrant Neighbourhoods in the Capital of Latin America." In *Tourism, Ethnic Diversity, and the City*, edited by Jan Rath, 164–80. Abingdon, UK: Routledge.

Aparicio, Frances R., and Susana Chávez-Silverman, eds. 1997. *Tropicalizations: Transcultural Representations of Latinidad*. Hanover, N.H.: Dartmouth College Press.

Ashworth, Gregory J. 1994. "From History to Heritage: From Heritage to Identity: In Search of Concepts and Models." In *Building a New Heritage: Tourism, Culture and Identity in the New Europe*, edited by Gregory J. Ashworth and Peter J. Larkham, 13–30. London: Routledge.

Balmaseda, Liz. 2018. "From Harlem to Miami: Chef Marcus Samuelsson Falls for 'the Modern American City.'" *Palm Beach Post,* February 28.

Barton, Alan W., and Sarah J. Leonard. 2010. "Incorporating Social Justice in Tourism Planning: Racial Reconciliation and Sustainable Community Development in the Deep South." *Community Development* 41 (3): 298–322.

Bell, David. 2007. "The Hospitable City: Social Relations in Commercial Spaces." *Progress in Human Geography* 31 (1): 7–22.

Boyd, Michelle. 2000. "Reconstructing Bronzeville: Racial Nostalgia and Neighborhood Redevelopment." *Journal of Urban Affairs* 22 (2): 107–22.

Boyd, Michelle. 2008. *Jim Crow Nostalgia: Reconstructing Race in Bronzeville*. Minneapolis: University of Minnesota Press.

Brulotte, Ronda L., and Michael A. Di Giovine, eds. 2014. *Edible Identities: Food as Cultural Heritage*. Burlington, Vt.: Ashgate.

Canham, Hugo, and Rejane Williams. 2017. "Being Black, Middle Class and the Object of Two Gazes." *Ethnicities* 17 (1): 23–46.

Chang, T. C., Simon Milne, Dale Fallon, and Corinne Pohlmann. 1996. "Urban Heritage Tourism: The Global-Local Nexus." *Annals of Tourism Research* 23 (2): 284–305.

Chronis, Athinodoros. 2012. "Between Place and Story: Gettysburg as Tourism Imaginary." *Annals of Tourism Research* 39 (4): 1797–1816.

City of Miami. 2015. SEOPW Community Redevelopment Agency. Meeting Minutes, December 14. http://egov.ci.miami.fl.us/.

Coakley, Liam. 2007. "'Sea, Sail, Steam and Emigration': The Imagining of a Heritage Tourist Town in the Republic of Ireland." *Geography* 92 (1): 13–24.

Connolly, N. D. B. 2014. *A World More Concrete: Real Estate and the Remaking of Jim Crow South Florida.* Chicago: University of Chicago Press.

Cresswell, Tim. 1996. *In Place / Out of Place: Geography, Ideology, and Transgression.* Minneapolis: University of Minnesota Press.

Di Giovine, Michael A., and Ronda L. Brulotte. 2014. "Introduction: Food and Foodways as Cultural Heritage." In *Edible Identities: Food as Cultural Heritage,* edited by Ronda L. Brulotte and Michael A. Di Giovine, 1–28. Burlington, Vt.: Ashgate.

Dluhy, Milan, Keith Revell, and Sidney Wong. 2002. "Creating a Positive Future for a Minority Community: Transportation and Urban Renewal Politics in Miami." *Journal of Urban Affairs* 24 (1): 75–95.

Dunn, Marvin. 1997. *Black Miami in the Twentieth Century.* Gainesville: University Press of Florida.

Dunn, Marvin, and Alex Stepick III. 1992. "Blacks in Miami." In *Miami Now! Immigration, Ethnicity, and Social Change,* edited by Guillermo J. Grenier and Alex Stepick III, 41–56. Gainesville: University Press of Florida.

E. L. Waters and Company. 2018. "2018 Redevelopment Plan Update." Southeast Overtown / Park West Community Redevelopment Agency. http://www.miamicra.com.

Esperdy, Gabrielle. 2002. "Edible Urbanism." *Architectural Design* 72: 44–50.

Gotham, Kevin Fox. 2005. "Tourism Gentrification: The Case of New Orleans' Vieux Carre (French Quarter)." *Urban Studies* 42 (7): 1099–1121.

Gotham, Kevin Fox. 2011. "Reconstructing the Big Easy: Racial Heritage Tourism in New Orleans." *Journal of Policy Research in Tourism, Leisure and Events* 3 (2): 109–20.

Hackworth, Jason, and Neil Smith. 2001. "The Changing State of Gentrification." *Tijdschrift voor economische en sociale geografie* 92 (4): 464–77.

Herring, Chloe. 2018. "His Restaurant Helped Renew Harlem. Will His New One Do the Same for Overtown?" *Miami Herald,* February 20.

hooks, bell. 1992. *Black Looks: Race and Representation.* Boston: South End.

Hyra, Derek S. 2006. "Racial Uplift? Intra-racial Class Conflict and the Economic Revitalization of Harlem and Bronzeville." *City and Community* 5 (1): 71–92.

Inwood, Joshua F. J. 2010. "Sweet Auburn: Constructing Atlanta's Auburn Avenue as a Heritage Tourist Destination." *Urban Geography* 31 (5): 573–94.

Jackson, John L., Jr. 2001. *Harlem World: Doing Race and Class in Contemporary Black America.* Chicago: University of Chicago Press.

Judd, Dennis R., and Susan S. Fainstein, eds. 1999. *The Tourist City.* New Haven, Conn.: Yale University Press.

Lentin, Alana, and Gavan Titley. 2011. *The Crises of Multiculturalism: Racism in a Neoliberal Age.* London: Zed Books.

McKittrick, Katherine. 2006. *Demonic Grounds: Black Women and the Cartographies of Struggle.* Minneapolis: University of Minnesota Press.

Mohl, Raymond A. 1993. "Race and Space in the Modern City: Interstate-95 and the Black Community in Miami." In *Urban Policy in Twentieth-Century America,* edited by Arnold Richard Hirsch and Raymond A. Mohl, 100–158. New Brunswick, N.J.: Rutgers University Press.

Molz, Jennie Germann. 2007. "Eating Difference: The Cosmopolitan Mobilities of Culinary Tourism." *Space and Culture* 10 (1): 77–93.

Reese, Ashanté. 2019. *Black Food Geographies: Race, Self-Reliance, and Food Access in Washington, D.C.* Chapel Hill: University of North Carolina Press.

Rose, Harold M. 1989. "Blacks and Cubans in Metropolitan Miami's Changing Economy." *Urban Geography* 10: 464–86.

Roy, Ananya. 2018. "Racial Banishment: A Postcolonial Critique of the Urban Condition in America." Presentation at (anti)Blackness in the American Metropolis, Baltimore, Md., November 2–3.

Safransky, Sara. 2018. "Land Justice as Historical Diagnostic: Thinking with Detroit." *Annals of the American Association of Geographers* 108 (2): 499–512.

Timothy, Dallen J., and Amos S. Ron. 2013. "Understanding Heritage Cuisines and Tourism: Identity, Image, Authenticity, and Change." *Journal of Heritage Tourism* 8 (2–3): 99–104.

Waitt, Gordon. 2000. "Consuming Heritage: Perceived Historical Authenticity." *Annals of Tourism Research* 27 (4): 835–62.

Wilson, David. 2018. *Chicago's Redevelopment Machine and Blues Clubs.* New York: Palgrave Macmillan.

Yancy, George. 2008. *Black Bodies, White Gazes: The Continuing Significance of Race*. Lanham, Md.: Rowman & Littlefield.

Zukin, Sharon. 1991. *Landscapes of Power: From Detroit to Disney World*. Berkeley: University of California Press.

Zukin, Sharon. 2010. *Naked City: The Death and Life of Authentic Urban Places*. New York: Oxford University Press.

7

"PRESERVE AND ADD FLAVOR"

Barbecue as Resistance in Memphis

Kimberly Kasper

• • •

"Where there's smoke, there's fire, but you got to remember one
thing. If you got a lot of smoke, the blaze ain't just gone raise
up and consume anything." Gill Erby paused. "You see, that
fire is just like life. Things blaze up, but they can't take hold
if you don't give them air. Smoke signals go up in your life . . .
sure, you got a problem. But, guess what? Smoke can't consume
nothing. It don't burn nothing. . . . From the work with the
barbecue, you know more about what else smoke can do?" The
boy thought about what his father could be asking. Finally, the
message came through. "Preserve and add flavor." A full and
tired, but proud, old man looked at his only son in the moon-
light. . . . "You gone have problems, but smoke don't consume
nothing. It just shows you the heat and that something's going
on in your life. Our fire ain't gone blaze up tonight, too much
smoke."

—Dwight Fryer, *The Legend of Quito Road*

Dwight Fryer, an African American resident of western Tennessee,
exemplifies the intersections between the historicity, materiality,
and cultural symbolism of barbecue in his historical novel *The Legend of Quito Road*. Fryer's family has lived in western Tennessee
for more than 175 years, since his great-great-grandmother, Jane
Dickins, was enslaved on the Fanny Dickins plantation in Fayette

County in western Tennessee. His familial legacy has helped shape African American lifeways, particularly those tied to foodways, in this region and beyond. As highlighted in the above narrative from Fryer's novel, which is based on his own life and experiences, African American barbecue culture (and the smoke associated with it) serves as an insightful analogy and a window into the past. The passage draws attention to the shaping of ancestral ideologies and practices of cultural cohesion in overcoming hardship, obstacles, oppression, and white supremacy in everyday life. It is within these dynamic cultural intersections that we can come to recognize and understand the role of barbecue and how it can "preserve and add flavor" from the past to the present in racialized foodscapes.

Memphis, which is the urban hub of this traditional agriculturally based landscape in western Tennessee, is one of the hungriest and most obese cities in the United States. In the last several years, community stakeholders have been working toward solving these pressing food-based inequalities by reviving a local food system that bolsters small-scale farmers and increases low-income access to associated agricultural products (vegetables, fruits, and meat). However, in this chocolate city with a 64 percent African American population (Memphis is considered a chocolate city due to its majority African American population and/or leadership), these initiatives often overlook the historically centered cultural practices and persistence from slavery onward and how they influence the present landscape. This historical knowledge gap often stalls or halts the efficacy of community solutions that seek to (re)shape this vibrant but turbulent, racialized foodscape.

Through a community-based project, I attempt to rectify that fissure in the knowledge base through intentionally engaging the historical and contemporary spheres via historical ethnography that blends oral histories, written records, and material culture (Beaudry 1988; Wilkie 2000, 2003; Singleton 2009; Battle-Baptiste 2011; Weik 2012; Moyer 2015). Through the lens of Black geographies, intersectionality, and cultural memory (Crenshaw 1991; McKittrick and Woods 2007; McKittrick 2011; Araujo 2014; Hancock 2016; Hill Collins and Bilge 2016; Sharpe 2016), I deconstruct the role of barbecue and the complexity of race, place, and community from slavery to the contemporary. In alignment with this volume's theme, I seek to demonstrate how and why barbecue matters (Twitty 2017) and is more than just food (Broad 2016). I highlight how generations of African Americans shaped barbecue and maintained their community cohesion and culture but also critically acknowledge its cultural appropriation. With this integrative framework, we, more specifically food justice stakeholders, can use barbecue's historicity, materialities, and symbolism to gain a deeper understanding of it as a tool of cultural, economic, and political unity and resistance in the region. Fundamentally, the story of barbecue within African American communities can help empower and bolster more intersectional food-based solutions within the social justice landscape.

Background

Since my arrival in Memphis in 2011 (coming from the slow food "Happy Valley" of western Massachusetts), I have been exposed to and engaged with a variety of farmers and ranchers. I even purchased a half hog from a local pig farmer in Stanton, Tennessee, who was a descendant of a nineteenth-century enslaver and fellow anthropologist, to learn more about barbecue via pork processing and cooking preparation. In the half-hog experience, I have to admit I made a major blunder while bringing out raw baby back ribs one day on a motorboat excursion up the Mighty Mississippi River. I just thought that we would slather the local barbecue sauce that I brought with me that day. NO WAY! My friends laughed in unison as I told them that my engineer-oriented father, who I consider to be a grill master of steaks and burgers, always cooked them that way. My friends labeled him a "Yankee Rib Cooker" due to a lack of meat prep and the ubiquitous lathering of over-the-counter Kraft barbecue sauce immediately before and after cooking his raw ribs on the grill. At this juncture, I humbly learned the difference between grilling and barbecuing. Barbecuing involves a slow, circumvented unit of hot air with the lid closed (typically for long periods of time), while grilling is done with the lid up and the heat source directly on the bottom of the food item instead of all around the source.

Needless to say, in these last few years, I learned that food in the South is not just a way that individuals feed themselves. It is often *who* you are. (Southern) food cultures are so heavily embedded in identities, whether they are tied to their regional, racial, gender, or sexual identity (Fischler 1988). And as Zora Neale Hurston describes, they are an explanation of why you eat and how that changes over time with improvisation (Opie 2015). It was within those intersections that I sought to better understand the role of barbecue in creating the spatial, racial, and cultural geographies of the chocolate city of Memphis (Hunter and Robinson 2018, 5).

To explore the intersections between the plantation landscape of slavery and our contemporary foodscapes, Rhodes College students, staff, and faculty and community partners have initiated the Southern Food Heritage and Equity Project. Our investigation is one of the first in the United States that integrates archaeological, historical, and ethnographic data from rural and urban regions to create material and symbolic connections between past and present foodways. Within this project, stakeholders from academic, nonprofit, and public arenas are engaging in a three-pronged research, teaching, and community-based project that uses the following: (1) historical data gathered from Memphis and western Tennessee, specifically from Fayette, Hardeman, and Shelby Counties; (2) archaeological data excavated from households of enslaved African Americans from a nineteenth-century plantation, Ames Plantation, in western Tennessee during the 2012–18 Rhodes Archaeological Field School; and (3) ethnographic data collected from the Overton Park Community Farmers Market (which my students and I initiated at Rhodes; I am also the faculty market manager), other regional farmers markets, and additional local food entities (such as barbecue restaurants and the Memphis in May Barbecue Fest).

The foodways of the southern United States are overwhelmingly saturated with historical themes with tendrils of interconnected practices and symbolism. Within many southern cities, like

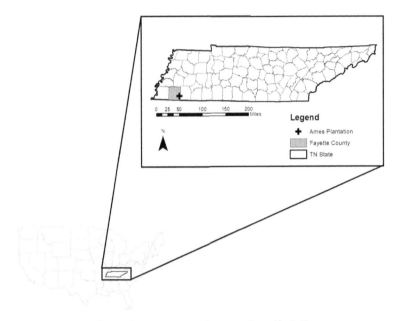

Figure 7.1. Location of Ames Plantation in western Tennessee. Created by C. Norton.

Atlanta and Memphis, certain cuisines blend different food practices of Native Americans, Africans, and settlers to create a spectrum of soul food, different varieties of barbecue, and even the more contemporary emergence of veganism. I had always been entranced with the plant-oriented practices of past societies and focused the vast majority of my research, teachings, and personal life around exploring and understanding how past humans used plants for both medicine and food. Thus, upon arriving in Memphis, I threw myself into conducting historical research (census records, overseer accounts, diaries of enslaved African Americans) and also excavating historical landscapes of enslaved African Americans (which I had focused on during my undergraduate years majoring in history and anthropology in New York City) to trace the origins of southern food. Through several field schools, we started the excavation of enslaved African American houses to better understand food access, cultural survivance, and the origins of food inequality in our region from the historical past to the present. At Ames Plantation, we also participated in an annual community-based event, the Heritage Festival, that highlighted more than 150 folk artists, community partners, reenactors, and musicians and which included demonstrations about stencil painting, quilt making, blacksmithing, tobacco farming, and the barbecue of a whole hog. We also ran a "mock" archaeological dig tied to a nineteenth-century plantation and discussed with attendees how the foodways of the past plantation landscapes were connected to current food systems.

Alongside those archaeological engagements, I also began to heavily participate as a food justice stakeholder in the "local food scene" in Memphis. I, along with my Rhodes College students, became involved in the local farmers markets, which seemed to be the only spaces that sold and promoted local foodstuffs beyond just the typical industrial commodity crops (soy, corn, wheat, rice, tobacco, and cotton). It is within this space that we were able to actively highlight and promote the historical knowledge tied to our archaeological work while also working side by side with community stakeholders to increase food access in historically Black neighborhoods in Memphis.

In 2012 we initiated a community-based farmers market, the Overton Park Community Farmers Market (OPCFM, originally called the Evergreen Farmers Market), which was housed in two on-campus locations. In 2015 we moved to Overton Park, a more publicly accessible space in the heart of Midtown Memphis. At this time, we also were awarded a USDA Farmers Market Promotion Grant to help run operations, conduct research, and create better access for low-income residents of Memphis. We inherently serve and work for, by, and with low-income individuals and families, which tend to be African American families because they make up 77 percent of the total number of individuals who are considered living below the poverty line (which is 27 percent of the total population of Memphis) (Delevaga 2017). We accomplished that through the implementation of a Supplemental Nutrition Assistance Program / Electronic Benefits Transfer (SNAP/EBT) produce membership with our community partner, Bring It Food Hub, and the Fresh Savings program (a money-doubling program for SNAP/EBT purchases that AARP helps oversee). Since starting the OPCFM in 2015, there has been a 6,672 percent increase in SNAP/EBT and Fresh Savings transactions.

The OPCFM is an opportunity to capitalize on the strengths of several unique community partners to bolster the historical elements of African American traditional cuisine, such as with weekly cooking demonstrations and associated recipes with the Tennessee Nutrition and Consumer Health Program (SNAP-Ed) and the National Program of Expanded Food and Nutrition Education. Alongside our community stakeholders, we held active demonstrations and used traditional African and African American vegetables and fruits grown by our market vendors (e.g., black-eyed peas, varieties of greens, and watermelon) to (re)create traditional recipes. Additionally, our market team worked hard at maintaining at least one pork-based vendor each week out of our more than fifteen vendors to increase access to local meat products. And at our market table where we conducted OPCFM and SNAP/EBT token transactions, we were always open to having more discussions about the region's cuisine as we sold vegetables and fruits (okra, greens, watermelon, different varieties of peas, and many more) grown from our own Rhodes College Heritage Garden. Historically, these items would have been cultivated and eaten from nineteenth- to twentieth-century African American gardens in the region (Yentsch 2009; Bowes 2011; Twitty 2017). Through these participatory platforms at Ames Plantation and the OPCFM, we unearthed the historical underpinnings of the local cuisine (which included barbecue and associated dishes) and used that knowledge to promote comprehensive community responses to local food and health issues.

Theoretical (and Spatial) Framework of Barbecue

The above three-prong historically situated project provides a powerful avenue to promote transformative thinking about the gastronomic heritage of the region while creating a larger network of historical involvement and awareness around race and food. It is through these methodological and theoretical lenses of history, archaeology, and ethnography that we can deconstruct, acknowledge, and understand how to (re)shape our present and future foodscapes. According to M. K. Goodman (2015), foodscapes are "more than food" and often highlight the nature of eating and politics and the vital (re)materializations of food's cultural geographies. It is within these foodscapes that you can observe the intersections of nature and culture and how different cultural groups—in this case African Americans—create, shape, and navigate the terrain.

In recent years, Memphis's foodscape has been labeled one of the barbecue capitals of the world largely due to a barbecue cooking contest that began in 1978 as part of the Memphis in May (MEM) International Festival (Veteto and Maclin 2011; Chamberlin 2016). When it started, only 28 teams participated, but now more than 230 teams from more than 25 states and several foreign countries participate and more than 100,000 people attend the four-day festival. It is considered the world's "Superbowl of Swine" (Memphis in May n.d.).

Unfortunately, in western Tennessee and at MEM, what is often missing from present barbecue entrepreneurship is the "place-making" and "geography" elements associated with African American communities from slavery to the present day. In essence, barbecue as practiced by people of different races within this regional landscape, even more so in other areas of the United States, seems to have overlooked and/or lost its "Black connection." This is not surprising, given that "physical geographies are bound up in, rather than simply a backdrop to, social and environmental processes. It follows that the materiality of the environment is racialized by the contemporary demographic patterns as shaped by historic precedents" (McKittrick and Woods 2007, 3). Memphis and its surrounding geographies, both urban and rural, have such a deep, deep history of commodity farming of cotton tied to the slave trade; it is projected to have been within the top five areas of production by the start of the Civil War (Hillard 1972, 1984). In this racialized landscape, the notion of "space" of the colonized and enslaved cannot be separate from the contemporary cultural processes. That history of slavery and cotton plantations and all the processes tied to those legacies are continuously tied to Black histories, bodies, and experiences. Contemporary barbecue culture, as explicitly mentioned in Texas, embodies a model of multiculturalism that has overlooked that situated knowledge of African American communities and their contributions (Haraway 1988; Walsh 2016; Horne 2019). It seems that little is different on the national scene of white chefs, cooks, and restaurateurs who continue to push away or avoid how these barbecue geographies are substantial political, economic, and social representations of African American narratives, lived experiences, and situated knowledge (Walsh 2016; Jackson 2017; Shahin 2017).

As a nation, whiteness has consumed barbecue and its seemingly associated multicultural practices. As a cuisine, it has been reclaimed by "backyard bros" (such as a Williamsburg, Brooklyn, restaurant foodie or a young, white, middle-class corporate Memphis in May participant), displacing African Americans and demarcating a new set of power relations tied to its contemporary manifestation. Barbecue has been exploited, claimed, dominated, and segregated by those in power, leaving very little room for stewardship, economic gains, and social justice with, for, and by African American communities.

However, inserting "black geographies back into our worldview and our understanding of spatial liberation and other emancipatory strategies can perhaps move us away from territoriality, the normative practice of staking a claim to place" (McKittrick and Woods 2007, 5). "Barbecue geographies" can highlight struggles, resistance, and maintenance of the identity of African American communities tied to their associated "chocolate maps" (Hunter and Robinson 2018). Those "chocolate maps" include narratives and experiences, such as enslaved African Americans cooking on antebellum plantations and establishment Jim Crow–era barbecue joints, and also feeding civil rights leaders and communities to the contemporary day (Veteto and Maclin 2011; Cooley 2015; Opie 2017). Marcus Anthony Hunter and Zandria Robinson advocate for evaluating how Black people made and live with their own [chocolate] maps, whether in response to or in spite of institutional discrimination. . . . [Those] chocolate maps are a living geography, whose areas and regions are always actively being constructed, mirroring and defined by the movement of Black Americans across the United States over time. (2017, 19)

Hunter and Robinson want us to think outside the traditional rigid regionalism and the geographic framework (North, South, Midwest, East, and West) that have permeated cultural studies in the last several decades. The study of barbecue and its culture manifestations across the United States is no different in terms of its use of "regionalisms." We tend to recognize the role of the Great Migration in the proliferation of barbecue across the United States (Auchmutey 2019) but then soon push aside the role of enslaved African American food cultures and their foundational influence as specific regionalisms develop. For example, western Tennessee and Memphis are home to a specific type of barbecue—they are famous for wet and dry ribs, pulled pork sandwiches, and perhaps even barbecue spaghetti (Simpson 2019). Maybe it is time to reevaluate how we create boundaries that divide through these regionalisms and instead create landscapes of association, community, and power.

Within these barbecue geographies, we can further analyze those associations, communities, and power dynamics of race and place through the use of intersectionality. As highlighted by Patricia Hill Collins and Sirma Bilge (2106, 25–30), this is a way of identifying and exploring the intricacies of the human experience through the interconnected facets of social inequality, authority, relationality, social context, complexity, and social justice. It is a magnificent analytical tool to better engage in critical inquiry and critical praxis, especially for our project that intertwines race and place. When these intersections are connected to cultural memories and oral histories (Battle-Baptiste 2011; Shackel 2011; Ford and Strauss 2019), which include autobiographical fiction (Hurston 1935, 1937; Fryer 2006), we can "document" how the past is connected to the present and continues to shape our future (Wilkie 2015).

The use of an anthropological and even archaeological-oriented, intersectional framework is imperative, especially for our project that seeks to engage contemporary food-based inequalities. We are not just excavating enslaved African American households and running farmers markets. We use the historical and archaeological information and contextualization of racialized foodways, which include barbecue, to create more effective understandings and solutions for our food-based practice in the contemporary. In essence, we seek to connect the past to the present and illustrate the wake of slavery in our current landscapes (Sharpe 2016). In the following sections, I will dive deeper into why the historicity, materiality, and symbolism of barbecue "matter."

The Historicity of Barbecue

One of the things most surprising about the conversations and connections in our food-based project is the lack of awareness, particularly with white individuals, that the contemporary version of barbecue today was originated by Native Americans and then bolstered by enslaved Africans and African Americans in the southern United States (Yentsch 2009; Twitty 2017; Auchmutey 2019). Although barbecue is present within our contemporary landscapes—from mom-and-pop shops in small rural towns to larger chain restaurants, with more than five in Memphis alone of a combined number of more than twenty-five locations and more than twelve independently owned—there appears to be an erasure of African Americans from the mainstream historicity of this cuisine. Historicity, which refers to the cultural perceptions (knowledge) of the past, often embodies structures, such as "rituals that people use to learn about the past, the principles that guide them, and the performance and genres in which the information about the past can be presented" (Stewart 2016, 79). What is problematic about the Western-centric viewpoint is that it improperly, if at all, narrates the historicity of barbecue cuisine within, among, and between African American communities in the southern United States. Decoding the historicity of barbecue can help decipher the African American historical experience, relationship(s) the individuals establish to the past, and expectations of the future (Koselleck 2004; Wentzer 2014). Claude Lévi-Strauss's (1966) dichotomous categorization of the range of societies ("hot" and "cold"/"raw" and "cooked") demonstrates that indeed there is "factuality" within communities, but there are different cultural frameworks for perceiving and representing the past, thus highlighting power relations tied to different possible interpretations to the past and the overall historicity. Furthermore, W. E. B. Du Bois (1940) argued that it was essential to restore that sense of historicity to Africans (and in our case, African Americans) to frame the daily experience and a shared history outside the European perspective and establish an anticolonial gaze.

Barbecue has its deep roots in many Indigenous communities prior to the fifteenth century. Andrew Warnes (2008) argues that *barbacoa, barbicu, barbikew,* or *barbeque* (regardless of spelling) referred to the smoked foods of Native peoples of the Americas. However, for Europeans it also conjured foods that were barbarous, primitive, crude, and tied to methods used by Indigenous ancestors. During the seventeenth and eighteenth centuries, the "invented tradition" of barbecue (similar to its practice as we know it today) was imagined by white settler populations and Europeans as it became desirous to abandon civilization and restore connections to "nature" or the frontier past (Lewis 1998; Ferris 2014). In mainstream society, it became associated with primitiveness, independence, masculinity, and strength (Warnes 2008). It was less tied to the Indigenous cultural practices of the Arawakan but more tied to the fabricated colonial representations that deeply sought to demonstrate those cultures as barbaric and the antithesis of European progressive models of evolution (Warnes 2008).

During the late eighteenth into the nineteenth century, barbecue became integral in slave-based diets in the United States, becoming part of African American identity as a special occasion foodstuff (Harris 2011). Although many Africans were not formally introduced to pigs before being enslaved in the United States, they approached this Old World animal with traditional African culinary traditions, using the entire "body" model for consumption

(Covey and Eisnach 2009; Whit 2009). Stomachs, ears, feet, intestines, brains (primarily in head cheese), ribs, back fat, and hocks were used in different culinary dishes as what has been labeled soul food (Ferris 2014). Barbecue and soul food are such a blend of foodstuffs and practices from Native American, African, and European cultures (Warnes 2008; Covey and Eisnach 2009; Ferris 2014; Wallach 2015). Michael Twitty remarks:

> We Africans in the Americas have not just been adopters, we are border crossers and benders. We have always been at play with what was presented to us. The Atlantic world has been an incredible experiment in how an enslaved population could get away with enslaving the palates of the people who enslaved them. (2017, 15)

Diligently and for their own survivance, African Americans collected, prepared, and provisioned Indigenous and imported foodstuffs for the main house and also their own personal consumption (Bowes 2011). Food was one way they were able to express themselves. Many slaves grew their own gardens near their quarters at many plantation farms (Whit 2009; Bowes 2011). Anne Yentsch (2009, 69) states that barbecue was a celebratory food that was part of highly public performance and notes that there are many unanswered questions around the intersections of its presence, accompanying foods, gender roles, and power dynamics on plantation systems.

To fully deconstruct and understand the historicity of this cuisine within this region, Rhodes College has been excavating plantation sites, particularly enslaved African American houses, in an annual field school at an antebellum plantation in Fayette County, West Tennessee. The sites can be found within the modern land aggregate called Ames Plantation, fifty miles from Memphis. This 18,650-acre land base, which is operated by the Hobart Ames Foundation (very fitting for an archaeological project since he is the famous shovel maker), contains more than 250 registered prehistoric and antebellum plantation sites. Considering this region's fertile soil, which has been used ever since the beginnings of the plantation system, this area served as one of the highest-producing zones of cotton during the antebellum period (Hillard 1984).

In the last seven years, the field research has centered around the excavation of slave houses and a manor house on the historical Dickins Plantation (established in the 1840s and abandoned in the late 1860s). The Dickins Plantation is one of five plantation farms owned by women during this time and was roughly 446 acres (a mid–small size plantation for the region). Fanny Dickins was a widow but bought the plantation and decided to participate in the cotton and slave industry on her own after her husband died— this was more common than previously thought, as more white women were able to gain power and resources within the heavily patriarchal capitalist society (Jones-Rogers 2019). From 2010 to 2013, we excavated the Dickins manor house and then shifted our focus from 2013 to 2018 to the excavation of three enslaved African American houses (one of which was significantly excavated and explored). At the enslaved house site, there is evidence of communal preparation and eating, as there are no fireplaces located inside the homes but they are thought to have been outside. There is also the presence and evidence for processing of pig bones, which will be further discussed in the next section. This house was most likely the home of the ancestors of Dwight Fryer, the community stakeholder introduced at the beginning of this chapter.

Within Fryer's historical narrative, barbecue holds a deep (ancestral) memory and establishes a historicity of hope, belonging, and adaptability. The father teaching his son how to smoke meat is tangible evidence of how barbecue processing and culture were passed down from generation to generation. Over the years, Fryer has pursued the connections branching out of his great-great-grandparents, former slaves Jane Dickens and her husband, Squire Hunt, and was often mesmerized listening to his mother's and father's storytelling of the dynamic landscapes tied to the winding journey of his enslaved migration from Kentucky and Virginia across North and South Carolina to Tennessee and Mississippi. The storytelling about the loving, struggling, starving, and killing often included visits to the modern-day eighteen-thousand-acre collection of dozens of smaller antebellum plantations four miles from Fryer's home in Grand Junction, Tennessee—very close to the Fanny Dickins plantation. Fryer muses about the mythical mentions of his enslaved great-great-grandmother Jane (who lived to be 104); her four children who lived to adulthood as freedmen; and the slave husband, Squire, who was sold, never to be heard from again. Even though Fryer's ancestors had to contend with overcoming life-and-death obstacles at the Fanny Dickins plantation, they still were able to create a historicity around culinary traditions, such as barbecue, to shape and maintain familial cohesion and survival in antebellum and postantebellum landscapes.

Within the historicity of this dynamic foodscape, rural foods, particularly barbecue, have influencedand continue to influence urban systems. Memphis was not a burgeoning city until the end of the nineteenth century, and rural towns, such as the nearby "social capital" of La Grange (four miles from the Fanny Dickins site), held a significant place (for additional resources and also social interactions) in the everyday lives of both the enslavers and the enslaved (such as Fryer's great-great-grandmother Jane) before and after emancipation. For example, two Black, generationally owned barbecue restaurants in Memphis, Cozy Corner and the BBQ Shop, have spoken about how the rural (preparative techniques and materialities) has influenced their own ways of showcasing their delicious barbecue to the urban sensibilities of Memphis residents. As discussed by Robinson (2014), the notion of country cosmopolitanism (Blackness that addresses the embattled notion of racial authenticity by engaging in and modernizing rural, country tropes) fully embodies what appears to be occurring within barbecue spaces in and around Memphis. The rural influences the urban and thus regionalization occurs, blending rural values and urban sensibilities within the production, consumption, and distribution of barbecue. This phenomenon has created an integrated, not divided, historicity of barbecue for African Americans in Memphis and the surrounding areas.

Agency and the Historical Materialities of "Barbecue"

With further investigation into the archaeological data and other comparative material collected from the Ames land base, we are able to understand how the slave communities negotiated broad inequality and overcame oppression through distinctive material tactics and then adapted to their surrounding cultural systems. It is thought that Africans and African Americans lacked agency (choice) within their households as to which types of foodstuffs they may have consumed. However, Paul Mullins discusses how the consumption that occurred in African American communities was a

> process by which consumers used material culture to see themselves as or opposed to racial subjectivities. Rich with symbolic possibilities and carrying a tacit promise of citizenship, material goods provided a seemingly innocuous, yet meaningful mechanism to reposition African Americans in opposition to racialized inequalities. (1999, 18)

In essence, consumption, particularly tied to barbecue and other African American foodways, could have been politicized and challenged the power relations while also fueling racial stereotyping and discontent. In this investigation, material culture is in fact a reflection of identity and includes choices within the social, economic, and political structures at play (Wilkie 2000; Battle-Baptiste 2011). The material culture tied to barbecue on the plantation and to the contemporary landscape in African American communities can help us imagine new social possibilities and reconcile lived contradictions, offering new relationships between the producer, consumer, and society and allowing futuristic narratives of who they wish to be to emerge (Mullins 1999).

By the time barbecue reached western Tennessee, it was already a 150-year-old "American" tradition (Moss 2011). It was in the colony of Virginia that barbecue was used not as a cooking technique but as a "social institution." It soon spread as those Virginians (and their enslaved populations) migrated down the Eastern Seaboard of the Appalachians into the Carolinas and Georgia. Many settlers pushed westward from North Carolina into Tennessee as the University of North Carolina was awarding land grants to those individuals who wished to civilize the western front.

Within these western Tennessee plantation landscapes, enslaved populations served as the pit masters for many of the barbecue events on plantations, political campaigns, and community gatherings to celebrate holidays and other events (Moss 2011; Auchmutey 2019). Preparation would have occurred days in advance as the animals were brought to the site of the event and slaughtered. Enslaved African Americans in western Tennessee were thought to have participated in their own community barbecue gatherings (although this was more often supervised). These celebratory events were very much prized by the enslaved African Americans hosting them; they called them a "ray of sunlight in their darkened lives" (Moss 2011, 31).

It is within the enslaved households at the Fanny Dickins archaeological site that you can see the material remains of barbecue and the adaptations or modifications that enslaved individuals and families may have made. We have recovered ceramics (for both consumption and storage) and metal utensils. We also have recovered numerous fragments of charred bone, including pig teeth, leading us to believe that there was some level of smoking of meats, not just pig but small mammals and rodents, in the vicinity of the house structures. These meats were most likely not smoked within a typical smokehouse operation on the plantation but within an open-air setup, as these structures were located in what could be labeled "field locations" and not close to the manor house.

In conjunction with the archaeological evidence of pig processing, according to the 1850 census records, Dickins reported more than fifty-five hogs within her inventory for her more than forty slaves (Tennessee Agricultural Census 1850). This was comparable to the holdings of many of her plantation neighbors (more than twenty-four plantations that ranged in size from three hundred to four thousand acres). They certainly were part of the overall wealth of the plantation (Hillard 1984). At her plantation, as well as others around her, hogs were a large part of the plantation's inventory and seem to have been consumed at both the manor and the enslaved African American houses. It is hard to decipher, based on the census data, whether they were just salted or used for barbecue. It is more likely that both happened within these plantation landscapes.

We also have accumulated a vast number of personal artifacts (e.g., bone hair combs, glass beads, tobacco pipes, lead bullets) and other materialities (such as nails, metal hardware tied to horse caretaking, and ceramics), which have signaled a dynamic material consumption within the African American occupants and cohesive familial household. What we are finding, not only within the archaeological record but through the oral narratives of the region (which included Fryer's autobiographical familial stories), is that African Americans—men, women, and children— were making specific choices to engage in the consumption of barbecue, shaping their familial households and possibly gendered practices. For example, barbecue was thought to be primarily a masculine-associated activity within the plantation and postantebellum landscapes, as can be seen in Figures 7.2 and 7.3, of a large-scale pig-processing event for barbecue and salt procurement completed by men, led by the African American manager, Jimmy Bryan, at Ames during the 1950s.

According to Hurston, the method of barbecuing a whole hog had not been modified in centuries and the creation of the barbecue pit (sometimes six feet long and often two feet deep) appeared to be more of a male activity, as "there was a group of men under the supervision of a pit master" (Opie 2015, 97). Also, making charcoal was essential, as it helped create the smoke, as mentioned in Fryer's earlier account. Pit masters are known to burn down hardwoods (oak, pecan, black cherry, fruit woods, or hickory, the latter of which was preferred) until they have a pit full of red-hot glowing coals. The wood is known to make a difference in the taste and possibly even the tenderness of the meat (Opie 2015; Twitty 2017). A long process of basting and saucing is also crucial to the tenderizing process (what my dad was actually missing from his Yankee ribs). Those recipes could/can be as simple as "butter, pepper, sail and vinegar" or a more complex combination of herbs and "hot stuff" (Opie 2015, 100).

In our discussion of the gendered roles, we also need to discuss the role of women in providing the structural framework for the associative foodstuffs tied to barbecue within African American communities. Almost all cooks who worked in the "big house"

Figure 7.2. Pork processing (dehairing and scalding) at Ames Plantation in western Tennessee during the 1950s. Pictured far left is Jimmy Bryan, manager and later superintendent and known pit master. Courtesy of the Ames Plantation Historical Society.

Figure 7.3. Pork processing (cooling of carcasses) at Ames Plantation in western Tennessee during the 1950s. Courtesy of the Ames Plantation Historical Society.

were enslaved African Americans and presented menus that were rich, highly seasoned, and often complicated (Sharpless 2010; Harris 2011; Tipton-Martin 2015). Women honed enormous skills to prepare food on an open hearth and mastered the tastes of their enslavers and own family (Fox-Genovese 1988). Women often were the keepers of the barbecue sauce recipes and preparation methods (Fryer 2006, 112–16). As Psyche Williams-Forson states, in the kitchen, you can also find "black women's acts of self-definition and imagination alongside cultural hegemony, food politics and demarcations of power" (2006, 2). The same could be said for the gendered roles of barbecue tied to plantation systems and beyond. Both men and women worked in tandem to provide the material output of the barbecue and the associative foodstuffs. Fundamentally, they actively participated in a "material" process to create a generational tradition that can still be seen in the African American barbecue restaurants that populate both the urban and rural systems of western Tennessee.

Whose Heritage Is It? The Symbolism of Barbecue

Barbecue is one of the most overlooked racialized cuisines in the United States, perhaps even the world. As demonstrated in this chapter, barbecue is deeply tied to African Americans on the plantation landscape and onward, but unlike other foodstuffs, such as fried chicken (Williams-Forson 2006), watermelon, and more broadly soul food, it has become co-opted by white Americans and catapulted into mainstream society (Shahin 2017). In a YouTube video tied to the release of his book *Cooked,* Michael Pollan (2013, 2014) advocates that barbecue transcends race. Within his narration, he embraces a postracial foodscape of multiculturalism that perpetuates a neoliberal ideology that barbecue can break down racial barriers and is everyone's heritage (2014). Even Frederick Douglass Opie (2015) states that no single ethnic group can claim its community members were the first barbecue pit masters (although many would argue that Native Americans were in fact the first pit masters—e.g., Twitty 2017; Auchmutey 2019). However, what is evident is that barbecue did in fact develop as a national tradition through the sweat of African American men and women in the nineteenth to twenty-first centuries.

This heritage and symbolism are often forgotten and in some instances continue to be a divider across race and can even highlight white supremacy. In 2017 the *New Yorker* documented how white supremacy "power" players in North Carolina promoted specific political and racial agendas through barbecue (Collins 2017). Even within Memphis, barbecue has become racialized not just socially or politically but also economically. In the civil rights movement, restaurants that served barbecue and soul food were seen as locales of resistance and safe spaces within the sanitation workers' strike of 1968 (Shahin 2016; Biggs 2018). However, soon thereafter began an economic and cultural transformation that further propagated boundaries between African Americans and the white residents of the city. During the late twentieth century, the cuisine became the sole focus of the famous, Greek-run Rendezvous restaurant (which collaborated with FedEx to ship its BBQ anywhere in the world—the first entrepreneurial example of this type), the Jewish-run Tops BBQ franchise, and other establishments run by non–African American individuals, such as the Central BBQ franchise. However, the pit masters for these three highly successful commercial BBQ franchises are predominately African American and are often given kudos for their mastery. But that does not mean that these pit masters or other African Americans were given the economic mobility opportunities in comparison with other non–African American restaurants in Memphis. When I asked the owners of one of the generationally run African American restaurants why they did not expand, their response was that they "never could get a loan" even though their restaurant is one of the most frequented barbecue joints in Memphis.

In 1978 we also had the start of the barbecue fest at Memphis in May, which predominantly caters to white participants around the United States and their associated teams. Each team has to pay a heavy entrance fee from $675 to $5,000 (dependent on placement near the Mississippi River) that typically is out of the price range for the vast majority of our city residents. Even Fryer, when attending the 1998 Memphis in May BBQ fest, noted that he was one of the few nonwhite attendees and it was "like stepping back into 1964" (Fryer, interview by the author, May 23, 2019). These examples highlight how barbecue has become a much wider, cultural spectacle that often excludes African Americans and pedestals the economic success of appropriated ventures.

In many ways in Memphis and beyond, there are still deep-seated racism and social, political, and economic constraints around the patterns of procurement, production, and consumption. In spite of those constraints, barbecue has such rich historicity, material culture, and symbolic elements in African American culture that one cannot deny its ability to continually build community and cohesiveness. Some may say that we are at a turning point when it comes to overcoming the lack of economic mobility of those who produce this cuisine and have been left out. Continual recognition of how food heritage needs to be part of the contemporary dialogue is needed, especially when assessing the losers and winners in the political, economic, and social capital tied to this pecific cuisine. Without that recognition, we will continue to overlook African American contributions to past, present, and future foodscapes.

Conclusion: Barbecue "Matters"

This investigation has helped offer a more nuanced picture of barbecue and material underpinnings of the African American gastronomic heritage within this region. All the examples given here highlight the cultural complexity of the regionalization of barbecue in Memphis and beyond. In order for barbecue to become "more than just food" and to "matter," we need to recognize the agency and historical networks tied to the origins of this cuisine while attempting to break our past food taboos that created and continue to birth deeper segregation within our foodscapes (i.e., white or African American restaurants) (Cooley 2015). This historical influence of that culinary erasure and segregation can still be seen within the contemporary urban and rural landscapes of the South (Opie 2017). We need to promote intersectional methods, as highlighted here, within our modern-day food movements from farmers, restaurants, school lunch programs, farmers markets, and supermarkets to recognize that Black food "matters" and acknowledge the autonomy that exists in the foodscape from past to present.

We view this work as a bridge to a multiyear, longitudinal community-based project. We have just begun to scratch the surface of the structural influences and producer/consumer agency to better understand the historical implications of the barbecue in our contemporary landscapes. We look forward to continual collaborations with local stakeholders in an interdisciplinary fashion that includes ventures related to nature/culture, conservation, food, African American studies/archaeologies, and social justice. With further investigation into these arenas, we will broaden our understandings and can create more awareness for how African American communities overcame broad inequality though unique material tactics and continue to impact the current food and cultural systems. What we can come to grasp is that the gastronomic heritage of barbecue is giving way to new practices propelled by modernity and consumerism. This cuisine is dependent on a blend of past and present local knowledge in conjunction with technological advancement. As Fryer's passage highlights, this heritage should in no way be considered static and never should the fire overtake the meat. The fire should be present to preserve and add flavor—provide resistance, perseverance, and survivance. There is no greater time than now to recognize that Black food matters with all its rich historicity, materialism, and symbolism in the southern United States and more broadly within our global foodscapes.

Bibliography

Araujo, Anna Lucia. 2014. *Shadows of the Slave Past: Memory, Heritage, and Slavery.* New York: Routledge.

Auchmutey, Jim. 2019. *Smokelore: A Short History of Barbecue in America.* Athens: University of Georgia Press.

Battle-Baptiste, Whitney. 2011. *Black Feminist Archaeology.* New York: Routledge.

Beaudry, Mary. 1988. "Words for Things: Linguistic Analysis of Probate Inventories." In *Documentary Archaeology in the New World,* edited by Mary Beaudry, 43–50. New York: Cambridge University Press.

Biggs, Jennifer. 2018. "Soul Food Restaurants Fed Bellies and Souls in Civil Rights Movement." *Commercial Appeal,* April 2.

Bowes, Jessica. 2011. "Provisioned, Produced, Procured: Slave Subsistence Strategies and Social Relations at Thomas Jefferson's Popular Forest." *Journal of Ethnobiology* 31 (1): 89–109.

Broad, Garrett M. 2016. *More than Just Food: Food Justice and Community Change.* Oakland: University of California Press.

Chamberlin, Chris. 2016. "The Best BBQ in America: Top 15 Cities." *Conde Nast Traveler,* April 7.

Collins, Lauren. 2017. "America's Most Political Food." *New Yorker,* April 24.

Cooley, Angela Jill. 2015. *To Live and Dine in Dixie: The Evolution of Urban Food Culture in the Jim Crow South.* Athens: University of Georgia Press.

Covey, Herbert C., and Dwight Eisnach. 2009. *What the Slaves Ate: Recollections of African American Foods and Foodways from the Slave Narratives.* Santa Barbara, Calif.: Greenwood.

Crenshaw, Kimberlé Williams. 1991. "Mapping the Margins: Intersectionality, Identity Politics, and the Violence of the Women of Color." *Stanford Law Review* 43 (6): 1241–99.

Delevaga, Elena. 2017. "Memphis Poverty Fact Sheet: 2017 Update." 2016 American Community Survey. http://www.memphis.edu.

Du Bois, W. E. B. 1940. *Dusk of Dawn: An Essay Toward an Autobiography of a Race Concept.* New York: Oxford University Press.

Ferris, Marcie Cohen. 2014. *The Edible South: The Power of Food and the Making of an American Region.* Chapel Hill: University of North Carolina Press.

Fischler, Claude. 1988. "Food, Self and Identity." *Social Science Information* 27 (2): 275–92.

Ford, Dionne, and Jill Strauss, eds. 2019. *Slavery's Descendants: Shared Legacies of Race and Reconciliation.* New Brunswick, N.J.: Rutgers University Press.

Fox-Genovese, Elizabeth. 1988. *Within the Plantation Household: Black and White Women of the Old South.* Chapel Hill: University of North Carolina Press.

Fryer, Dwight. 2006. *The Legend of Quito Road.* Toronto: Kimani.

Goodman, M. K. 2015. "Food Geographies I: Of Relational Foodscapes and the Busy-ness of Being More-than-Food." *Progress in Human Geography* 40 (2): 257–66.

Hancock, Ange-Marie. 2016. *Intersectionality: An Intellectual History.* New York: Oxford University Press.

Haraway, Donna. 1988. "Situated Knowledges: The Science Question in Feminism and the Privilege of Partial Perspective." *Feminist Studies* 14 (3): 575–99.

Harris, Jessica. 2011. *High on the Hog: A Culinary Journey from Africa to America.* New York: Bloomsbury.

Hillard, Sam Bowers. 1972. *Hog Meat and Hoecake: Food Supply in the Old South, 1840–1860.* Carbondale: Southern Illinois University Press.

Hillard, Sam Bowers. 1984. *Atlas of Antebellum Southern Agriculture.* Baton Rouge: Louisiana State University Press.

Hill Collins, Patricia, and Sirma Bilge. 2016. *Intersectionality.* Cambridge, UK: Polity.

Horne, Shontel. 2019. "These Black Pitmasters Are Hustling to Preserve Barbecue's Roots." *Huffington Post,* June 24. http://www.huffington post.com.

Hunter, Marcus Anthony, and Zandria F. Robinson. 2018. *Chocolate Cities: The Black Map of American Life.* Oakland: University of California Press.

Hurston, Zora Neale. 1935. *Mules and Men.* Philadelphia: J. B. Lippincott.

Hurston, Zora Neale. 1937. *Their Eyes Were Watching God.* New York: HarperCollins.

Jackson, Lauren Michele. 2017. "The White Lies of Craft Culture: How the World of Small Batch, Single Origin, and Totally Artisanal Erases the People of Color Who Made It Possible." *Eater,* August 17. http://eater.com.

Jones-Rogers, Stephanie. 2019. *They Were Her Property: White Women as Slave Owners in the American South.* New Haven, Conn.: Yale University Press.

Koselleck, Reinhart. 2004. *Futures Past: On the Semantics of Historical Time.* Translated by Keith Tribe. New York: Columbia University Press.

Lévi-Strauss, Claude. 1966. *The Savage Mind.* Chicago: University of Chicago Press.

Lewis, George. 1998. "The Maine Lobster as Regional Icon: Competing Images over Time and Social Class." In *The Taste of American Place: A Reader on Regional and Ethnic Foods,* edited by Barbara G. Shortridge, 65–84. New York: Rowan & Littlefield.

McKittrick, Katherine. 2011. "On Plantations, Prison, and a Black Sense of Place." *Social and Cultural Geography* 12 (8): 947–63.

McKittrick, Katherine, and Clyde Woods, eds. 2007. *Black Geographies and Politics of Place.* Cambridge, Mass.: South End.

Memphis in May. n.d. "Our History." Accessed March 6, 2020. https://www.memphisinmay.org.

Moss, Robert. 2011. "A History of Barbecue in the Mid-South Region." In *The Slaw and the Slow Cooked: Culture and Barbecue in the Mid-South,* edited by James R. Veteto and Edward M. Maclin, 25–42. Nashville: Vanderbilt University Press.

Moyer, Teresa S. 2015. *Ancestors of Worthy Life: Plantation Slavery and Black Heritage at Mount Clare.* Gainesville: University Press of Florida.

Mullins, Paul. 1999. *Race and Affluence: An Archaeology of African America and Consumer Culture.* New York: Kluwer Academic.

Opie, Frederick Douglass. 2015. *Zora Neale Hurston on Florida Food: Recipes, Remedies and Simple Pleasures.* Charleston, S.C.: American Palate.

Opie, Frederick Douglass. 2017. *Southern Food and Civil Rights: Feeding the Revolution.* Charleston, S.C.: American Palate.

Pollan, Michael. 2013. *Cooked: A Natural History of Transformation.* New York: Penguin Books.

Pollan, Michael. 2014. "How BBQ Transcends Race." YouTube, June 9. Posted by Big Think. www.youtube.com/watch?v=aq1wlRtMGhA.

Robinson, Zandria. 2014. *This Ain't Chicago: Race, Class, and Regional Identity in the Post-Soul South.* Chapel Hill: University of North Carolina Press.

Shackel, Paul. 2011. "Public Memory and the Search for Power in American Historical Archaeology." *American Anthropologist* 103 (3): 655–70.

Shahin, Jim. 2016. "They Fed the Civil Rights Movement. Now Are Black-Owned Barbecue Joints Dying?" *Washington Post,* February 22.

Shahin, Jim. 2017. "This Is the Future of Barbecue: No Regions, No Rules, Lots of Innovation." *Washington Post,* May 14.

Sharpe, Christina, 2016. *In the Wake: On Blackness and Being.* Durham, N.C.: Duke University Press.

Sharpless, Rebecca. 2010. *Cooking in Other Women's Kitchens: Domestic Workers in the South, 1865–1960.* Chapel Hill: University of North Carolina Press.

Simpson, Teresa. 2019. "What Is Memphis Style Barbecue?" *TripSavvy,* June 4. http://tripsavvy.com.

Singleton, Theresa A., ed. 2009. *The Archaeology of Slavery and Plantation Life.* New York: Routledge.

Stewart, Charles. 2016. "Historicity and Anthropology." *Annual Review of Anthropology* 45:79–94.

Tennessee Agricultural Census. 1850. Hardeman Public Library.

Tipton-Martin, Toni. 2015. *The Jemima Code: Two Centuries of African American Cookbooks.* Austin: University of Texas Press.

Twitty, Michael. 2017. *The Cooking Gene: A Journey through African American Culinary History in the Old South.* New York: HarperCollins.

Veteto, James R., and Edward M. Maclin, eds. 2011. *The Slaw and the Slow Cooked: Culture and Barbecue in the Mid-South.* Nashville: Vanderbilt University Press.

Wallach, Jennifer Jensen, ed. 2015. *Dethroning the Deceitful Pork Chop: Rethinking African American Foodways from Slavery to Obama.* Fayetteville: University of Arkansas Press.

Walsh, Robb. 2016. "How Texas BBQ Boom Marginalizes Its African-American Roots." *First We Feast,* June 16. http://firstwefeast.com.

Warnes, Andrew. 2008. *Savage Barbecue: Race, Culture and the Invention of America's First Food.* Athens: University of Georgia Press.

Weik, Terrance M. 2012. *The Archaeology of Antislavery Resistance.* Gainesville: University Press of Florida.

Wentzer, Thomas Scharwz. 2014. "'I Have Seen Königsberg Burning': Philosophical Anthropology and the Responsiveness of Historical Experience." *Anthropological Theory* 14 (1): 27–48.

Whit, William. 2009. "Soul Food as a Cultural Creation." In *African American Foodways: Explorations of History and Culture,* edited by Anne L. Bower, 45–58. Urbana: University of Illinois Press.

Wilkie, Laurie A. 2000. *Creating Freedom: Material Culture and African American Identity at Oakley Plantation, Louisiana, 1840–1950.* Baton Rouge: Louisiana State University Press.

Wilkie, Laurie A. 2003. *The Archaeology of Mothering: An African-American Midwife's Tale.* New York: Routledge.

Wilkie, Laurie A. 2015. "Documentary Archaeology." In *The Companion to Historical Archaeology,* edited by Dan Hicks and Mary Beaudry, 13–33. Cambridge: Cambridge University Press.

Williams-Forson, Psyche A. 2006. *Building Houses out of Chicken Legs: Black Women, Food, and Power.* Chapel Hill: University of North Carolina Press.

Yentsch, Anne. 2009. "Excavating the South's African American Food History." In *African American Foodways: Explorations of History and Culture,* edited by Anne L. Bower, 59–98. Urbana: University of Illinois Press.

8
SISTERS OF THE SOIL
Urban Agriculture in Detroit
Monica M. White

• • •

This chapter analyzes an overlooked innovative experience led by Black women activists who participate in urban agriculture as a strategy to reconnect with and reassess their cultural roots and reclaim personal power, freed from the constraints imposed by consumerism and marketing, on the supply of food in the city of Detroit. By participating in food production, they demonstrate agency and self-determination in their efforts to rebuild a sense of community. Using an ecofeminist perspective, I examine the relationship between women's resistance and the environment. By focusing on women's urban gardening, the chapter broadens the definition of resistance to include less formal but no less important forms.

This chapter focuses first on the implementation of the project launched by the members of the Detroit Black Community Food Security Network (DBCFSN). Governmental statistics and secondary research provide the backdrop for the economic problems in Detroit that triggered the community response. I then present Black women farmers' attempts to transform vacant land to create a community-based food system. These activists created the farm as a community safe space, which operates as a creative, public, outdoor classroom where they nurture activism and challenge the racial and class-based barriers to accessing nutrient-rich food. In addition to improving access to nutrient-rich food by repurposing vacant land, they are transforming their communities into safe and green spaces.

For years, upon my return to my hometown of Detroit, I attended meetings of DBCFSN. Progressively becoming more and more committed to the vision as a volunteer, I contributed my skills to the work of the organization, thus making this a participatory research design. Extensive interactions led them to trust me to tell their stories. I interviewed both members of the organization and leadership. This chapter draws on the interviews of eight Black women farmers who were highly active in farm operations of DBCFSN at what is known as D-Town, as demonstrated by the volunteer records. The respondents range in age from thirty-one to sixty and include occupations such as community organizers, city government employees, educators, and those currently unemployed. These Black women farmers define themselves as activists and fight for causes such as food justice, prisoner's and prisoner's families' rights, community-based and citizen's education, digital justice, and environmental rights. Their work, as they conceptualize it, all moves toward the liberation of African people; however, they are all brought together in the struggles for food justice and security. The political ideology of the organization, and subsequently many of its members, is undeniably influenced by the tenets of Black nationalism. While not all respondents would identify themselves as Black nationalists, many of the founding members of the organization and its philosophy demonstrate the influence of the radicalism of the 1960s. Many still consider themselves freedom fighters against capitalist and racist oppression.

The Detroit Context: Food Insecurity

Detroit's social and economic ills have been well documented. Some scholars argue that the city's underdevelopment and overall economic decline are a result of housing discrimination and racial segregation; business, tax, and capital flight to the more affluent suburbs (Darden et al. 1987; Sugrue 1996); and a combination of race relations and urban and labor conflict (Thompson 2001). The transformation of the automobile industry, along with the subsequent shrinking of the working and middle classes, has left

Detroiters mired in poverty-induced challenges, including reduced city services; poor-quality education; and high rates of unemployment, crime, and housing foreclosures, leaving them with little to no access to healthy food.

Detroit's economic "depression" existed for several years before the U.S.-wide economic downturn of 2008 (Kaza 2006). Detroit's high unemployment rate, according to 2006–8 census estimates, is approximately 30 percent, or almost three times the national average.[1] For those who lack access to a vehicle (estimated at one in five urban residents), or those with unreliable transportation, many of whom are also single-parent heads of household, life in the city is particularly difficult. Transportation not only is a critical prerequisite to accessing employment, particularly in a city that lacks a reliable public transportation system but is necessary to access resources such as health care, healthy food, and other essentials (U.S. Census Bureau 2006–8).

Numerous studies have documented racial and economic disparities in access to food outlets in cities. These findings suggest that lower-income and African American neighborhoods have fewer supermarkets and greater access to liquor and convenience stores with lower-quality food and limited access to more expensive, healthy food options (Baker et al. 2006; Andreyeva et al. 2008; Franco et al. 2008; Beaulac, Kristjansson, and Cummins 2009; Larson, Story, and Nelson 2009).

Shannon Zenk et al. (2005) found that African American–majority communities are on average 1.1 miles farther from a supermarket than are predominantly white neighborhoods. Now many areas within Detroit are designated as "food insecure" (Gallagher 2007, 2). Eighty percent of the city's residents must purchase their food at the more than one thousand fringe food retailers, such as "liquor stores, gas stations, party stores, dollar stores, bakeries, pharmacies, convenience stores and other venues" (Gallagher 2007, 5). These stores offer few, if any, healthy food choices and often charge higher prices for poorer quality than comparable stores in the suburbs (Brown 2003; Dowie 2009). Zenk et al. (2006) also found that these fringe food retailers or independent stores that are more likely found in Detroit's impoverished neighborhoods are directly linked to a decline in the consumption of fruits and vegetables for African American women and children in Detroit.

Inadequate food supply to underserved communities has long been viewed as a problem by planners and food activists. While the suburbs attract food markets and national chains, the lack of political pressure leaves impoverished communities with few food options (Pothukuchi 2005). Add to this the abundance of fast-food outlets, and the result is a perfect storm of food insecurity and subsequent diet-related illnesses for poor people in Detroit.

Black women's health is especially negatively impacted by inadequate access to healthy food options. According to the National Health and Nutrition Examination Survey 2005–6 (NHANES), 52.9 percent of Black women are defined as obese, one of the precursors for other diet-related illnesses, compared to 37.2 percent of Black men and 32.9 percent of white women. Black women are two to three times more likely than their white female counterparts to be diagnosed with hypertension, which often leads to cardiovascular disease (Lackland and Keil 1996). Additionally, Black women are diagnosed with type 2 diabetes at twice the rate of white women and 1.4 times that of Black men (Cowie et al. 2006).

In response to the lack of access to healthy and affordable food in Detroit, agriculture has been suggested as a major initiative to develop community food security for citizens. Community food security is defined as "a condition in which all community residents obtain a safe, culturally acceptable, nutritionally adequate diet through a sustainable food system that maximizes community self-reliance and social justice" (Hamm and Bellows 2003, 37). According to a feasibility study conducted by Kathryn Colasanti, Charlotte Litjens, and Michael Hamm (2010), the City of Detroit has the capacity to provide "31% and 17% of the seasonally available vegetables and fruits, respectively" (41). Using the approximately 44,085 acres, or the equivalent of 7.6 square miles of vacant land within the city, would increase the health outcomes of city residents by providing healthy, sustainable, locally grown fruits and vegetables. It would also provide much-needed employment opportunities and green spaces within the city.

What follows is an examination of the farmers of one such organization, the Black women members of DBCFSN, and their involvement in farming as a strategy to exercise political agency and bring about community transformation and, in the process, alleviate the food crisis and demonstrate social and political transformation. Formed to address food insecurity in the Black community, DBCFSN represents the majority African American population and is motivated by the belief that successful community change is led by leaders from within its own community (DBCFSN n.d.). Nevertheless, this organization strives to improve access to quality food to all residents of Detroit as it organizes to improve the city's future. The activities of the DBCFSN can be viewed as a first step in building partnerships with other community-based organizations, as well as public agencies, so residents can work to rebuild their city.

DBCFSN uses mobilization, education, policy advocacy, and the physical improvements in neighborhoods to increase the food supply and prevent malnutrition, thereby enhancing the health of its residents, revitalizing neighborhoods through shared activities that also improve and strengthen the community's local economy and build a sense of justice, equity, and community self-determination.

Members of DBCFSN farm for several reasons. They are concerned about neighborhood beautification and increasing Detroit residents' access to healthy food; they consider themselves stewards of the environment and engage in farming for the purpose of reallocating vacant land within the city for green purposes while meeting the needs of the local community. They also conceptualize their efforts as a resistance strategy in providing a replacement for the vanishing community centers that were once prevalent in African American communities. Through a strategy of engaging the environment, communities that have been polluted and abandoned show agency by rebuilding themselves while restoring their environment.

Theoretical Framework: Ecofeminism

Ecofeminism, coined by French feminist Françoise d'Eaubonne (1974), is a philosophy that examines feminism in relation to the natural environment and lobbies for women's ability to engage with the earth and respond to and solve ecological crises. In an attempt to understand and deconstruct oppressive relationships between men and women and between humans and nature, ecofeminism argues that a masculinist paradigm perpetuates the status quo where "women, or rather women's work and lives, like the natural world, are externalized and exploited by the valued economy" (Mellor 2006, 139). Given traditional and contemporary gender roles, women continue to be largely responsible for the "mental and manual labor of food" (Allen and Sachs 2007, 1). Women's traditional roles of providing sustenance for the family enhance their dependence on the earth along with their vulnerability to the ecological degradation caused by multinational corporations that, these scholars argue, exploit the environment in order to increase profit. Women's vulnerability is exacerbated by ongoing deforestation, desertification, water and land pollution, blocked access to clean water and fertile land, toxins, and the harmful effects of hazardous wastes. Vandana Shiva casts women's commitment to the environment as necessary for their own survival: "Women's involvement in the environmental movement has started with their lives and with severe threat to the health of their families. From the perspective of women, environmental issues are quite directly, and clearly, issues of survival" (1994, 4).

Although ecofeminism offers a theoretical framework from which to understand oppression, it also has a practical component that includes participation in social movements and, especially, women's resistance. Scholars have typically applied ecofeminism to cases of resistance against multinational corporations that are allegedly responsible for ecological disasters. Women's resistance has been documented as an international concern (Steady 1998), ranging from rural Himalayan women challenging multinational corporations (Guha 1989), to Micronesian women fighting nuclear weapons testing, English women protesting against the storage of nuclear missiles (Krauss 1993; Kirk 1997), rural Kenyan women planting trees in order to conserve soil and water, and women protesting flooding in the Chipko Mountains brought about by corporate deforestation (Shiva 1994).

Patricia Hill Collins discusses the importance of safe spaces in understanding Black women's political consciousness and mobilization. She argues that safe spaces "represent places where black women could freely examine issues that concerned us" and are "one mechanism among many designed to foster black women's empowerment and enhance our ability to participate in social justice projects. . . . Their overall purpose most certainly aims for a more inclusionary, just society. . . . [These safe spaces] foster the conditions for black women's independent self-definitions" (2004, 110–11).

Ecofeminism and the work of Black women farmers in Detroit emphasize women's traditional gender roles as food providers in ways that encourage oppressed communities, especially women, to participate in the food system in greater numbers and for political, liberatory reasons. This application also endorses a human collaboration with nature as opposed to the domination of nature. Black women, in this case, engage the environment and transform vacant land into urban/community gardens and in so doing ensure that these spaces operate as a safe space where they are able to define their behavior as a form of resistance, one in which their resistance is against the social structures that have perpetuated inequality in terms of healthy food access, and one where they are able to create outdoor, living, learning, and healing spaces for themselves and for members of the community.

Farming, for them, is an opportunity to work toward food security and to obtain more control of the food system that impacts their daily lives. Food security is one goal in the direction of self-determination and self-reliance. Their transformation of the food system is an example of what can happen when the community controls those social institutions with which it comes into contact, such as with community-controlled education, community-based policing, and so on.

Black Women, Resistance, and Farming as Self-Determination

Black women activists engage in urban/community gardening as a strategy to increase access to nutrient-rich foods in communities that have been defined as food insecure. In doing so, they partici-pate in gardening as a strategy of resistance, one that demonstrates self-determination and political agency. They also argue that the Earth is an ally in the struggle for liberation by providing a living learning space and a refuge for communities that experience racial and economic apartheid.

Gardening in Detroit, for these women activists, is a dem-onstration of self-reliance and self-determination. While mem-bers of the community face harsh economic realities, gardening becomes an exercise of political agency and empowerment. In-stead of petitioning the city government to increase their access to fresh food, or lobbying for more grocery stores and markets to locate in the city, they transform vacant land into a community-based healthy food source where they are able to feed themselves and their families and provide an example to their community of the benefits of hard work. In addition to this, food becomes a point of entry to discuss how African Americans might gain control over other aspects of their lives, including access to afford-able housing, clean water, community policing, and decent public education.

If food is life, as these women activists suggest, then the ability to control the quality of food and increase access to healthy food in Detroit's predominantly Black community is an essential aspect of the struggle for self-determination and self-reliance. Lewa, one of the women in DBCFSN, suggests that the importance of healthy food access is essential for recognizing the difference between a community in control versus one that is being controlled: "Who-ever controls the food, controls the people, controls everything. Farming and sharing food with one another, potlucks and building community dinners slaps in the face of the systemic ways we've come to think about food. In so many ways farming is active self-determination, self-reliance, and empowerment."[2] Abiba agrees: "If you can control the food supply you can control the people; you don't need guns."

Ebun elaborates the importance of control of the food source and portrays the gardens as essential to survival when she de-scribes what can happen when citizens rely on others to meet their needs.

> The reality that at any moment on any given day the folks who control the grocery stores can say, "You know what? We tired of y'all. We are going to make our money somewhere else, or we are not going to sell what you want us to sell." You need to be able to feed yourself rather than waiting, you need to know how to grow it yourself instead of waiting on somebody down the street to sell it to you or choose not to.

Some of the farmers see self-reliance as larger than control over the food supply. Ebun suggests that farming, as an act of self-determination, is specifically what attracted her.

> The reason I'm engaged in farming is self-determination. It is important for us to create for ourselves and define our own realities, and the reasons that we should be doing anything when it comes to businesses, housing, anything, we should be in control of that. Being in Detroit, a predominantly Black city, it's important for us to determine, for those of us who know, to be in control of the food system in Detroit because there are a lot of us who don't know.

Most of these women farmers live in areas where food security is compromised. Major-chain grocery stores and supermarkets joined the exodus from the city for more economically affluent suburbs; this phenomenon is obvious to them. Ngozi comments on the importance of location in determining food security: "In the suburbs, there's a fruit market on every other corner. There's someplace to get fresh produce—to get fruit and vegetables." They farm in response to their initial feelings of abandonment and helplessness by exercising their own political agency. Involvement in community gardening came in response to a feeling of being abandoned by retailers who left the city during the economic downturn. Abiba describes this: "Particularly in Detroit, our grocery stores have been woefully inadequate in terms of clean food. The major grocery store chains have all left our city, and a lot of people felt very abandoned and almost helpless." Lina also describes inaccessibility of healthy food as the exigency for becoming involved in urban gardening: "There are no markets in our area; therefore, people are not able to shop in their immediate area for healthy food, or fresh vegetables, as opposed to canned foods or fast-food restaurants, so the need is what directed me towards going out and helping out in a community garden."

Gardens as Resistance

Women farmers view gardening as an act of resistance. For them, gardening offers an opportunity to work against systems and structures that have oppressed them. They envision their work in the areas of food sovereignty, food security, and community development as a recent manifestation of an agrarian tradition of African people and a legacy of African Americans who have connected food to life, liberty, and justice. For Ebun, her work in urban gardening is connected to a history of food justice and resistance of African people in the area of food.

> Resistance [and food] started before enslavement ended. When our ancestors were kidnapped and brought over here, they stowed seeds that were native to their land, that we now know were native to the areas that they were taken from. These foods are staples in our diet. . . . They were holding on to their culture. They were holding on to home. That right there was resistance.

Tisha suggests that for her, contemporary gardening in the city is an undeniable, everyday act of resistance.

> Gardening in the City of Detroit is saying, "Fuck it!" It says, I can grow my own food *and* I can feed my community. You are dealing with a majority [African American] population that has been scarred, battered, and bruised. The first step to rebuilding a culture is agriculture.

While not all who engage in gardening and farming identify their behaviors as resistance, the women of DBCFSN clearly do. They characterize their gardening as resistance against multinational corporations who attempt to "colonize their plate." They articulate their struggle as one that includes decisions about where grocery stores and supermarkets should be located based on profit, instead of based on people's need, as an indicator of oppression. They articulate their strategies of sustainable, eco-friendly agriculture as an act of defiance against genetically modified food, the harmful toxins that are sprayed as pesticides and fertilizers, and the damaging effect these chemicals have on people and on the environment. Their work is also connected to the local food movement. They argue that it is important to know your farmer and to contribute to the economic well-being of people in their community. They conceptualize their work as contributing to a much larger cause. Their work is an effort to demonstrate their own voice in being able to grow food that goes to feed their families but also as an example of a community-based solution to food insecurity.

Rabia articulates the complex issues that, for her, gardening challenges, thus:

> You resist when you grow. Gardening resists the corporations that are knowingly putting things that we can't even pronounce into our foods. You resist those things when you grow wholesome foods or when you buy wholesome foods. There is so much genetically altering of things now and you don't even really know what it is. When you grow a tomato, you know that tomato is not something that was created in a laboratory because you grew it from organic seeds. You resist the whole corporate factory farm type of thing.

While agribusiness is coupled with modern technology to offer the convenience of stored, canned, boxed, and highly processed foods that are plentiful in many urban corner and convenience stores, these women believe that their involvement in urban agriculture is an act of resistance against these unhealthy food choices. Abiba resists the prevalence of convenience and prepackaged foods that are high in sugar, salt, fat, and that contribute to diet-related illnesses that plague the African American community, most significantly Black women.

I'm resisting everything that's in the grocery stores, that's on TV that's bombarding me. Everything in the media bombarding me about what I should eat, medicines I should take. I'm resisting commercials [for convenience foods] that are out there and I'm creating my own food. I feel powerful when I'm doing this with other like minds. When I'm at the farm with the farm manager or the irrigation manager, it feels like resistance. I am not engaging in commercialisms, not engaging in consumerism. The choice I'm making is to engage in the farm.

Lewa relates her resistance to a larger context, one that opposes not only large agricultural operations but pharmaceutical and insurance companies that she argues benefit from disease and ill health as well. She sees her work as a visible example of the ability to directly influence the health and food system.

You are resisting the "colonization of your plate." Monocrops, plantations, controlled environments are not natural. Fruits and vegetables don't resemble what they used to. [Gardening allows you to] educate your palate . . . gardening is actively pushing against the health care industrial complex, manufactured diseases, dietary-related diseases . . . realizing the collective power to influence the food system by holding accountable grocery stores, or school lunches.

Through farming, these women activists argue, they can produce their own food, invest in their communities, and assist community members to learn much-needed survival skills and impact the quality of life through improving the quality of food.

The Garden as a Safe Space for Women in the Community

Through this intimate relationship of preparing the land to grow healthy food, women of DBCFSN have begun to see the environment and their relationship to the earth in a different light, as a safe or community space. Elsewhere I argue that urban/community gardens have filled the void left behind by the cost-cutting act of closing community centers that once offered services for the citizens of the city.

> Farmers have established alternative communal and social spaces where intergenerational relationships are nurtured and maintained and where citizens have access to a safe space for physical exercise. Additionally, these gardens are centers where people learn about healthy eating, access healthy food, and receive health screenings and services. (White 2011, 412)

In addition to community centers, these women farmers argue that the community garden is an earthen sanctuary. As a demonstration of their agency, they have created the farm as a safe space, a community space where they are able to develop meaningful relationships with their neighbors, an outdoor learning center, and even a healing space, a location where they are able to exercise, reflect, meditate, and farm as a stress reliever.

Contrary to the assumption that African Americans avoid farming as a result of the historical memory of slavery and sharecropping, these women are appropriating this activity and its negative connotations from a painful reference and creating spaces that are cathartic, political, and liberatory. Lewa speaks specifically to the farm's role in urban communities.

> Black women create the safe space of the garden. Gardens operate as a place for conversation and for healing, as a safe space, a place where we can give birth to ideas, give birth to concepts, and to new ways of doing and being. It's about healing as it relates to our historical wounds and perceptions around farming and gardening.

Not only is the farm conceptualized as a place for healing, but Abiba describes the farm as a safe space where she can transform her powerlessness into empowerment.

> I feel more empowered by growing my own. I have experienced not having it, and I felt powerless. They [grocery stores] can come

and go. . . . If I grow it myself, I know what's going to happen. I get more peace of mind knowing that I can grow it, freeze it, dry it. Even if there were a grocery store that consistently provided fresh produce [in my neighborhood], I would still participate because I need to be able to control it myself.

Relatedly, Rabia describes working in the garden as a stress reliever.

When you come out there you can clear your mind. We talk, we vent. . . . The garden is a gathering place. It's like the earth takes up your problems . . . you're weeding the earth and it's like you're pulling out problems in your mind. You are venting your anger and it feels like you leave it there. Healing, positive energy, nothing like solving your problems with weeding. Gotta go out and weed; it's a stress reliever.

In mourning the passing of her father, Lewa was counseled by some of the founding women members.

My father had just passed and I came out to D-town. The women told me, "You need to get in the dirt." [They told me] I needed to literally get my hands, connect with the mother [Earth], the original mother. This is the spiritual quality to gardening. What I learned gave me a way to be alone with my thoughts, a safe space to get with my thoughts. Women were all around me; they saw a satisfaction to it. I saw a direct connection from the pain of mourning my father to what I was planting. I planted that whole [row] of collard greens; look at me go. What a sense of satisfaction.

This lesson of viewing the farm as a cathartic space was so powerful for Lewa that she insisted that her children experience the farm's healing potential: "I knew that getting out in the garden would be good for their soul. As a mother I was doing a good thing."

These women activists also see the farm as an easily accessible, outdoor, living classroom. Lewa argues, "Growing your own garden is the most popular form of popular education, learning by doing, place based, spiritual, all those things in one and its resistance." Tisha also sees the garden as a place to teach and learn resistance, especially for young people. She argues that the farm is a space where political engagement begins and they learn agency. Not only do they learn how to grow food; they also learn the power of their own voices.

> To ask children for their opinion in designing something that's a permanent fixture in a community, and that's powerful. Their faces are illuminated and when they see the results, "I wanted the tomatoes there and they're there." That's empowering. I want children to know that they are powerful. That they are in the position to change things and that they are worthy of being heard. Their voices are worth being heard and it makes sense. A lot of times they don't feel like they make sense.

Another healing benefit of farming and gardening is the ability to, through ecologically sustainable techniques, grow fruits and vegetables that are healthy. Rabia sees genetically modified, chemically treated food as a link to disease but gardening and increasing access to healthy food as a source of healing. For her, growing her own food becomes another form of treatment.

> Healthy food is healing. I've had health issues and there was not a link. . . . I would ask the doctors how did I acquire this illness, and they wouldn't really know. This is not a hereditary thing, so I really had to think. This was what I ingested either from the environment or from the food that I ate. If I can have peace of mind, if I can put love into the food that I grow, then hopefully it can have some healing effect on me. There's power over what you put into and take out of your food. The decisions that you make about what you take into your body is very important to your longevity and your health and that's a powerful thing.

Conclusion

Participation in urban gardening for these women functions as protest, not only one where their energies feed their families and their communities healthy food but also one that feeds their need to be the change agent in their communities. The farm operates as a space where they are able to work and relieve the stressors of their everyday lives and create a food system that is community-based, environmentally responsible, and an example of the potential transformation from rust belts to green belts.

In response to the race and class distinction in accessing healthy food for citizens in the City of Detroit, Black women activists engage in farming as a strategy of resistance against capitalism, corporatism of the food system and agribusiness, and its use of environmentally unsustainable food production practices. These new spaces teach communities the power of a different kind of inwardly focused resistance that produces creative and productive spaces in the neighborhood.

These findings are significant for several reasons. The application of ecofeminism to the work of Black women farmers in Detroit broadens the utility of this theoretical model to include instances of race and class as well as proactive mobilization efforts. Previous theoretical applications often focus on women's resistance in reaction to threats or actions of environmental destruction and degradation. The work of the women of DBCFSN demonstrates how a relationship between the land and members of an oppressed group can lead to an expression of resistance before or without threats of destruction. This case study illustrates the importance of an ecofeminist analysis to explain how a group of Black women farmers proactively engage the environment, emphasizing the symbiotic relationship between activist and earth, prior to ecological destruction, in the interests of mutual liberation.

Ecofeminist scholars often discuss resistance strategies that involve more formal means of confrontation with the oppressive social structure, such as boycotts, formal protests, and pickets to draw attention to the struggle to protect the land and ultimately save the lives and communities of those who live closest to the earth. For Detroit women activists, transforming public spaces resists the social, economic, and gendered oppression that complicates the accessibility of healthy food for poor people and the communities of color who have not left the impoverished city.

Instead of petitioning the city government to demand greater access to healthy food, these women turn their strategies inward. These findings suggest that through their work, they connect the oppression and pollution of the earth with their own oppression and view the earth as an ally in the respective liberation struggles.

This case study allows us to apply the ecofeminist theoretical perspective to Global North communities and includes the work of African American and urban activists in the efforts to work toward more sustainable communities, whose work in the environmental justice and sustainability movements is often overlooked. In their struggle for increasing food access, these women see the pollution of the earth and the environment as directly related to pollution of their bodies and the community as united concerns. Given the intersection of race, class, and gender, they see themselves as structurally located to understand and connect with the earth to respond.

Notes

1. This does not include those who are no longer looking for work, those who are working part-time but are seeking full-time employment, or those who are underemployed. If these groups are included, the city's unemployment rate is 44.8 percent of adults who otherwise are able to work (Wilkinson 2009). Joblessness is another measure of the intensity of unemployment. According to the Bureau of Labor Statistics, in 2009 the jobless rate, at 7.3 percent in the Detroit Metropolitan Statistical Area, represented the highest increase of any metropolitan area in the nation. Relative to long-term unemployment, among men ages twenty to sixty-four in the city of Detroit who did not have a job in 2008, the rate of joblessness is estimated at 48.5 percent (Wilkinson 2009).

2. Unless otherwise noted, all quotes from respondents are verbatim. I have used pseudonyms for the respondents.

Bibliography

Allen, Patricia, and Carolyn Sachs. 2007. "Women and Food Chains: The Gendered Politics of Food." *International Journal of Sociology of Food and Agriculture* 15 (1): 1–23.

Andreyeva, Tatiana, Daniel M. Blumenthal, Marlene B. Schwartz, Michael W. Long, and Kelly D. Brownell. 2008. "Availability and Prices of Foods across Stores and Neighborhoods: The Case of New Haven, Connecticut." *Health Affairs* 27 (5): 1381–88.

Baker, Elizabeth A., M. Schootman, Ellen Barnidge, and Cheryl M. Kelly. 2006. "The Role of Race and Poverty in Access to Foods That Enable Individuals to Adhere to Dietary Guidelines." *Preventing Chronic Disease* 3 (3): A76.

Beaulac, Julie, Elizabeth Kristjansson, and Steven Cummins. 2009. "A Systematic Review of Food Deserts, 1966–2007." *Preventing Chronic Disease* 6 (3): A105.

Brown, Katherine H. 2003. *Urban Agriculture and Community Food Security in the United States: Farming from the City Center to the Urban Fringe.* Portland, Ore.: Community Food Security Coalition.

Colasanti, Kathryn, Charlotte Litjens, and Michael Hamm. 2010. "Growing Food in the City: The Production Potential of Detroit's Vacant Land." C.S. Mott Group, June. http://fairfoodnetwork.org.

Cowie, Catherine C., Keith F. Rust, Danita D. Byrd-Holt, Mark S. Eberhardt, Katherine M. Flegal, Michael M. Engelgau, Sharon H. Saydah, Desmond E. Williams, and Edward W. Gregg. 2006. "Prevalence of Diabetes and Impaired Fasting Glucose in Adults in the U.S. Population." *Diabetes Care* 29 (6): 1263–68.

Darden, Joe, Richard Hill, June Thomas, and Richard Thomas. 1987. *Detroit: Race and Uneven Development.* Philadelphia: Temple University Press.

Detroit Black Community Food Security Network (DBCFSN). n.d. Accessed November 18, 2010. http://detroitblackfoodsecurity.org/.

Dowie, Mark. 2009. "Urban Farming in Detroit and Big Cities Back to Small Towns and Agriculture." *Whiskey and Gunpowder,* November 3. https://dailyreckoning.com.

Eaubonne, Françoise d'. 1974. *Le féminisme ou la mort.* Paris: P. Horay.

Franco, Manuel, Ana V. Diez Roux, Thomas A. Glass, Benjamin Caballero, and Frederick L. Brancati. 2008. "Neighborhood Characteristics and Availability of Healthy Foods in Baltimore." *American Journal of Preventive Medicine* 35 (6): 561–67.

Gallagher, Mari. 2007. *Examining the Impact of Food Deserts on Public Health in Detroit.* Chicago: Mari Gallagher Research & Consulting Group.

Guha, Ramachandra. 1989. *The Unquiet Woods: Ecological Change and. Peasant Resistance in the Himalaya.* Delhi: Oxford University Press.

Hamm, Michael W., and Anne C. Bellows. 2003. "Community Food Security and Nutrition Educators." *Journal of Nutrition Education and Behavior* 35 (1): 37–43.

Hill Collins, Patricia. 2004. *Black Feminist Thought: Knowledge, Consciousness, and the Politics of Empowerment.* New York: Routledge.

Kaza, Greg. 2006. "Michigan's Single-State Recession." *National Review,* October 18. https://www.nationalreview.com.

Kirk, Gwyn. 1997. "Ecofeminism and Environmental Justice: Bridges across Gender, Race, and Class." *Frontiers* 18 (2): 2–20.

Krauss, Celene. 1993. "Blue-Collar Women and Toxic Waste Protests: The Process of Politicization." In *Toxic Struggles: The Theory and Practice of Environmental Justice,* edited by R. Hofrichter, 107–17. Philadelphia: New Society.

Lackland, Daniel T., and Julian E. Keil. 1996. "Epidemiology of Hypertension in African Americans." *Seminars in Nephrology* 16 (2): 63–70.

Larson, Nicole I., Mary T. Story, and Melissa C. Nelson. 2009. "Neighborhood Environments: Disparities in Access to Healthy Foods in the U.S." *American Journal of Preventive Medicine* 36 (1): 74–81.

Mellor, Mary, 2006. "Eco-feminist Political Economy." *International Journal of Green Economics* 1 (1): 139–50.

Pothukuchi, Kameshwari. 2005. "Attracting Supermarkets to Inner-City Neighborhoods: Economic Development outside the Box." *Economic Development Quarterly* 19 (3): 232–44.

Shiva, Vandana. 1994. *Close to Home: Women Reconnect Ecology, Health and Development Worldwide.* London: Taylor and Francis.

Steady, Filomina Chioma. 1998. "Gender Equality and Ecosystem Balance." *Race, Gender & Class* 6 (1): 13–32.

Sugrue, Thomas 1996. *The Origins of the Urban Crisis: Race and Inequality in Postwar Detroit.* Princeton, N.J.: Princeton University Press.

Thompson, Heather Ann. 2001. *Whose Detroit? Politics, Labor, and Race in a Modern American City.* Ithaca, N.Y.: Cornell University Press.

White, Monica M. 2011. "D-Town Farm: African American Resistance to Food Insecurity and the Transformation of Detroit." *Environmental Practice* 13 (4): 406–17.

Wilkinson, Mike. 2009. "Nearly Half of Detroit's Workers Are Unemployed." *Detroit News,* December 16.

U.S. Census Bureau. 2006–8. "Selected Social Characteristics in the United States: 2006–2008: Detroit City." American Community Survey 3-Year Estimates. http://data.census.gov.

Zenk, Shannon N., Amy J. Schulz, Teretha Hollis-Neely, Richard T. Campbell, Nellie Holmes, Gloria Watkins, Robin Nwanko, and Angela Odoms-Young. 2006. "Fruit and Vegetable Intake in African Americans: Income and Store Characteristics." *American Journal of Preventive Medicine* 29 (1): 1–9.

Zenk, Shannon N., Amy J. Schulz, Barbara A. Israel, Sherman A. James, Shuming Bao, and Mark L. Wilson. 2005. "Neighborhood Racial Composition, Neighborhood Poverty, and the Spatial Accessibility of Supermarkets in Metropolitan Detroit." *American Journal of Public Health* 95 (4): 660–67.

9

RACE, LAND, AND THE LAW

Black Farmers and the Limits of a Politics of Recognition

Willie J. Wright, Tyler McCreary, Brian Williams,
and Adam Bledsoe

•   •   •

On December 8, 2010, President Barack Obama signed into law—before an audience of Cabinet members, lawmakers, aides, and advocates—House Resolution 4783, also known as the Claims Resolution Act of 2010. The law gave the United States Treasury Department permission to distribute financial payments to claimants within the second iteration of the class-action lawsuit *Pigford et al. v. Glickman* (USDA, Civil Action no. 97-1978, Dist. Court, Dist. of Columbia (1997)) (Pigford I). As a result of the initial consent decree, 15,749 of 22,889 eligible class members were approved to receive a total of roughly $1.06 billion in financial compensation (Cowan and Feder 2013). However, there were concerns about the high rejection rate, with nearly a third of claims denied, and the large number of claimants who were unable to have their cases heard because they did not meet the filing window. According to Obama, a settlement for the second Pigford case (*Pigford et al. v. Glickman,* 127 F. Supp. 2d 35, Dist. Court, Dist. of Columbia (2001)) (Pigford II) was warranted because

> for many years, African American farmers claimed they were
> discriminated against when they applied for federal farm loans—
> making it more difficult for them to stay in business and maintain

their farms. In 1999, a process was established to settle these claims. But the process was implemented poorly and tens of thousands of African American families who applied after the deadline were denied their chance to make their case. (Obama 2010, 3:22)

Recognizing the injustice of the constrained claims resolution process—an inept advertising campaign by the United States Department of Agriculture (USDA) failed to clearly explain whether the due date for claims was the date upon which they were to be received or postmarked—the government approved the appropriation of another $1.25 billion to extend this remedy to a larger claimant group. The president's speech left the impression that a simple stroke of the pen would amend the governmental wrongdoings committed between 1984 and 1997, the period of discrimination covered by Pigfords I and II.

> Here, in America, we believe that all of us are equal. And that each of us deserves the chance to pursue *our own version of happiness*. It's what led us to become a nation. It's at the heart of who we are as a people. And our history is defined by the struggle to fulfill this ideal—to build a more perfect Union, to ensure that all of us, regardless of our race or religion, our color or creed, are afforded the same rights as Americans and fair and equal treatment under the law. I think all of us understand that we haven't always lived up to those ideals. When we've fallen short, it's been up to ordinary citizens to stand up to inequality and unfairness wherever they find it. That's how we've made progress. That's how we've moved forward. And that's why we're here today—to sign a bill into law that *closes* a long and unfortunate chapter in our history. (Obama 2010, 2:11, emphasis added)

Obama begins his speech by thoughtfully recognizing all those present as Americans, Black farmers and their advocates included, with shared investments in American ideals. He then acknowledges that the government failed to uphold these ideals. Lauding the contribution of Black farmers, as ordinary citizens charged with correcting government misconduct, he rhetorically positions wrongdoing in the past. Thus, approving the Claims Resolution Act works to restore the perfection of the Union. Bracketing injustice within the past, Obama portrays racial injustice as a discrete event that can be acknowledged and transcended. However, the speech occludes—as does the lawsuit itself (*Pigford et al. v. Glickman* 1997)—the possibility that there are injustices occurring in the present that may require remediation. Discrimination is presented as an aberrant singularity rather than a structural feature of America's brand of governance. Obama frames financial recompense in Pigfords I and II as closing a quest for justice initiated by Black farmers long before Black agrarians had legal rights within the nation. However, the Pigford settlement does not provide the justice demanded by Black farmers but reflects the limited justice that the U.S. government was willing to offer.

The prevalence of "liberal" media discourse denouncing the excessiveness of the Pigford compensation highlights the depth of U.S. commitments to anti-Blackness (see LaFraniere 2013). While the average compensation of $67,000 in Pigford I surpassed the expectations of many commentators, it does not replace the lost lands and livelihoods of Black farmers. During the mediations, absent were discussions of Black farmers' connections to the land and how this connection has been impacted by the USDA's injustices. Rural landownership has been said to foster a number of positive qualities among Black rural residents (e.g., cultural retention, desire to till and tend to the earth, self-determination, personal and mental health, and intergenerational transfer of wealth) (Salamon 1979).

Furthermore, the Pigford settlements could not disrupt the policies embedded within the USDA that help foster the displacement of Black farmers. The USDA's policies privilege commercial farms and direct support to large operations with production oriented to global commodity markets. The prioritization of large-scale commodity production for private profit has often been irreconcilable with local food needs and community development. Rarely is this more evident than in the history of plantation cotton production in the U.S. South. Throughout the Mississippi Delta and the Black

Belt, high rates of hunger have existed in spite of agricultural policies that encourage productivity. At the same time, less capitalized and locally oriented Black-owned farms become systemically marginalized by structural and communal impediments (Woods 1998). Today, Black farmers represent just under 50,000 of the nation's 3.5 million farm operators, and the average age is sixty (Census of Agriculture 2017). Nevertheless, it is against the conditions of Black farmer displacement and systemic Black hunger that groups like the Nation of Islam (NOI) and the Pan African Orthodox Christian Church struggle to produce a secure food and farming system separate from the dictates of the USDA (McCutcheon 2013). As the NOI is well aware, locating justice within the frames of the racial state stymies the production of alternative social projects beyond the fiscal logics of the U.S. government.

With this intervention, we aim to resituate Pigford within a broader account of the Black farmers' movement. Rather than celebrate the Pigford settlements, as was common during its litigation (Martin 2013), we argue for an approach that recenters land ownership and refuses financial compensation for dispossession as an end goal of struggle. We have organized our argument into four subsequent sections. First, we begin with a critical review of the Pigford litigation, highlighting how lawyers and politicians transformed the injustice of land dispossession into a case about financial compensation. Second, in order to disrupt the notion of federal malfeasance as bookended within a finite timespan, as the lawsuits mandate, we highlight a history of Black resistance that predates the post–Civil Rights era. Third, drawing on Indigenous and postcolonial critiques of regimes of recognition, we address how the forms of recognition affected by liberal legal orders normalize commodified social relations and foreclose more radical visions of Black liberation.

Finally, while we support Black farmers' acceptance of financial compensation, we argue that a radical Black agrarian politics must look beyond the teleological finality of compensation and the individualistic notions of landownership to which it is tied. We conclude the chapter with an epilogue that returns to Pigford and positions compensation claims as a tactical but not a strategic recourse, with the goal of agrarian struggle being land restitution and the development of communal forms of Black land use and ownership.

Pigford et al. v. Glickman

The initial Pigford claim was a culmination of more than four hundred Black farmers who argued that racial discrimination by USDA officials, primarily at the county level, resulted in their not receiving fair assistance from farm support agencies. Responsible for providing financial, technical, and agricultural aid to farmers and rural landowners in need, county-level agencies of the USDA, such as the Farmers Home Association (now Farm Service Agency) and the Cooperative Extension Service (CES), have the authority to determine whether an applicant is eligible for assistance. In Pigford I, the plaintiffs argued that employees of these county-level agencies had discriminated against Black farmers, intentionally delaying and denying their applications (CRAT 1997).[1]

Without access to timely funding, Black applicants were unable to get their crops planted in season or at all, forcing many farmers into bankruptcy. At bankruptcy sales, it was common for neighboring white farmers to purchase once Black-owned farms and farming equipment at a discount. However, the Pigford litigation targeted only the discrimination in the distribution of farm aid. Land transfers through bankruptcy proceedings, while exacerbating racial inequalities, were left unchallenged. These forced land sales impact America's agri-food industry in a number of ways. First, many of the applicants impacted by the USDA's practices were engaged in commercial monocultural production, which meant they were responsible for growing a variety of crops consumed and worn by Americans (e.g., peanuts, soybean, cotton, tobacco, and sweet potatoes). Second, despite their contribution to food security, this community of Black agrarians seems to receive far less concern from the nation and food studies scholars than urban growers and consumers (Winne 2008, 2010a, 2010b; Gottlieb and Anupama 2010; Allen 2012; Rose 2013). This lopsided interest in the future of farming furthers an urban/rural agricultural divide rather than a vision of "the food movement as polyculture" (Alkon and Agyeman 2011, 1).

Third, the forced decline of Black farmers and future farmers has had a direct impact on the desire and ability of rural Black youth and young adults to follow the footsteps of their forebears. In a study of rural poverty, Kenneth Deavers and Robert Hoppe state that as a result of the decline of Black farm operators in the twentieth century, "most Blacks who remain in rural areas are not involved in farming" (1992, 6). Thus an argument can be made that in some ways, rural youth and young adults are as disconnected from agricultural production as their urban equals. Fourth, the generational disconnect between aging Black farmers and Black youth has contributed to a gap in the transfer of agricultural knowledge between experienced rural growers and urban growers in search of agricultural livelihoods and in need of fertile lands. Consider the potential economic, agricultural, and cultural benefits of land transfers between aging Black farmers and Black urban growers who have the desire and skill to farm but lack the financial capital to acquire arable lands.[2] Last, as expressed by Mark Winne (2018) and Willie Wright (2013), overlooking the plight of the Black farm community will result in a missed opportunity for multilateral alliances between various segments of America's agri-food movement.

Not long after the filing of Pigford I, Secretary Dan Glickman instituted a moratorium on all farm foreclosures, pausing the confiscation of scores of farmland, homes, equipment, and other assets owned by indebted Black applicants. He also called for the creation of a Civil Rights Action Team (CRAT) to investigate claims of discrimination (CRAT 1997). The CRAT conducted twelve listening sessions in eleven states throughout the southern United States, resulting in a damning report, "Civil Rights and the USDA." The report documented that the USDA was fully aware that its county-level agents provided assistance to Black and white farmers unequally based on race (CRAT 1997). These findings echoed those established three decades earlier by a United States Commission on Civil Rights investigation into inequalities in the distribution of farm aid. As the earlier report documented, white farmers control county governance processes, and the locally administered structure of USDA programs was "[being] used in the South to establish and maintain racial differentials in the kinds and amounts of Federal aid available to farmers" (United States Commission on Civil Rights 1965, 102). Rather than rectify this concern, the USDA maintained this structure of institutional racism, leaving vastly unequal services between white and Black farm families.

The literature on the effects of structural racism on Black land-ownership and the decline of Black farmers is damning (Gilbert, Sharp, and Felin 2002; Gilbert, Wood, and Sharp 2002; Grant, Wood, and Wright 2012; Wood and Ragar 2013). According to Carmen Harris, a systematic belief in Black inferiority permeated the USDA.

> The popular belief in African-American inferiority and pragmatic political compromises aimed at creating a bureaucracy serving the nation's agricultural constituency and ensuring its longevity, led to a conscious marginalization of African-American interests within the program. Federal extension officials not only tolerated, but actively supported, discrimination within the southern branches of the service. (2008, 193)

Perhaps the most explicit example of federal malfeasance occurred during the tenure of former secretary of agriculture Earl Butz. Butz's remarks regarding Black men's sexual proclivities, initially published in a *Rolling Stone* article, demonstrated his racist views and his comfort with expressing them publicly (R. Goldstein 2008; Noah 2008; Grant, Wood, and Wright 2012).[3] The *Rolling Stone* exposé prompted Butz's resignation, but not before his legacy was forever stamped into U.S. farm policy, the American farm-scape, and USDA institutional policies and procedures. His mantras "adapt or die" and "get big or get out" are widely credited with heralding the decline of small farms and the rise of agribusiness (Philpott 2008; Allen 2012; Byrne 2014). Yet rarely are they linked to his inveterate racism or opposition to the implementation of equal rights laws at the USDA (Daniel 2013).

Though the prevalence of discrimination within the USDA has been extensively investigated (USCCR 1967; CRAT 1997; Harris 2008; Wood and Ragar 2013), along with the decline of Black farmers and landownership (Wadley and Lee 1974; USCCR 1982; Wood and Gilbert 2000; Gilbert, Sharp, and Felin 2001; Gilbert, Wood, and Sharp 2002), too little has been said by scholars on the strategies used by Black farmers to resist institutionalized racism within the USDA (Wright 2007, 2013; Grant, Wood, and Wright 2012). Notably, Pete Daniel (2013) touches upon the importance of the Pigford lawsuit in the post–Civil Rights era but fails to discuss the limitations of an approach based in a politics of recognition. In order to develop such a critique, it is necessary to present other accounts of Black agrarian struggle.

A Brief History of Black Agrarians' Modes of Resistance

Black agrarian struggles need to be interpreted within the *longue durée* of struggles for Black autonomy in the United States. In this section, we stress three important lessons from the history of Black agrarian resistance. First, the struggle for freedom counters white supremacist mythologies regarding Black resistance traditions. Second, the creation of Black geographies of freedom—through escape, marronage, and land reclamations—has been central to the development of Black visions of liberation. Third, freedom is won, not granted.

Whether one begins with the point of contact in Africa, the forced transatlantic voyage, or the antebellum era, Africans and their progeny in the Americas resisted enslavement (Du Bois 1935; Douglass 1997; Equiano 2004; Smallwood 2007; Hartman 2007). Although historical records were maintained by white authorities and often excluded acts of resistance, Black radicalism is evident in the margins of these records, particularly in the white anxieties shared regarding the looming threat of slave rebellions. As Angela Davis argues, the limited existing records of these events should be read as evidence of a broader dynamic of resistance.

The few uprisings—too spectacular to be relegated to oblivion by racism of ruling class historians—were not isolated occurrences. . . . The reality, we know now, was that these open rebellions erupted with such a frequency that they were as much a part of the texture of slavery as the conditions of servitude themselves. And these revolts were only the tip of an iceberg: resistance expressed itself in other grand modes and also in the seemingly trivial forms of feigned illness and studied indolence. (1972, 86)

Histories of revolt and the micropolitics of everyday resistance informed one another, as well as other efforts to actualize Black freedom. A central means to achieve freedom from enslavement in rural areas was to escape the plantation. J. Blaine Hudson's work on the Underground Railroad in the Kentucky borderlands is a unique analysis of the resistance tactics of fugitive slaves.

Although slave escapes are often equated with the Underground Railroad in the public mind, most early escapes and probably the majority of the later escapes were largely unaided. In other words, there were fugitive slaves with or without the Underground Railroad, but there could have been no Underground Railroad without fugitive slaves. (2002, 4)

Hudson's take on the Underground Railroad and abolitionism presents this freedom movement as an ethic and practice deriving from enslaved men and women—an autonomous desire that did not rely on the visions of northern white liberal reformers. Moreover, the establishment of spaces of Black autonomy played a key role in fostering dreams of freedom and the reassertion of Black humanity. Marronage played a key role in Black abolitionist struggle, as enslaved Africans engaged in fugitive movements to separate themselves from the brutal realities of racial slavery (Du Bois 1935; Hall 1985; Hudson 2002; Sayers, Burke, and Henry 2007; Sayers 2008, 2015; Roberts 2015). Clyde Woods describes marronage as "a way of life, a permanent state of being, and an institution with its own sites and networks" (2017, 13). In most cases, the result of marronage, which often took hold in remote, difficult terrains, was the creation of "a parallel social order" (Woods 2017, 13). In concert with dejected landscapes, fugitive slaves developed visions of Black life opposed to what Daniel Sayers calls a "capitalist enslavement mode of accumulation" (2015, 56).

As Clyde Woods (2017) describes in his analysis of two centuries of struggle by Black agrarians in the Mississippi Delta, via cultural forms such as the blues, Black communities established a distinct epistemology that enabled them to share social-political critiques and cultivate dreams of a future where Black communities could be independent of white supremacist designs. The continued circulation of this knowledge of resistance was central to the perpetuation of Black struggle for liberation well into and beyond the civil rights and Black Power movements (Williams 1962; Kelley 1990; Jeffries 2009; Umoja 2013).

These alternative histories of Black mobilization show that Black agrarians did not always turn the other cheek (or to recognition) when confronted with structural racism. Rather, they made tactical choices about how to best advance the cause of Black liberation in their place and time.

Pigford's Politics of Recognition

In this section, we emphasize the disjuncture between this legacy of Black agrarian struggle and the contemporary politics of recognition as articulated through Pigford. Drawing on Indigenous critiques of the politics of recognition, we highlight the need to differentiate a politics of recognition from the aims of struggles for self-determination. The U.S. government's offer of recognition is an effort to capture a liberatory movement within a logic of multicultural liberal democracy. In the place of the autonomous forms of knowledge, relations to land, and the struggle of movements for freedom, the state offers bureaucratic processes to evaluate claim-worthiness, to determine financial compensation, and to grant (or deny) government recognition. While we support both Black and Indigenous claims to justice, it is vital that the meaning of justice be defined by those within those social movements and through the process of struggle. While justice as participation in liberal democracy normalizes the commodified relations of American agricultural capitalism (e.g., individual landownership, land dispossession, and labor exploitation), more radical visions of justice present the possibility of alternative relations.

The 2010 Claims Resolution Act linked historic injustices perpetrated against Black farmers and Indigenous peoples. In addition to extending compensation to additional Black farmers associated with the Pigford case, the legislation advanced resolution of the class-action lawsuit *Cobell v. Salazar.* Originating in 1996, this lawsuit brought by Elouise Cobell of the Blackfeet Confederacy along with other Native American representatives asserted that the Department of Interior and the Department of the Treasury mismanaged Indian trust funds. Settled for $3.4 billion, the case was one of the largest in U.S. history—splitting the funds between payments to the plaintiffs and funds to repurchase dispossessed Indigenous land interests and return them to communal tribal ownership.

Although legislators linked Black farmers and Indigenous communities via a politics of recognition, not much of the research on Black farmers in the United States has tended to focus on such similarities, separating Black farmers from the anti- and postcolonial struggles for land by Indigenous peoples in the Americas and those of the broader Black diaspora. In this section, we seek to place these land struggles into dialogue, drawing upon works by Indigenous scholars to theorize how regimes of legal recognition seek to capture the politics of Black liberation within the individualized and racialized logics of capitalism, an argument with strong parallels to the recent work of Alyosha Goldstein (2014, 2018). As a new politics of recognition that registers the collective claims of historically disadvantaged communities has emerged in liberal democracies, decolonization theorists have critiqued equating recognition from colonial authorities with the goal of struggle. Drawing on the foundational anticolonial theories of Frantz Fanon ([1952] 2008; [1961] 2004), Glen Sean Coulthard (2014) has argued that beneath the patina of liberal inclusion, modern regimes of recognition perpetuate colonial forms of misrecognition. In *Mohawk Interruptus,* Audra Simpson (2014) also critiques politics of misrecognition. The asymmetries produced by ongoing dynamics of racial oppression distort the recognition of Black and Indigenous humanity. For Fanon ([1952] 2008; [1961] 2004) and Coulthard (2014), the colonized can achieve self-consciousness only by struggling against and ultimately overthrowing white supremacist colonial regimes. For Indigenous scholars, seemingly consensual workings of settler colonial law are said to frame Indigenous claims within a legal structure that obscures the possibility of autonomy from the existing colonial racial order (Borrows 1999; Povinelli 2002; Christie 2005; Coulthard 2014; McCreary 2014; Simpson 2014; Moreton-Robinson 2015).

Today, multiple examples from Latin America demonstrate the shortcomings and pitfalls of relying on a politics of state recognition to address legacies of anti-Black land dispossession. In the past three decades, state governments in Latin America have legally codified measures aimed at ameliorating the long-term effects of discrimination by granting land rights to Afro-descendant populations. Brazil, Colombia, Ecuador, Guatemala, Honduras, and Nicaragua have land rights legislation for Afro-descendant communities (Hooker 2008). While such legislation nominally acknowledges the historic and contemporary spatial agency of Afro–Latin American groups, case studies from these countries demonstrate how a politics of state recognition may further marginalize the very groups it claims to support.

After gaining state recognition of their land title in 2010, the once autonomous artisanal gold mining people of La Toma, Colombia, became beholden to state-imposed taxes and royalties on their small-scale extractive way of life (Vélez-Torres 2014). Taxes and royalties displaced traditional practices of extraction in La Toma and placed new expectations of "rational" production as well as unprecedented debts on the people of the community (Vélez-Torres 2014). Following the reception of land titles in 2004, the communal governance structure of the rural Afro-Brazilian community of Rio das Rãs was supplanted by a legally recognized governing association, and the community was forced to undertake state-imposed development projects (Amorim and Germani 2005). Relatedly, Pablo Lapegna (2013) notes that agrarian movements in Argentina often undergo demobilization, and movement leaders, entering rights-based relations with state actors, end up in clientele-like positions with institutional actors. Therefore, a politics of recognition results in the attenuation of peasants' self-determination and self-sufficiency (Lapegna 2016). These examples from Latin America demonstrate some ways in which a politics of recognition can undermine the struggle to secure Black territorial self-determination.

Most pertinently, Alyosha Goldstein (2014, 2018) has sought to develop an analysis of how the politics of financial compensation shape the possibilities and limitations of the Claims Resolution Act. Goldstein calls attention to an important contradiction: the debts of a deeply rooted history of racial discrimination cannot be settled through the bureaucratic workings of a state that is constitutionally founded upon and committed to institutional practices of colonial racism and dispossession. Goldstein argues that "standard juridical doctrines of discrimination and their attendant forms of redress are ultimately insufficient for substantively reckoning with the economies of dispossession[s]" that Pigfords I and II and Cobell ostensibly challenge (2018, 84). With Pigford, the settlement was portrayed by state actors as a means of closure: a decisive statement "that federally institutionalized racial inequality was now past, finished, and resolved" (Goldstein 2014, 50).

Yet Pigfords I and II were far from adequate. They did not represent a settlement of past debts accrued by the nation prior to 1984. Nor did the settlement provide the opportunity to return to farming for many Black farmers (Goldstein 2014). As Eddie Carthan, a former farmer and current county supervisor in Holmes County, Mississippi, emphasizes, these loans do not begin to address the broader history of the theft of Black land, of which loan discrimination was just a part.

> The damage that they had done over the years, in terms of making Blacks whole, that wasn't a drop in the bucket; you couldn't buy a tractor for $50,000. Most of them had already lost land, some of them still losing the land. Those who were able to get the loans, they gave it to them late, you know, intentionally. . . . If you're supposed to plant in March, April, May, and you don't

get your money until June, July, you're already 50 percent a failure because farming is a seasonal thing, it's a timely thing. You can't plant cotton in July and expect it to pay your debts off and make money. (Eddie Carthan, interview with Brian Williams, Tchula, Miss., July 6, 2012)

As Black farmers were burdened with accumulating debts, they were locked into forms of financial bondage that constricted their agency. The financial structures not only pressed Black farmers into bankruptcy but also constricted the practice of Black farming to market production in order to service loans. Even those farmers who escaped bankruptcy lost a significant degree of autonomy.

Instead of truly accounting for the compounded debts of the USDA, Pigfords I and II mobilized a language of discrimination and redress, which deflects attention from the historical and ongoing centrality of racialized dispossession to the workings of the contemporary state (Goldstein 2014). This focus on discrimination obfuscates the systematic relationship between instances of discrimination and "broader structural inequities" (Goldstein 2018, 85). Goldstein argues that the Claims Resolution Act indicates the possibilities of judicial action, but it simultaneously "throws into relief the inadequacies of legal redress and colonial reconciliation" (2014, 57). He cautions against the limitations of a legal case built purely upon discrimination, which treats the racial logics of agrarian dispossession as exceptional rather than foundational (Goldstein 2018). Antidiscrimination legislation can serve the important purpose of strategically challenging the gap between "liberal de jure norms and de facto practices," but it "ultimately reinforces the legitimacy of such institutions and social and economic norms predicated on the racialized logics of possessive individualism more broadly" (Goldstein 2018, 99).

Pigfords I and II exposed the USDA's implicit bias and set in motion a series of steps toward retribution for past acts of discrimination. However, a politics of recognition-based redress underwritten by the state normalized the nation's commodified relations of racial capitalism and foreclosed more radical visions of Black liberation. While securing financial redress for historic discrimination can create greater space for select Black farmers to maneuver, this is the case only if those within the Black farmers' movement recognize the disjuncture between a vision of justice articulated by the courts and Black farmers' long struggle for spatial autonomy and economic self-determination.

Toward an Agrarian Politics of Difference

In this section, we argue for the recovery and recentering of a vision of Black spatial autonomy and economic self-determination. This is a clarion for a politics of difference within the Black farmers' movement and the Black farming community that continues the long trajectory of struggle for freedom from racial capitalism that refuses to subjugate the conditions of Black being to the normalized relations of white supremacy. Making this call, we continue our deference to land-based movements across the Black diaspora as well as to critical dialogues between Black and Indigenous movements. Doing so, we argue for tactical engagements with the law rather than the subjugation of radical strategic horizons to the racial state.

Robert Knox (2012) usefully parses the terms *tactic* and *strategy*—the former referring to a pragmatic intervention to win a local or immediate victory and the latter a movement's structural objective for change. Thus, thinking through Pigford, it is necessary to distinguish the tactical from the strategic. While Black farmers' use of the law in Pigford has regularly been framed—by politicians, the media, and representatives of the Black farmers' movement—as effecting a resolution or end to the issue of racial discrimination in agriculture, we want to refuse this notion of the end to struggle. In opposition to the suggestion by Obama, we want to insist that the struggle continues, and the relationship between past, present, and future remains open. It is necessary to hold the legacy of Black struggle against injustice as unfinished in order to bring about the possibility of an agrarian future different from the past. In order to do so, claims-making in the courts must be resituated as a tactic (i.e., a means) rather than as a strategy (i.e., an end).

Scholars are engaging in analyses of the effective use of legal approaches to gain and retain access to land and territory in Latin America (Wolford 2010; Reyes and Kaufman 2011; Zibechi 2012) and Palestine (Quiquivix 2013/14). A central concern of these studies is the difference between the use of legal maneuvers and whether they facilitate social change or foster the appropriation of social movements. Raúl Zibechi (2012) discusses these anxieties in his treatise on the origins and political philosophies of Latin American land-based social movements. As Latin American countries shifted from a Fordist/Taylorist mode of production to a neoliberal economy that further devalorized workers and their labor, communities have shifted from a politics of recognition that sought to join the state to a self-affirming politics of difference that seeks separation from the state. According to Zibechi, "It is within these new territories that the movements are collectively building a whole new organization of society" (2012, 38).

The use of the law as a tactic of resistance for the expansion of autonomous territory emerges in Wendy Wolford's (2010) study with the Movimento Sem Terra (MST, Landless Workers' Movement) in Brazil. The MST's use of the law in order to access property rights was a tactic through which the MST was able to legally acquire territory and reproduce its communal ways of life (Wolford 2010, 14). The MST's use of the legal process as a way to hold the government accountable to the needs and demands of its communities allowed for a two-pronged attack — a politics of recognition grounded in a politics of difference.

Alvaro Reyes and Mara Kaufman (2011) argue that although the Zapatistas have made use of Mexico's legal system for the recognition of their rights, they have not externalized their right of authentication to the state. The Zapatistas use the legal field as a tactic toward the self-reproduction of Zapatista subjectivity and territory and a subversion of the state's desire for the socio-spatial and political-economic homogenization of society.

Transplanting diasporic tactics within the context of the United States, it becomes apparent that if used as a strategy, Black farmers' attempts to gain recognition of their rights and subjectivity from a state responsible for their past and present marginalization run the risk of reifying the state's control rather than withering it. If rights claims are applied as a measure toward a greater, more collective goal, a politics of representation could serve as a catalyst for the maturation of a separate politics altogether.

Pigford: An Epilogue

This chapter sought to explain limitations of Black farmers' usage of a class-action lawsuit to acquire justice for generations of federally facilitated discrimination at the behest of the USDA. In doing so, we argued that Black farmers' use of Pigfords I and II as a strategy of resistance left the movement vulnerable to co-optation through a politics of state recognition and reformation. Drawing from literature in Indigenous studies on the limitations of using a politics of recognition and research on agrarian movements in Latin America, we suggested that Pigfords I and II were best used as a tactic toward the production of alternative agrarian politics, particularly ones based in a communitarian ethic. Thus, rather than accept state recognition of their ills and supposed resolution, we propose Black farmers present unique agrarian politics of difference that promote alternative land-use options, forward-thinking agricultural modes of production, and collective economic enterprises.

Rather than the normalization of private property and the individual pursuit to succeed or fail in competitive (and clearly unequal) economic markets, Black farmers in the United States might draw inspiration from more collective attempts at spatial autonomy and economic self-determination in the United States and abroad. Examples of collective agrarian practices exist in the United States. In the early 1980s, the largest Black landowner was not a privately held farm but a cooperative—New Communities Inc. (NCI). Created as a community land trust, NCI established a distinct model of Black spatial and economic justice. However, like many Black farmers throughout the United States, NCI eventually went bankrupt as a result of the USDA's discriminatory practices. In the wake of the Pigford settlements, NCI has been revitalized as a model for transformative agrarian justice. Using the financial capital available as a result of the Pigford case, NCI's founding members, including Shirley Sherrod, a well-known advocate for Black farmers, have sought to leverage the compensation provided through a politics of recognition to support the rearticulation of a politics of Black agrarian difference based on the collective construction of their agrarian futures (Shirley Sherrod, personal communication, October 10, 2013).

NCI is but one example of a reimagining and revitalization of Black farming through a politics of difference. Others have included the work of the Mississippi-based Freedom Farms Cooperative during the heart of the civil rights movement (White 2017a), the contemporary urban agricultural additions of D-Town Farms (White 2011a, 2011b, 2017b), and the Cooperative Community of New West Jackson (Flanders 2014; Wright 2019). The agro-economic and spatial relations embodied within these cooperative initiatives are models for how to transform the individualized capitalist logic of farmer compensation into a vision of collective Black agrarianism, one that extends the dreams of spatial autonomy and self-determination from the past into the present.

Notes

1. We use the phrase *would-be farmers* because a number of claimants within Pigfords I and II were applicants who sought to become farmers but could not attain the funds necessary to purchase equipment and implements.

2. This concept has come out of conversations between Willie Wright, Ashanté Reese, and food justice advocate Dara Cooper.

3. An unedited version of Secretary Butz's remarks is published in Noah 2008.

Bibliography

Alkon, Alison Hope, and Julian Agyeman. 2011. "Introduction: The Food Movement as Polyculture." In *Cultivating Food Justice: Race, Class, and Sustainability,* edited by Alison Hope Alkon and Julian Agyeman, 1–20. Cambridge, Mass.: MIT Press.

Allen, Will. 2012. *The Good Food Revolution: Growing Healthy Food, People, and Communities.* New York: Gotham Books.

Amorim, Itamar Gomes, and Guiomar Inez Germani. 2005. "Quilombos Da Bahia: Presença Incontestável." *Anais do X Encontro de Geógrafos da América Latina,* 796–812.

Borrows, John. 1999. "Sovereignty's Alchemy: An Analysis of *Delgamuukw v. British Columbia.*" *Osgoode Hall Law Journal* 37 (3): 537–98.

Byrne, Dave. 2014. "Ground Down to Molasses: The Making of an American Folk Song." *Boston Review,* July 2. http://bostonreview.net.

Census of Agriculture. 2017. "Race/Ethnicity/Gender/Profile." https://www.nass.usda.gov.

Christie, Gordon. 2005. "A Colonial Reading of Recent Jurisprudence: *Sparrow, Delgamuukw* and *Haida Nation.*" *Windsor Yearbook of Access to Justice* 23 (1): 17–53.

Civil Rights Action Team (CRAT). 1997. "Civil Rights at the United States Department of Agriculture: A Report by the Civil Rights Action Team." Washington, D.C.

Coulthard, Glen Sean. 2014. *Red Skin, White Masks: Rejecting the Colonial Politics of Recognition.* Minneapolis: University of Minnesota Press.

Cowan, Tadlock, and Jody Feder. 2013. "The *Pigford* Cases: USDA Settlement of Discrimination Suits by Black Farmers." Congressional Research Service, Washington, D.C., May 29.

Daniel, Pete. 2013. *Dispossession: Discrimination against African American Farmers in the Age of Civil Rights.* Chapel Hill: University of North Carolina Press.

Davis, Angela. 1972. "Reflections on the Black Woman's Role in the Community of Slaves." *Massachusetts Review* 13 (1/2): 81–100.

Deavers, Kenneth, and Robert Hoppe. 1992. "Overview of the Rural Poor in the 1980s." In *Rural Poverty in America,* edited by Cynthia M. Duncan, 3–20. Westport, Conn.: Auburn House.

Douglass, F. 1997. *Narrative of the Life of Frederick Douglass, an American Slave.* New York: Laurel Books.

Du Bois, W. E. B. 1935. *Black Reconstruction: An Essay toward a History of the Part Which Black Folk Played in the Attempt to Reconstruct Democracy in America, 1860–1880.* New York: Harcourt, Brace.

Equiano, Olaudah. 2004. *The Interesting Narrative of the Life of Olaudah Equiano, or, Gustavas Vassa, the African.* New York: Modern Library.

Fanon, Frantz. (1952) 2008. *Black Skin, White Masks.* Translated by Richard Philcox. New York: Grove.

Fanon, Frantz. (1961) 2004. *The Wretched of the Earth.* Translated by Richard Philcox. New York: Grove.

Flanders, Laura. 2014. "After Death of Radical Mayor, Mississippi's Capital Wrestles with His Economic Vision." *YES!,* April 2. http://www.yesmagazine.org.

Gilbert, Jess, Gwen Sharp, and M. Sindy Felin. 2001. "The Decline (and Revival?) of Black Farmers and Rural Landowners: A Review of the Research Literature." Land Tenure Center, University of Wisconsin–Madison.

Gilbert, Jess, Gwen Sharp, and M. Sindy Felin. 2002. "The Loss and Persistence of Black-Owned Farms and Farmland: A Review of Research Literature and Its Implications." *Southern Rural Sociology* 18 (2): 1–30.

Gilbert, Jess, Spencer Wood, and Gwen Sharp. 2002. "Who Owns the Land? Agricultural Land Ownership by Race/Ethnicity." *Rural America* 17 (4): 55–62.

Goldstein, Alyosha. 2014. "Finance and Foreclosure in the Colonial Present." *Radical History Review* 2014 (118): 42–63.

Goldstein, Alyosha. 2018. "The Ground Not Given: Colonial Dispositions of Land, Race, and Hunger." *Social Text* 36 (2 (135)): 83–106.

Goldstein, Richard. 2008. "Earl L. Butz, Secretary Felled by Racial Remark, Is Dead at 98." *New York Times,* February 4.

Gottlieb, Robert, and Joshi Anupama. 2010. *Food Justice.* Cambridge, Mass.: MIT Press.

Grant, Gary, Spencer Wood, and Willie Wright. 2012. "Black Farmers United: The Struggle against Power and Principalities." *Journal of Pan African Studies* 5 (1): 3–22.

Hall, N. A. T. 1985. "Maritime Maroons: 'Grand Marronage' from the Danish West Indies." *William and Mary Quarterly* 42 (4): 476–98.

Harris, Carmen V. 2008. "The Extension Service Is Not an Integration Agency: The Idea of Race in the Cooperative Extension Service." *Agricultural History Society* 82 (2): 193–219.

Hartman, Saidiya. 2007. *Lose Your Mother: A Journey along the Atlantic Slave Route.* New York: Farrar, Straus and Giroux.

Hooker, Juliet. 2008. "Afro-Descendant Struggles for Collective Rights in Latin America: Between Race and Culture." *Souls* 10 (3): 279–91.

Hudson, J. Blaine. 2002. *Fugitive Slaves and the Underground Railroad in the Kentucky Borderland.* Jefferson, N.C.: McFarland.

Jeffries, Hasan. 2009. *Bloody Lowndes: Civil Rights and Black Power in Alabama's Black Belt.* New York: New York University Press.

Kelley, Robin D. G. 1990. *Hammer and Hoe: Alabama Communist during the Great Depression.* Chapel Hill: University of North Carolina Press.

Knox, Robert. 2012. "Strategy and Tactics." *Finnish Yearbook of International Law* 21: 193–229.

LaFraniere, Sharon. 2013. "U.S. Opens Spigot after Farmers Claim Discrimination." *New York Times,* April 26.

Lapegna, Pablo. 2013. "Social Movements and Patronage Politics: Processes of Demobilization and Dual Pressure." *Sociological Forum* 28 (4): 842–63.

Lapegna, Pablo. 2016. *Soybeans and Power: Genetically Modified Crops, Environmental Politics, and Social Movements in Argentina.* New York: Oxford University Press.

Martin, Roland. 2013. "'It's Better to Eat, Than Starve': John Boyd on the Black Farmers Settlement." *Tom Joyner Morning Show,* August 6. http://www.nationalblackfarmersassociation.org.

McCreary, Tyler. 2014. "The Burden of Sovereignty: Court Configurations of Indigenous and State Authority in Aboriginal Title Litigation in Canada." *North American Dialogue* 17 (2): 64–78.

McCutcheon, Priscilla. 2013. "'Returning Home to Our Rightful Place': The Nation of Islam and Muhammad Farms." *Geoforum* 49: 61–70.

Moreton-Robinson, Aileen. 2015. *The White Possessive: Property, Power, and Indigenous Sovereignty.* Minneapolis: University of Minnesota Press.

Noah, Timothy. 2008. "Earl Butz, History's Victim." *Slate,* February 4. http://www.slate.com.

Obama, Barack. 2010. "Claims Resolution Act of 2010." C-Span, December 8. https://www.c-span.org.

Philpott, Tom. 2008. "A Reflection on the Lasting Legacy of 1970s USDA Secretary Earl Butz." *Grist,* February 8. https://grist.org.

Povinelli, Elizabeth. 2002. *The Cunning of Recognition: Indigenous Alterities and the Making of Australian Multiculturalism.* Durham, N.C.: Duke University Press.

Quiquivix, Linda. 2013/14. "Law as Tactic: Palestine, the Zapatistas, and Global Exercises of Power." *al-Majdal,* no. 55 (Winter).

Reyes, Alvaro, and Maura Kaufman. 2011. "Sovereignty, Indigeneity, Territory: Zapatista Autonomy and the New Practices of Decolonization." *South Atlantic Quarterly* 110 (2): 505–25.

Roberts, Neil. 2015. *Freedom as Marronage*. Chicago: University of Chicago Press.

Rose, Shayna A. 2013. "Seed Is Good." *Los Angeles Magazine,* July.

Salamon, Lester M. 1979. "The Time Dimension in Policy Evaluation: The Case of the New Deal Land Reform Experiments." *Public Policy* 27 (2): 130–83.

Sayers, Daniel. 2008. "Diasporan Exiles in the Great Dismal Swamp, 1630–1865." *Transforming Anthropology* 14 (1): 10–20.

Sayers, Daniel. 2015. *A Desolate Place for a Defiant People: The Archaeology of Maroons, Indigenous Americans, and Enslaved Laborers in the Great Dismal Swamp*. Gainesville: University Press of Florida.

Sayers, Daniel, Brendan Burke, and Aaron Henry. 2007. "The Political Economy of Exile in the Great Dismal Swamp." *International Journal of Historical Archaeology* 11 (1): 60–97.

Simpson, Audra. 2014. *Mohawk Interruptus: Political Life across the Borders of Settler States*. Durham, N.C.: Duke University Press.

Umoja, Akinyele. 2013. *We Will Shoot Back: Armed Resistance in the Mississippi Struggle*. New York: New York University Press.

United States Commission on Civil Rights (USCCR). 1965. "Equal Opportunity in Farm Programs: An Appraisal of Services Rendered by Agencies of the United States Department of Agriculture." February 27.

United States Commission on Civil Rights (USCCR). 1967. "Equal Opportunity in Federally Assisted Agricultural Programs in Georgia." Georgia State Advisory Committee, August.

United States Commission on Civil Rights (USCCR). 1982. "The Decline of Black Farming in America." February.

Vélez-Torres, Irene. 2014. "Governmental Extractivism in Colombia: Legislation, Securitization and the Local Settings of Mining Control." *Political Geography* 38: 68–78.

Wadley, Janet K., and Everett S. Lee. 1974. "The Disappearance of the Black Farmer." *Phylon* 35 (3): 276–83.

White, Monica. 2011a. "D-Town Farm: African American Resistance to Food Insecurity and the Transformation of Detroit." *Environmental Practice* 13 (4): 406–17.

White, Monica. 2011b. "Sisters of the Soil: Urban Gardening as Resistance in Detroit." *Food Justice* 5 (1): 13–28.

White, Monica. 2017a. "'A Pig and a Garden': Fannie Lou Hamer and the Freedom Farms Cooperative." *Food and Foodways* 25 (1): 20–39.

White, Monica. 2017b. "Voices of the Food Movement in Detroit." *Journal of Agriculture, Food Systems, and Community Development* 7 (2): 5–7.

Williams, Robert. 1962. *Negroes with Guns.* New York: Third World.

Winne, Mark. 2008. *Closing the Food Gap: Resetting the Table in the Land of Plenty.* Boston, Mass.: Beacon.

Winne, Mark. 2010a. "African American Farmers Go Organic, Bring Healthy Food to the Southeast." *Resilience,* April 7, 2010. https://www.resilience.org.

Winne, Mark. 2010b. *Food Rebels, Guerrilla Gardeners, and Smart-Cookin' Mamas: Fighting Back in an Age of Industrial Agriculture.* Boston: Beacon.

Winne, Mark. 2018. *Stand Together or Starve Alone: Unity and Chaos in the U.S. Food Movement.* Santa Barbara, Calif.: Praeger.

Wolford, Wendy. 2010. *This Land Is Ours Now: Social Mobilization and the Meanings of Land in Brazil.* Durham, N.C.: Duke University Press.

Wood, Spencer, and Jess Gilbert. 2000. "Returning African American Farmers to the Land: Recent Trends and a Policy Rationale." *Review of Black Political Economy* 27 (4): 43–64.

Wood, Spencer, and Cheryl R. Ragar. 2013. "Institutional Discrimination in the Civil Rights Violations of Black Farmers." *Journal of Pan African Studies* 5 (6): 16–36.

Woods, Clyde. 1998. *Development Arrested: The Blues and Plantation Power in the Mississippi Delta.* New York: Verso.

Woods, Clyde. 2017. *Development Drowned and Reborn: The Blues and Bourbon Restorations in Post-Katrina New Orleans.* Edited by Jordan T. Camp and Laura Pulido. Athens: University of Georgia Press.

Wright, Willie Jamaal. 2007. "Upside Down from the Word Go": Kentucky's Black Farmers Speak Out on the Issue of Land Loss." Master's diss., University of Louisville.

Wright, Willie. 2013. "The Black Farmers' Struggle and Its Importance to the Local Food Movement." *Sustain: A Journal of Environmental and Sustainability Issues,* no. 27 (Fall/Winter): 49–54.

Wright, Willie Jamaal. 2019. "The Public Is Intellectual." *Professional Geographer* 71 (1): 172–78.

Zibechi, Raúl. 2012. *Territories in Resistance: A Cartography of Latin American Social Movements.* Translated by Ramor Ryan. Oakland, Calif.: AK Press.

10

THE MANGO GANG AND NEW WORLD CUISINE

White Privilege in the Commodification of Latin American and Afro-Caribbean Foods

Judith Williams

• • •

Miami is a hot destination for hipster foodies anxiously seeking the ultimate in culinary experimentation and exoticized ethnic flavors. South Florida's distinctive use of "traditional" and "rustic" cooking techniques and ingredients commonly found in the Caribbean, South America, and Central America, fused with "classic" European cooking methods, is known as New World cuisine.[1] In the late 1980s, a white male chef named Norman Van Aken, who had relocated to South Florida from the Midwest, took credit for "discovering" this new cuisine (Van Aken 1997; Maze 2018).[2] Van Aken and three of his white male colleagues became known as the Mango Gang after they developed a cultlike following for their bold, contemporary fare that primarily fused Latin American and Afro-Caribbean cooking with classic European styles.

Capitalizing on South Florida's immigrant communities of traditional Haitian, Jamaican, and Cuban cooks, the Mango Gang appropriated Latin American and Afro-Caribbean cooking methods and recipes, then whitewashed and rebranded these foods as New World cuisine. While this appropriation seemed to be focused on food, it was the underlying appropriation of culinary knowledge and labor that was most crucial to their success. After eating at Caribbean-owned eateries in Little Haiti, Little Havana, and other immigrant neighborhoods, members of the Mango Gang replicated the Caribbean culinary flavors and techniques, incorporating them into their menus with little modification. While a plate of *vaca frita* with *boniato* (a traditional Cuban dish of shredded beef with yam) might cost ten dollars from a cafeteria in Hialeah, it cost three times as much presented as "*Vaca Frita* with a Tropical Tuber Hash Cake" at one of the Mango Gang's high-end New World cuisine restaurants. Lauded by industry experts as daring visionaries, whose "discovery" of New World cuisine put Miami on the culinary map, each of the original Mango Gang chefs went on to build a portfolio of successful business interests based on their appropriated and reinvented Latin American and Caribbean food.

There has been much scholarly debate surrounding the concept of "cultural appropriation," what it means, and when it should apply. Merriam-Webster's *Collegiate Dictionary* (2017) defines "to appropriate" as "to take or make use of without authority or right." Some scholars view cultural appropriation as the use of another culture's symbols, rituals, and artifacts, regardless of intent or motive (Shugart 1997; Rogers 2006). Others argue that cases of appropriation must be classified according to the "social, economic and political contexts in which they occur" (Rogers 2006, 476; see also Wallis and Malm 1984; Ziff and Rao 1997; Rodriquez 2006). In this chapter, I use the term *culinary appropriation* to refer to the unauthorized use of Latin American and Afro-Caribbean foods, recipes, and cuisines, as well as the intellectual and physical exploitation of Latin American and Afro-Caribbean cooks. I contend that in the case of the Mango Gang and New World cuisine, culinary appropriation is a phenomenon based on the relationships and power dynamics within the racial hierarchy of white chefs and the nonwhite people whose food, ideas, and labor they appropriate. The appropriation I discuss in this chapter was of significant benefit to the white chefs who had little concern for the social, economic, or political welfare of the people whose food and culture were being appropriated.

In this chapter, I compare Van Aken's "discovery" of New World cuisine to Christopher Columbus's "discovery" of the Americas. I use the term *discovery* to reflect the parallels between Columbus and Van Aken, who both stumbled across unfamiliar terrain—or foods, in the case of Van Aken—and claimed it as their own unique discovery. Van Aken is the self-proclaimed founding father of New World cuisine, a fact that I metaphorically interpret as his "discovery" of New World cooking (Balcomb Lane 1991; Van Aken 1997; Maze 2018). With an understanding that Columbus did not in fact "discover" the New World, I dispute Van Aken's "discovery" of New World cuisine. I argue that the foods and flavors used in the creation of New World cuisine were not new to most South Florida residents. They were a repackaged amalgamation of Afro-Caribbean and Latin American foods, formerly invisible to the white American culinary imagination. Using the framework of racial capitalism, as well as narratives in line with Cedric Robinson's Black radical tradition, I argue that the consumption and promotion of New World cuisine was a modern-day colonization of Miami's darkest, poorest, and most vulnerable immigrants. After a brief discussion of racial capitalism, I describe my own position and present two anecdotes from my personal experience that illustrate the ways in which this exotification and exploitation directly affect those working in the restaurant kitchens. Then I discuss the Mango Gang and their discovery of New World cuisine, followed by an examination of the Mango Gang's invisible authority to essentialize and usurp Latin American and Caribbean food and flavors and present them as their own. I explore how authority was fortified by the use of nonwhiteness as culinary capital, focusing on how the "discovery" of New World cuisine led to the formation of a culinary Other, which was both exotified and exploited in a city that relied heavily on ideas of multiculturalism for its economic success. This is followed by an examination of nonwhiteness as culinary capital and for white consumption. Finally, I discuss how New World cuisine and its offshoot, Nuevo Latino cuisine, bolstered the professional success of the Mango Gang and simultaneously whitened the image of Miami's dominant Latinx community in the local and national imagination.

Racial Capitalism and the Black Radical Tradition

For this analysis, I frame my discussion using the Black radical tradition. Originating in a critique of Marxism, Cedric Robinson's theory of racial capitalism argues that all capitalism is racial, because race has been historically embedded in European society since the Medieval period and the age of feudalism. Robinson uses the racialization of other Europeans, such as the Irish and working-class British, to argue that racialism has always been a means of establishing social hierarchies and order in both Europe and Europe's colonies (Robinson 1983; Meyerson 2000). Although racism has been a constant social force shaping European politics and the development of capitalism, the ways in which race was deployed expanded globally during slavery and colonialism. Long-distance trade extended capitalism's reach, and the business model of low-cost racialized immigrant labor was foundational to its success.

In his historical analyses of race, Robinson disputes the presumption that "the social and historical processes that matter, which are determinative, are European" (1983, 67–68). Instead, he draws our attention to the untold stories of resistance and Black radicalism, steeped in the legacy of African cultures, habits, beliefs, and morality.

> Marx had not realized fully that the cargoes of laborers also contained African cultures, critical mixes and admixtures of language and thought, of cosmology and metaphysics, of habits, beliefs and morality. These were the actual terms of their humanity. . . . African labor brought the past with it, a past that had produced it and settled upon it the first elements of consciousness and comprehension. (Robinson 1983, 121–22)

This rich African intellectual and cultural legacy was violently dismissed in practice and was silenced in historical accounts of slavery, colonialism, and American imperialism (Robinson 1983; Meyerson 2000; Kelley 2002). European identity relied on stereotypes of the racialized Other as ignorant, violent, hypersexed, and biologically inferior, a being from whom they could distinguish themselves as superior: both wiser and better (Spivak 1988). In the following sections, I will draw on Robinson's arguments to make a case that the invisibility of Afro-Caribbean culinary expertise in the development of New World cuisine was used to bolster the credibility and authority of the white chefs who are the self-proclaimed founders of New World cuisine. I will illustrate this with stories of resistance and contestation that draw attention to the ways that the Black radical tradition is engaged in Miami's racially segregated restaurant industry.

Reflexive Statement

What I perceive as important in the stories shared in this chapter is informed by who I am, where I live, and where I come from. I was born and raised in Kingston, Jamaica. In 1981 I migrated to Miami with my mother, brother, and sister, and I have lived mostly in South Florida since then. By nationality and culture, I am Jamaican. However, having lived in the United States for most of my life, I strongly identify as a Black woman and, like most people of color, I am highly attuned to both overt and covert anti-Black discrimination. I am also passionate about food and fascinated by the ways in which food shapes people's life experiences. I grew up in my mother's restaurant in Kingston and have spent most of my professional career working in the food service industry. My passion for food has taken me all over the world. I have studied cooking in Paris, taught cooking in China and Haiti, and learned that food can be a tool of social justice in Phnom Penh, Cambodia. These global experiences have shown me the centrality of food in every culture and taught me the importance of respecting and celebrating the diversity of our culinary palates. In this chapter, I share stories from my experiences working as a prep cook in a fine-dining restaurant in Miami in order to illustrate the complex racial beliefs and hierarchies that exist in the restaurant industry. I also use these stories to illuminate some of the ways that people of color resist and contest racial discrimination.

Mark's Place

It was 1993, in the middle of the Miami summer. The kitchen at Mark's Place was sizzling. The air-conditioning cooled the dining room, but it did not work very well back in the kitchen, so we kept the back door open to let out some of the stifling heat—though I am not sure how much that helped, given that temperatures outside were in the nineties. At least there was a screen to keep flies and mosquitos at bay. On that particular afternoon, the kitchen was more crowded than usual, and with so many people packed into that little space, the heat felt unbearable. We were fully booked that night. The dinner cooks had already arrived to set up their stations and we lowly prep cooks were in danger of being squeezed out of the kitchen. In our hierarchy, the dinner cooks were exalted. A brigade of white men and one white woman, the dinner cooks got to perform their culinary magic every night in an open kitchen, in front of a crowd of mesmerized diners. The *really* important cooks would meet with chef Mark Militello and his sous-chef to discuss the menu before the dinner service began: a ritual in which we prep cooks were never included.

Relations of power determine the social order and hierarchy of restaurant kitchens. In professional kitchens, these social stratifications are often formalized with a hierarchical military brigade system. In a culinary brigade, workers are ranked in order of importance with the chef at the helm and dishwashers at the bottom. At Mark's Place, this formal hierarchy often worked in tandem with an unwritten social contract to create concrete and abstract rules about power, authority, and social order. This unwritten social contract reflected local cultural dynamics and reinforced intersectional race, gender, and ethnic hierarchies. The Mango Gang could appropriate food, knowledge, and labor because it was understood that nonwhite, immigrant workers were subjugated to their white, male, American bosses. Therefore, when Mark or his sous-chef brought us some of our native food, such as yellow yam or breadfruit, we performed as expected and would cook it up just right, proud to share the culinary techniques that had been passed on to us over generations. Later, when the dinner cooks arrived and scooped up the gently sautéed chayote or yellow yam with garlic that we had spent all day prepping for them, we knew we had to silently make room for them. We had to give up our precious counter space and work with our cutting boards and knives precariously perched on top of gray Rubbermaid industrial trash cans. On that particular afternoon, I had wedged myself and my improvised trash-can workspace into a small corner at the end of the dish station. I was working quickly to finish my prep, so I could leave in time for my second job, waiting tables. Just as I was getting ready to leave, a case of live Maine lobsters arrived. The sous-chef handed them to me and told me to cook them, removing the meat but leaving the exoskeleton intact, so the head, claws, and tail could be restuffed and used as a garnish. Not an easy chore.

I glanced at the clock. It was 4:55 p.m. I spotted some boiling water on the stove. Working as fast as I could, I cooked the lobsters and then plunged them into an ice bath. At 5:30 p.m., I still had six left to prepare. I was starting to feel very nervous. My second shift would begin in only thirty minutes, and I still had to rid my body of kitchen funk, change clothes, and drive twenty minutes to the mall where the other restaurant was located. I could not risk being late for my second job, but I did not want to jeopardize this job either. I had just graduated from culinary school summa cum laude. Working as a prep cook for the famous Mark Militello was a coveted entry-level job, a stepping stone to higher opportunities. But I *had* to get to my second job on time. Reality set in as my stomach began to growl. I was famished. We were not allowed breaks and the chef did not feed us during the day. If I was going to last through my night shift waiting tables, I needed to leave now, so I could grab some breadsticks and salad before my shift. I mustered up the courage to approach the chef and nervously told him that I had to leave in order to arrive at my other job on time. He looked at me quizzically. "*Other* job?" he asked, as if the concept were unheard of. "How many children do you have?" His voice was dripping with condescension. "None," I said emphatically—pissed off that he had assumed I must be an uneducated woman with several kids, just because of my race and gender. I looked him in the eye and said, "I don't have any children.

I just graduated from culinary school. I can't live on what you pay me, which is nine dollars per hour." "Oh!" he said. And then he looked at me more closely and repeated it slowly, in what I hope was a dawning realization: "Ohhhhhh."

Resistance and the Black Radical Tradition

I usually arrived at the kitchen around 6:30 a.m., just after dawn. There were only a few of us around then: me, a few prep cooks, and the dishwashers. Most of the dishwashers were Haitian and most of the prep cooks were Jamaican. We were all Black, and I was the only woman. We arrived at work before any of the bosses or white workers showed up, so we could make ourselves a good hot meal that would sustain us throughout the day. By 8:00 a.m., we had eaten an authentic Caribbean fusion meal of Haitian fish, Jamaican brown stew chicken, rice and peas, sweet plantain, and cabbage, all washed down with recycled plastic cups of ice-cold Sprite. Sometimes we had to improvise, using whatever we could find in the walk-in cooler that we thought the chef would not notice the lack of—but, whatever we ate, it was always good. It reminded us of home—of our families and of our shared cultural connection as Black Caribbean Others.

The intersection of my gender, race, class, and nationality designated my rank in the racial hierarchy, as different both from that of my island compatriots and that of my white boss. In Andrea Queeley's (2010) examination of the Anglo-Caribbean diaspora in Cuba, she found that many Jamaicans used their colonial British heritage as a way to differentiate themselves as more sophisticated and better educated than other Black people on the island. While I was certainly guilty of this, and in wider society often consciously and subconsciously found ways to position myself differently from other Black people, with my coworkers I refrained. It was unnecessary. They treated me with a reverence and pride that I believe stemmed from their understanding of what it had taken for me to get to where I was. There was no sexual harassment; there were no weak woman jokes. Instead, they went out of their way to help me lift the heavy stock pots of boiling liquid off the stove, and when I sliced the tips of my fingers while peeling potatoes and yellow yam, they were quick to bring me antibacterial ointment and a bandage. We all understood that systemic racism meant that we had to work twice as hard to get half as far. It was not lost on my coworkers that my French training and culinary pedigree had only enabled me to progress to a position just beyond the dish pit.

Resistance to white dominance was part of daily life as a racialized Other working in a segregated kitchen. We heeded the old Jamaican saying, "Play fool to catch wise," and kept up a pretense of blind obedience in front of the chef and his surrogates (Scott 1990). When they were not around, we stole food and entertained ourselves with funny stories about their latest tirade. This resistance enabled us to challenge systemic social and racial inequality and reaffirm our self-worth, and connected us culturally, as Black immigrants. This form of resistance—using stolen and reappropriated food to nourish Black bodies—is rooted in African slave culture. It is reminiscent of the clandestine late-night and early-morning farming and cooking that slaves would engage in to keep their bodies and their families strong.

In the restaurant, we workers used various techniques to resist white dominance. None of these techniques were formally organized per se but instead in a "weapons of the weak" type of scenario generally involved a slowdown in production, people who disappeared for longer than usual when taking out the trash or cleaning up outside, and a feigned lack of understanding due to linguistic differences (Scott 2008). On one occasion, the chef hired a new white prep cook, a transplant from the Northeast who had taken a job slotted for a relative of one of the Haitian dishwashers. All the dishwashers gave him the cold shoulder and refused to speak English around him. Most of the time they would pretend they could not understand him. They called him "blan," the Haitian creole term for white man. They always washed his equipment last, which frustrated him so much that he often ended up washing his own pots and pans. On the white prep cook's last day, he walked out midshift, after the chef called him "a fucking incompetent ass" for overcooking asparagus in the steamer. The prep cook had been distracted by one of the dishwashers slowly and inefficiently washing his equipment. The next day, the white prep cook's slot was filled by a young, Black, Haitian man.

While the ultimate responsibility for hiring and firing rests with the chef and his surrogates, the Haitian workers' resistance demonstrates how those who are considered powerless find ways to retaliate, maintain their sense of dignity, and manage their situation. In this act of resistance, the Haitian dishwashers spoke as subalterns (Spivak 1988). Collectively, they used their language and the social perception of themselves as uneducated and scary people to manipulate and frustrate a white worker until he was driven to quit. This strategy of resistance guaranteed that the white prep cook would be summarily replaced with one of their own, which had been the dishwashers' aim all along. A position as a prep cook was a step up from the dish pit for a young Haitian man. It paid more, which in practical terms meant more consistent food and shelter for their families in the United States as well as in Haiti. This example of resistance is a contemporary reflection of Robinson's Black radical tradition. It demonstrates the wit, cunning, strength, and perseverance brought to bear by a group of people whose fight against systemic oppression was passed down by their ancestors and is deeply rooted in their DNA. It also demonstrates the quotidian ways in which resistance was deployed within a system of structural disenfranchisement to clandestinely curtail power in the restaurant.

The Mango Gang and Their "Discovery" of New World Cuisine

In the early 1990s, South Florida's chefs Norman Van Aken, Mark Militello, Douglas Rodriguez, and Allen Susser became known as the Mango Gang and achieved celebrity status for their acclaimed Latin American– and Caribbean-inspired fusion cuisine also known as "New World cuisine" (Chrissos 1996; Santiago 2011). The chefs first became the "Mango Gang" in 1991 when they coined the slogan as a corporate business identity for a cookbook they planned to collaboratively publish (Van Aken 2016).

Although the cookbook never came to fruition, the name "Mango Gang" was picked up by the media and became Miami's moniker for chefs Militello, Rodriguez, Susser, and Van Aken, who were widely lauded for putting Miami on the culinary map with their "innovative" and "bold" cuisine that featured "local ethnic" flavors (Hamersly 2001; Rossant 2011; Santiago 2011; Van Aken n.d.).

In a series of media reports, the Mango Gang discussed how they came to learn about and appreciate Latin American and Caribbean cuisine (Wilson 1992; M. Warren 2000; Martin 2013; Do Simon 2018). With the exception of Douglas Rodriguez, whose parents are Cuban immigrants, tropical flavors and cooking were new to them. Norman Van Aken stumbled across Cuban food in cheap bodegas while working as a painter in Key West (Van Aken 2016). A vocal aficionado of Caribbean and Latin American food, Van Aken describes his first encounter as follows:

> I went to the tiny restaurants and bodegas trying to understand the Cuban, Haitian, Bahamian and other influences around me and thinking about how I could work those influences into dishes at Louie's Backyard. Plantains were the thing that dropped me down the well. I was at a restaurant with these carpenter buddies of mine and they were serving roasted pork with black beans and rice and *maduros* [sweet plantains]. I thought, "Why are there bananas on my dinner plate?" But then I tasted them, and I went "Holy s***!" (Martin 2013)

Allen Susser and Mark Militello were on a quest for the freshest local products to use in their new positions as executive chefs and subsequently in their own restaurants. Susser contends that he sought out Miami because of the region's potential for "unique culinary combinations" and that "his dramatic translation of the bounty of South Florida's foodstuffs became New World Cuisine" (Susser n.d.). Militello has been described as having "a nearly psychotic obsession for the freshest, finest, ingredients" (Militello 2002). He was known for commissioning local farms and cottage farmers to grow exactly what he needed if he could not find it through traditional sources (Morgan 1994).

Van Aken's "discovery" of New World cuisine has many metaphorical parallels with Columbus's discovery and subsequent colonization of the New World. The most obvious of these is that the foods, flavors, and culinary techniques that the chefs "discovered" were not in fact new but had existed for decades, if not centuries, and were frequently used by people from ethnic cultures across Latin America and the Caribbean. Like Columbus, Van Aken and the Mango Gang chefs benefited greatly from the knowledge and labor of the locals they discovered on their New World journey. Foods that were central to New World cuisine such as plantains, mango, and black beans were already in wide use in South Florida's immigrant communities; however, these communities and their foods were largely invisible to American mainstream culture. The Mango Gang's production of New World cuisine introduced the flavors of Miami's immigrant culture to American fine-dining cuisine and simultaneously essentialized Caribbean and Latinx ethnicity, homogenizing the food and culture of dozens of countries and cuisines into two categories: Latin American and Caribbean. Their whiteness and the invisible authority that came with being white male chefs enabled them to appropriate the culinary knowledge and skill of their mostly immigrant prep cooks while working them long, hard hours, and paying them subpar wages. As I will show, this colonization of labor, culinary knowledge, and skills was not only evident in the racial segregation of their kitchens; it was crucial to their success. In presenting their "discovery," the Mango Gang exoticized the natives' food, thus reaffirming their own role as wise white chefs, whose knowledge of food and cooking was superior to that of the "natives."[3] The ethnic and racial stratification that resulted Othered the knowledgeable traditional cooks and ensured that Caribbean and Latin American foods could be legitimized only by white male chefs.

Douglas Rodriguez was the only Mango Gang chef who was raised in South Florida. As a second-generation Cuban American in late twentieth-century Miami, Rodriguez was a privileged member of the dominant local economic and political majority, the Cuban exile community. An estimated half-million Cubans migrated to Miami in the 1960s, following the 1959 overthrow of the U.S.-sponsored Cuban dictator, Fulgencio Batista (Mohl 1990). Unlike the Black Bahamian immigrants who also migrated to Miami at that time, Cuban immigrants to South Florida received significant aid from the U.S. government, through the federally funded Cuban Refugee Program. This program provided $1.3 billion in financial assistance, educational loans, health care, and child welfare services for Cuban migrants (Portes 1984; Grenier and Stepick 1992; Batalova and Zong 2017). Strong support from the U.S. government was a significant catalyst for the eventual political and economic ascension of Cubans in Miami, from which Douglas Rodriguez and his family benefited. Generous government aid allowed Cubans to establish themselves in ethnic enclaves, achieve cultural cohesion and economic success, and fortify their growing community.[4]

It should be noted that Cuban privilege upon migration was closely aligned with race, as most Cubans arriving in Miami were of a lighter complexion. Cuban cultural signifiers of Blackness such as Afro-Cuban music and religion were rejected by early Cuban migrants, further complicating local racial politics and tensions. Cubans were receiving government aid slated for Black people while simultaneously rejecting Blackness (Palmié 2013). The racial categories of Black and white in Miami became muddled when Cubans of various skin tones arrived. Their initial outsider status as immigrants as well as their intraracial diversity positioned them as nonwhite. However, as more and more Cubans with lighter complexions became successful and powerful, light-skinned Cubans were progressively included in the white racial category by white Americans and other light-skinned Cubans (J. Warren and Twine 1997; Bonilla-Silva and Embrick 2006). Douglas Rodriguez was included in this white racial category.

Unlike the other Mango Gang chefs, who considered Latin American and Caribbean food exotic, Cuban food was in Rodriguez's DNA. He grew up on the stuff—frijoles negros, plantanos maduros, and pernil (black beans, sweet plantains, and roasted pig)—and became so passionate about food and cooking that, by age thirteen, he had started working in restaurants as a cook.

Rodriguez went on to graduate from Johnson & Wales University, one of the two most prestigious U.S. culinary schools. Shortly after graduating, Rodriguez returned to Miami and opened Yuca, Miami's first fine-dining Cuban restaurant in Coral Gables, a prestigious neighborhood in Miami with a solid fine-dining restaurant row, which was home to a growing number of wealthy Cuban exiles and their families.

Rodriguez's choice of the name Yuca introduces another area of analysis. Yuca is a tuber used as a starch in Caribbean and Latin American cooking—and an acronym for "Young Urban Cuban Americans" who were more likely to appreciate Rodriguez's reinvented Cuban food than their first-generation parents. The name could be interpreted as Rodriguez's rejection of old-school traditional cuisine, and traditional ideas of Cuban identity, in favor of something more upscale and contemporary. Alejandro Portes and Min Zhou's theory of segmented assimilation for second-generation immigrants suggests that assimilation into American culture is segmented according to immigrants' access to middle-class resources, affinity with their national culture, and location in the racial and social hierarchy. Rodriguez uses his race, nationality, and privilege to access middle-class opportunities (Portes and Zhou 2012). Like many second-generation Cubans who benefited from Cuban hegemony in Miami, Rodriguez assimilated into middle-class whiteness while embracing his cultural and culinary heritage, a combination that catapulted him to fame and success. Unlike the other Mango Gang chefs, Rodriguez departed from the New World cuisine narrative and unapologetically called his style of cooking Nuevo Latino (New Latin) cuisine. Nuevo Latino cuisine eventually superseded New World cuisine and is more often credited as the culinary catalyst that made Latin American foods mainstream. It is no surprise that of the four Mango Gang chefs, Rodriguez, a white Cuban immigrant, acquired the greatest fame and most accolades (V. Fonseca 2005).

As a second-generation Cuban immigrant, Chef Douglas Rodriguez had several structural advantages. He was an elite member of the dominant group, who were also his target clientele. He appealed to their sense of self, their wistful nostalgia, and their memories of home—a winning combination (Kandiyoti 2006). His position as a white Cuban man gave him access to traditionally white spaces, such as the prime real estate of both his first restaurant in Coral Gables and his second on Lincoln Road in South Beach. Within the Latinx racial hierarchy of Miami's restaurant industry, his nationality and language also enabled him to recruit and maintain a solid staff of Black and Brown Latinx faces, whose knowledge and labor he admittedly drew upon to craft his Nuevo Latino cuisine (V. Fonseca 2005).

To many in Miami's Cuban exile community, Rodriguez represented the antithesis of communism and the embodiment of the American Dream: a successful capitalist with multiple businesses that relied on the exploitation of the proletariat for success. His Cuban pedigree ensured his access to other Latin American cuisines and protected him from claims of cultural appropriation. On the one hand, his skin tone, nationality, and Latino ethnicity gave him a cultural authority that the other Mango Gang chefs did not have. On the other hand, Rodriguez's race, nationality, and language intersected to put him in a place of power within a city and a community that celebrated both who he was and who they wanted him to be. Rodriguez's modern take on traditional Cuban cuisine reflected the Cuban exiles' reinterpretation of their own positionality in Miami and in the United States (M. Fonseca 2008). Like the New Cubans, Rodriguez's food was exciting, different, upscale, and elite, a formula that laid the foundation for a segue into a new hybrid Cuban American identity as privileged, elite, and white. The Mango Gang's cultural appropriations, as well as Van Aken's discovery of New World cuisine, contributed to a shift in Miami's discourse about Latinx identity and social position, to reflect new ideologies that whiten and depict Cuban Americans and Latinx people as sophisticated and elite.

Rodriguez's Nuevo Latino cuisine would prove to be one of the more sustainable offshoots of New World cuisine. It continued the rebranding of Latin American cuisine as both nostalgic and simultaneously exotic and upscale (V. Fonseca 2005; Beushausen et al. 2014). Eventually, Nuevo Latino cuisine became a national phenomenon whose consumption whitened and resignified Cuban and Latinx identity and culture as sophisticated and upper class (V. Fonseca 2005).

Invisible Authority

By the mid-1990s, South Florida was an established immigrant community. Cubans were in the majority, but Miami-Dade and Broward counties were also home to large numbers of Haitians, Jamaicans, Trinidadians, South Americans, Central Americans, and Puerto Ricans. Restaurants from every nationality and culture could be found throughout the city. State Road 7 in North Dade was a busy corridor filled with Afro-Caribbean markets and eateries. Further south, Miami's Northeast Second Avenue was lined by a string of bustling Haitian markets and restaurants. In the Cuban enclaves of Hialeah and Little Havana, there were Cuban restaurants, cafeterias, and bodegas on every corner. Outside these enclaves, too, Cuban culture permeated Miami. La Carreta and Pollo Tropical were well-established Cuban food chains with numerous restaurants scattered across South Florida. Versailles, one of the oldest Cuban restaurants in Little Havana, became a sought-after tourist destination. In 1992 Emilio and Gloria Estefan opened Lario's, a fine-dining Cuban establishment in South Beach. The flavors of the Caribbean and of Latin America could be found throughout the city, yet it was the Mango Gang chefs who were granted the power and authority to determine the tropical flavors and cooking techniques that would come to define New World cuisine.

While some would argue that their culinary pedigree conferred that authority upon them, I believe that it was the intersection of those chefs' race, gender, and socioeconomic identities, juxtaposed against the Latin Caribbean Other, that established them as Miami's authorities on multicultural cuisine (Cook and Crang 1996; Cook and Harrison 2003). Whiteness scholars have established that one of the defining features of white racial identity is that white people tend to avoid thinking about race or acknowledging their privilege (McIntosh [1988] 1992; Frankenberg 1993; Hartigan 1997; McDermott and Samson 2005). In her essay "White

Privilege: Unpacking the Invisible Knapsack," Peggy McIntosh writes: "I have come to see white privilege as an invisible package of unearned assets which I can count on cashing in each day, but about which I was 'meant' to remain oblivious" ([1988] 1992, 30). This obliviousness to or lack of acknowledgment of privilege is significant, as it permits white people's social acceptance of their role in constructing race discrimination. As McIntosh becomes aware of her race privilege and the many ways in which she takes that privilege for granted, she also comes to realize that the systems that privilege her must also hinder others.

Race privilege gave the chefs invisible authority and structural advantage, not just because they were white but because the people whose food and culture they appropriated were nonwhite and systematically disenfranchised and discriminated against. In our society's hierarchy, white male chefs are considered smarter, better, and wiser than nonwhite cooks. Similarly, foods from ethnic cultures are perceived as different from the accepted, routine cultural fare that dominates the day-to-day eating habits of the dominant, white racial group. Ethnic foods help solidify different aspects of national and ethnic identities in our collective imagination, especially by contrast with normalized whiteness (Mintz and Du Bois 2002). For example, there has been a surge in Thai/sushi fusion restaurants in America. Most people do not see this combination of two cuisines in one restaurant as problematic, because white Americans tend to lump all Asian countries into the same bracket. To them, they look and sound the same, so their food must be the same too (Nguyen 2005). Consuming the cuisines of different countries reaffirms our perceptions of the national identities of people from those countries and who they are as individuals (Flammang 2009). What other people eat—or what we think they eat—determines what we think of them, their social status, and their value to society (Mintz 2010). The Mango Gang used foods, labor, and knowledge from different people and places—in their case, New World cuisines—to distinguish themselves as daring, innovative, and globally oriented. Their ability to exploit and monetize the gastronomic intellect, skill, and labor of marginalized immigrant people in Miami positioned New World cuisine and the Mango Gang as tangible symbols of a cosmopolitan city that embraced diversity and multicultural cuisine while simultaneously reproducing race, gender, and class hierarchies.

Nonwhiteness as Culinary Capital

All four chefs benefited tremendously from their ability to master Latin American and Caribbean recipes. They all opened multiple restaurants, published cookbooks, and developed retail products such as tamarind barbecue sauce and mango ketchup, a slightly modified version of a chutney popular in Trinidad and Jamaica. All the chefs have received one or more awards from the coveted James Beard Foundation, the culinary equivalent of an Emmy, for their innovative New World cuisines.

Food and the ways in which it is consumed are markers of social class and signifiers of cultural capital (Bourdieu 1984). For example, fine-dining restaurants patronized by the elite have plush, comfortable chairs that encourage guests to linger and savor their meals. Meals are artistically presented on beautiful plates and the service is slow, considerate, and guest-centric. In fast-casual restaurants, the polar opposite of fine-dining establishments, the target market is working-class families. Service is efficient, and meals are presented wrapped in paper or in disposable service ware made of cardboard, plastic, or other materials. Guests have to participate in the low-cost dining experience by ordering their food at a counter, picking it up, and bringing it to their table. At the end of the meal, they are expected to take their dirty dishes and utensils to the allocated area for cleanup and disposal. At restaurants that cater to those of a lower socioeconomic status, guests are encouraged to dine quickly by ordering at the drive-through window. Those who choose to dine in the restaurant are subjected to harsh, bright lighting and hard seats, which effectively discourage them from lingering.

In their analysis of culinary capital, Peter Nacaratto and Kathleen Lebesco (2013) argue that society does not allocate a single, static value to particular foods, consumption patterns, or styles of service. Instead, culinary capital is perpetually changing, in accordance with value shifts across the culinary habitus, as relevant actors display, exchange, and usurp various levels of social, economic, and political power (Bourdieu [1986] 2011; Naccarato and Lebesco 2013). The Mango Gang's appropriation of Latin American and Afro-Caribbean foods to create New World cuisine demonstrates the ways in which their invisible white authority and structural advantages, such as access to wealthy investors and full-time public relations professionals, enabled them to shift the discourse around these foods, transforming these cuisines from underrated and insignificant cookery into expensive and exotic gastronomy. In other words, the "gourmetification" of these peasant foods perceived as nonwhite cuisine led to an increase in the culinary capital both of those innovative enough to use them in fine dining and of those adventurous enough to consume them in the safe, elite, white-dominated spaces the chefs provided (Naccarato and Lebesco 2013; Johnston and Baumann 2014).

More broadly speaking, the Mango Gang's use of these foods as culinary capital allowed them to align themselves with Miami's dominant immigrant community and reflected local cultural values of Cuban superiority and Latinx dominance. In the mid-1990s, when New World cuisine was popularized in Miami, the city was a Cuban powerhouse. Unlike other immigrant dominant cities across the United States, the Cuban community dominated Miami numerically, politically, and socioeconomically (Grenier and Castro 1999; Stepick 2003; Aranda, Hughes, and Sabogal 2014). Cuban scholars contend that Cuban power in Miami is so prodigious that Miami is the only city where white Americans endorse "reverse acculturation" (Stepick 2003, 148). New World cuisine reflects the shifting racial and cultural dynamics of Miami in the 1990s and may even suggest that the Mango Gang deferred to Cubanidad in an effort to maintain their social standing. When the chefs initially rolled out New World cuisine, they described it as one that incorporated "African influences" and frequently referred to foods from the Afro-Caribbean, such as Haiti, Jamaica, and the Bahamas. However, as time went on, they began to focus less on the Afro-Caribbean culinary connection and more on Latin American foods, especially the cuisines of Cuba, Peru, Argentina, and

Brazil. In this way, the racial connotations of New World cuisine became whitened in the local imagination, in which contemporary race formations of whiteness now included powerful, light-skinned Latinx immigrants (Bonilla-Silva 2006; Omi and Winant 2014; Ramírez 2015).

Fetishizing, Racializing, and Consuming the Other

In bell hooks's "Eating the Other: Desire and Resistance," the author argues that desire for the racial Other is heightened in the imaginations of the racially dominant because of stereotypes that mark encounters with the racial Other as intense, dangerous, sensual, and sexual. She states that "the commodification of Otherness has been so successful because it is offered as a new delight, more intense, more satisfying than normal ways of doing and feeling. Within commodity culture, ethnicity becomes spice, seasoning that can liven up the dull dish that is mainstream white culture" (hooks 2012, 308). She goes on to argue that "processes of commodification and consumption displace the Other and eradicate the Other's historical significance" (313). In her analysis of culinary tourism, Jennie Germann Molz builds on hooks's theory, arguing that white Western tourists "consume the Other through food, without acknowledging the complex histories, power relationships, mobilities or even the migrants . . . that make this food available" (Molz 2007, 82). For Molz, privileged consumption includes eating for fun and curiosity and positions national and ethnic differences as a novelty. This perception, in turn, reinforces the relational social statuses and relative hierarchies that separate the privileged from the Othered.

In earlier media interviews and reports on the Mango Gang and how they came to discover New World cuisine, each chef reflected on the significance of learning about Latin and Afro-Caribbean food and cooking directly from an immigrant community with firsthand knowledge of the food products, cooking methods, and culinary combinations involved (Balcomb Lane 1991; Gressette 1995; Hsiao-Ching 1998; V. Fonseca 2005; Martin 2013). The appropriation of knowledge and labor from Latin American and

Caribbean communities was vital to the chef's success. Without the aid of their immigrant cooks and workers, the chefs would not have been able to master Latin Caribbean cuisine, position themselves as experts, and incorporate these foods into their fine-dining repertoires. This creates an interesting paradox. The vibrant, inclusive, multicultural community in which immigrants are portrayed as American success stories is also the place where structural racism limits opportunities for low-wage immigrant labor and reproduces racial and social hierarchies. A similar paradox also plays out in the consumption of New World cuisine that relies on a white, elite, foodie culture that is positioned in opposition to the Other through class and race yet at the same time consumes the Other for pleasure and social capital, thus concurrently reinforcing the boundaries of difference: class and race. This consumption is further problematized by ideas of the Black aesthetic, an often-intangible idea of Blackness as cool, and Miami's appropriation and exotification of Blackness for neoliberal, multicultural marketing (Thompson-Summers 2018). Within this context, New World cuisine fetishizes nonwhite food by capitalizing on the white imagination of the racial Other.

There is no evidence to suggest that the chefs' intent with regard to New World cuisine was to spread feel-good multiculturalism or participate in cultural exchange and sharing as a means of promoting healthy and egalitarian cultural consumption (Pitcher 2014). Food is part of daily life. *Who* prepares, commodifies, and consumes food within specific spaces and *how* they do so both reflect the social stratification and racial politics of society at large. In the daily making and unmaking of racism, the Mango Gang's New World cuisine was a mechanism through which race and class privilege were reproduced and given credence (Santiago-Valles 2005; Johnston and Baumann 2014; Pitcher 2014).

Conclusion

In the mid-1990s, the Mango Gang chefs and their New World cuisine redefined South Florida's culinary landscape as the place for the best in upscale Latin American and Afro-Caribbean foods.

The group's New World cuisine incorporated many of the foods and flavors from Latin America and the Caribbean. They followed in the path of traditional immigrant cooks by primarily using fresh and seasonal products. The chefs responsible for "discovering" New World cuisine came to be known as the Mango Gang because of their use of "refreshing" and "startling" tropical flavors (Rossant 2011; Van Aken 2016). The exoticism of these foods stems from the white cultural imagination of immigrants as different or Other. The Mango Gang's use of these Othered foods inevitably made these foods more desirable in foodie culture (Johnston and Baumann 2014).

The consumption of food is layered with various sociocultural meanings of belonging and exclusion. Food is also a marker of social class and a signifier of cultural capital (Bourdieu 1984). In the case of New World cuisine, it became culinary capital for both the chefs who prepared and the diners who consumed the food. Broadly speaking, New World cuisine also served as culinary capital for Miami's dominant Cuban community. The chefs' use of these foods, during a time when Miami was experiencing Cuban hegemony, aligned them with the Cuban community. Nationally, New World cuisine symbolically whitened the cultural perception of Cuban and Latinx people through the presentation of Latin American food by white men as elite and sophisticated. Subsequently, New World cuisine segued into Nuevo Latino cuisine, reflected in the chefs' increasing gravitation toward foods from Central America and South America and away from any mention of Afro-Caribbean cuisine.

Finally, the issue of race and class is especially significant in this discussion of the Mango Gang and New World cuisine. Race privilege gave the chefs invisible authority to boldly appropriate, and then declare themselves authorities on, the reformed and appropriated food. It also gave them a structural advantage, which they leveraged for tangible power and authority in the kitchen. This leverage was important because they relied on low-wage immigrant labor, not just for production in their kitchens but also as tutors in Latin American and Afro-Caribbean cuisine. The chefs were adept at exploiting the materiality of racialism, their race privilege, and the contrasting racial disadvantage of others to accumulate social and economic capital. However, this type of racial oppression also led to resistance. Black Haitian and Jamaican workers drew upon their ancestral arsenal of clandestine resistance in a "weapons of the weak" sense to survive the brutal working conditions and secure jobs for their own people (Scott 2008).

Resistance to white dominance and racial segregation in Miami's restaurant industry continues today. Many restaurant cooks and chefs of color have left fine-dining establishments for self-employed work at farmers markets or on food trucks, or as personal chefs and caterers. More than two decades since the Mango Gang and New World cuisine dominated South Florida's culinary landscape, a network of Black food entrepreneurs has gradually developed, with the help of social media. The paltry representation of people of color at signature foodie events and awards is increasingly being questioned, and the intent behind the increased commodification of immigrant foods by nonimmigrant people is being challenged more frequently in the media. In 2018 the James Beard Foundation honored Nina Compton, the first Black female chef to ever win the prestigious award. Also for the first time in 2018, they brought together Afro-Caribbean chefs for an honorary dinner. Things are changing, but New World cuisine remains an appropriate term for capitalist, postcolonial, political structures within the restaurant industry that appropriate and exoticize the natives' food while concurrently exploiting their knowledge and labor to make a profit. Maybe it is time for reparations.

Notes

This chapter was developed based on content analysis of newspaper and media articles, interviews with informants who worked for the Mango Gang, and my own personal experiences as a chef coming of age in Miami in the 1990s.

1. This style of fusion cooking, which incorporated the local foods and flavors of Latin America and the Caribbean, is sometimes referred to as New Florida, New World, or Floribbean cuisine. In this chapter, I use the term *New World cuisine* to refer to South Florida's regional style of

cooking, which features the foods and flavors of the local immigrant community.

2. There is some debate as to which of the Mango Gang chefs can be considered the founding father of New World cuisine. Norman Van Aken is the self-proclaimed founder of New World cuisine and is most often credited as such by both local and national media. He has published two cookbooks directly related to New World cuisine—*Norman's New World Cuisine* (1997) and *New World Kitchen: Latin American and Caribbean Cuisine* (2003)—and he continues to speak to the media about New World cuisine and how it led to global "fusion" cuisine. However, in other culinary circles, Chef Allen Susser is considered the founding father of this style of cooking, on the basis that his book on the subject, *Allen Susser's New World Cuisine,* was published in 1995, before Van Aken's, and because of his continued advocacy of New World cuisine. I personally favor Van Aken's claim to have founded this style of cuisine and credit him as such.

3. The term *natives* is used allegorically as a parallel to Columbus's story of discovery.

4. Cuban Refugee Center Records, 1960–1994, University of Miami Cuban Heritage Collection, n.d.

Bibliography

Aranda, Elizabeth M., Sallie Hughes, and Elena Sabogal. 2014. *Making a Life in Multiethnic Miami: Immigration and the Rise of a Global City.* Boulder, Colo.: Lynne Rienner.

Balcomb Lane, Charlotte. 1991. "'New World' Cuisine: Expect the Unexpected." *Orlando (Fla.) Sentinel,* August 15, H1.

Batalova, Jeanne, and Jie Zong. 2017. "Cuban Immigrants in the United States." Migration Policy Institute, November 9. https://www.migrationpolicy.org.

Beushausen, Wiebe, Anne Brüske, Ana-Sofia Commichau, and Patrick Helber. 2014. *Caribbean Food Cultures: Culinary Practices and Consumption in the Caribbean and Its Diasporas.* Bielefeld, Germany: Transcript Verlag.

Bonilla-Silva, Eduardo. 2006. *Racism without Racists: Color-Blind Racism and the Persistence of Racial Inequality in the United States.* 2nd ed. Lanham, Md.: Rowman & Littlefield.

Bonilla-Silva, Eduardo, and David G. Embrick. 2006. "Black, Honorary White, White: The Future of Race in the United States?" In *Mixed*

Messages: Multiracial Identities in the "Color-Blind" Era, edited by David L. Brunsma, 33–48. Boulder, Colo.: Lynne Rienner.

Bourdieu, Pierre. 1984. *Distinction: A Social Critique of the Judgement of Taste.* Cambridge, Mass.: Harvard University Press.

Bourdieu, Pierre. (1986) 2011. "The Forms of Capital." In *Cultural Theory: An Anthology,* vol. 1, edited by Imre Szeman and Timothy Kaposy, 81–93. West Sussex, UK: Wiley-Blackwell.

Chrissos, Joan. 1996. "Chef Inc.: From Cookbooks to TV Appearances to Product Lines, South Florida's Celebrity Chefs Have a Lot More than Dinner Cooking." *Miami Herald,* March 7, 1E.

Cook, Ian, and Philip Crang. 1996. "The World on a Plate: Culinary Culture, Displacement and Geographical Knowledges." *Journal of Material Culture* 1 (2): 131–53.

Cook, Ian, and Michelle Harrison. 2003. "Cross over Food: Rematerializing Postcolonial Geographies." *Transactions of the Institute of British Geographers* 28 (3): 296–317.

Do Simon, Nila. 2018. "The Original Gangster." *Venice,* January 2. https://venicemagftl.com.

Flammang, Janet A. 2009. *The Taste for Civilization: Food, Politics, and Civil Society.* Urbana: University of Illinois Press.

Fonseca, Marcelo. 2008. "Understanding Consumer Culture: The Role of 'Food' as an Important Cultural Category." *Latin American Advances in Consumer Research* 2:28–33.

Fonseca, Vanessa. 2005. "Nuevo Latino: Rebranding Latin American Cuisine." *Consumption Markets & Culture* 8 (2): 95–130. https://doi.org/10.1080/10253860500112826.

Frankenberg, Ruth. 1993. *White Women, Race Matters: The Social Construction of Whiteness.* New York: Routledge.

Grenier, Guillermo J., and Max J. Castro. 1999. "Triadic Politics: Ethnicity, Race, and Politics in Miami, 1959–1998." *Pacific Historical Review* 68 (2): 273–92.

Grenier, Guillermo J., and Alex Stepick. 1992. *Miami Now! Immigration, Ethnicity, and Social Change.* Gainesville: University Press of Florida.

Gressette, Felicia. 1995. "'Chef Allen' Shares Latest Creation: A Cookbook." *Miami (Fla.) Herald,* March 9, 1E.

Hamersly, Kendall. 2001. "Fabulous Norman's Is Always an Adventure." *Miami (Fla.) Herald,* December 7, 37G.

Hartigan, John, Jr. 1997. "Establishing the Fact of Whiteness." *American Anthropologist,* n.s. 99 (3): 495–505.

hooks, bell. 2012. "Eating the Other: Desire and Resistance." In *Media and Cultural Studies: Keyworks,* edited by Meenakshi G. Durham and Douglas Kellner, 308–17. 2nd ed. Hoboken, N.J.: John Wiley & Sons.

Hsiao-Ching, Chou. 1998. "Taste of the New World—Florida Food Guru Norman Van Aken a Stickler about Fresh, Pure Ingredients." *Denver (Colo.) Post,* July 15, E-01.

Johnston, Josée, and Shyon Baumann. 2014. *Foodies: Democracy and Distinction in the Gourmet Foodscape.* New York: Routledge.

Kandiyoti, Dalia. 2006. "Consuming Nostalgia: Nostalgia and the Marketplace in Cristina García and Ana Menéndez." *MELUS* 31 (1): 81–97.

Kelley, Robin D. G. 2002. *Freedom Dreams: The Black Radical Imagination.* Boston: Beacon.

Martin, Lydia. 2013. "For Miami Chef Norman Van Aken, It's Been a Long Road to the Top." *Miami (Fla.) Herald,* September 7.

Maze, Jonathan. 2018. "How Norman Van Aken Developed His 'New World Cuisine.'" *A Deeper Dive,* September 26. https://www.restaurantbusinessonline.com.

McDermott, Monica, and Frank L. Samson. 2005. "White Racial and Ethnic Identity in the United States." *Annual Review of Sociology* 31 (1): 245–61.

McIntosh, Peggy. (1988) 1992. "White Privilege: Unpacking the Invisible Knapsack." In *Multiculturalism, 1992,* edited by Anna May Filor, 30–36. [Washington, D.C.]: Educational Resources Information Center.

Merriam-Webster's Collegiate Dictionary. 2017. 11th ed. Springfield, Mass.: Merriam-Webster.

Meyerson, Gregory. 2000. "Rethinking Black Marxism: Reflections on Cedric Robinson and Others." *Cultural Logic* 3 (2): 1–43.

Militello, Mark. 2002. "The Chef; Mark Militello." *New York Times,* June 5.

Mintz, Sidney W. 2010. "Food Enigmas, Colonial and Postcolonial." *Gastronomica* 10 (1): 149–54.

Mintz, Sidney W., and Christine M. Du Bois. 2002. "The Anthropology of Food and Eating." *Annual Review of Anthropology* 31 (1): 99–119.

Mohl, Raymond A. 1990. "On the Edge: Blacks and Hispanics in Metropolitan Miami since 1959." *Florida Historical Quarterly* 69 (1): 37–56.

Molz, Jennie Germann. 2007. "Eating Difference: The Cosmopolitan Mobilities of Culinary Tourism." *Space and Culture* 10 (1): 77–93.

Morgan, Curtis. 1994. "A Mark of Distinction." *Miami (Fla.) Herald,* August 14, 1J.

Naccarato, Peter, and Kathleen Lebesco. 2013. *Culinary Capital.* London: Bloomsbury.

Nguyen, Athena. 2005. "I'm Not a Racist, I Eat Dim Sims! The Commodification and Consumption of Asianness within White Australia." *Graduate Journal of Asia-Pacific Studies* 3 (2): 45–105.

Omi, Michael, and Howard Winant. 2014. *Racial Formation in the United States.* New York: Routledge.

Palmié, Stephan. 2013. *The Cooking of History: How Not to Study Afro-Cuban Religion.* Chicago: University of Chicago Press.

Pitcher, Ben. 2014. *Consuming Race.* New York: Routledge.

Portes, Alejandro. 1984. "The Rise of Ethnicity: Determinants of Ethnic Perceptions among Cuban Exiles in Miami." *American Sociological Review* 49 (3): 383–97.

Portes, Alejandro, and Min Zhou. 2012. "The New Second Generation: Segmented Assimilation and Its Variants." In *The New Immigration,* edited by Marcelo Suarez-Orozco, Carolo Suarez Orozco, and Desiree Qin, 99–116. New York: Routledge.

Queeley, Andrea. 2010. "Finos, Somos Negros, and Anglophone Caribbean." In *Global Circuits of Blackness: Interrogating the African Diaspora,* edited by Jean M. Rahier, Percy C. Hintzen, and Felipe Smith, 201–22. Urbana: University of Illinois Press.

Ramírez, Margaret Marietta. 2015. "The Elusive Inclusive: Black Food Geographies and Racialized Food Spaces." *Antipode* 47 (3): 748–69.

Robinson, Cedric J. 1983. *Black Marxism: The Making of the Black Radical Tradition.* Chapel Hill: University of North Carolina Press.

Rodriquez, Jason. 2006. "Color-Blind Ideology and the Cultural Appropriation of Hip-Hop." *Journal of Contemporary Ethnography* 35 (6): 645–68.

Rogers, Richard A. 2006. "From Cultural Exchange to Transculturation: A Review and Reconceptualization of Cultural Appropriation." *Communication Theory* 16 (4): 474–503.

Rossant, Juliette. 2011. "Miami's Mango Gang: Precursors to Today's Top South Florida Chefs . . ." *Mango World Magazine,* June 6. http:// mangoworldmagazine.blogspot.com.

Santiago, Fabiola. 2011. "The Four Who Put South Florida on the Culinary Map." *Miami (Fla.) Herald,* June 3.

Santiago-Valles, Kelvin. 2005. "Racially Subordinate Labour within Global Contexts: Robinson and Hopkins Re-examined." *Race & Class* 47 (2): 54–70.

Scott, James C. 1990. *Domination and the Arts of Resistance: Hidden Transcripts.* New Haven, Conn.: Yale University Press.

Scott, James C. 2008. *Weapons of the Weak: Everyday Forms of Peasant Resistance.* New Haven, Conn.: Yale University Press.

Shugart, Helene A. 1997. "Counterhegemonic Acts: Appropriation as a Feminist Rhetorical Strategy." *Quarterly Journal of Speech* 83 (2): 210–29.

Spivak, Gail C. 1988. *Can the Subaltern Speak? Reflections on the History of an Idea.* Basingstoke: Macmillan.

Stepick, Alex. 2003. *This Land Is Our Land: Immigrants and Power in Miami.* Berkeley: University of California Press.

Susser, Allen. 1995. *Allen Susser's New World Cuisine.* Text by Kathleen Gordon. New York: Doubleday.

Susser, Allen. n.d. "The Chef." Accessed March 4, 2020. http://restaurant.chefallens.com.

Thompson-Summers, Brandi. 2018. "Black Aesthetic/Aesthetic Black: Race, Space, and the Possibilities." *Public Seminar,* May 7. http://www.publicseminar.org.

Van Aken, Norman. 1997. *Norman's New World Cuisine.* New York: Random House.

Van Aken, Norman. 2003. *New World Kitchen: Latin American and Caribbean Cuisine.* With Janet Van Aken. New York: Ecco.

Van Aken, Norman. 2016. "Norman Van Aken: Reminiscing on the Mango Gang." *Edible South Florida,* November 25. http://ediblesouthflorida.ediblecommunities.com.

Van Aken, Norman. n.d. "Norman Van Aken, Biography." Accessed March 4, 2020. www.normanvanaken.com.

Wallis, Roger, and Krister Malm. 1984. *Big Sounds from Small Peoples: The Music Industry in Small Countries.* New York: Pendragon.

Warren, Jonathan W., and France Winddance Twine. 1997. "White Americans, the New Minority? Non-Blacks and the Ever-Expanding Boundaries of Whiteness." *Journal of Black Studies* 28 (2): 200–218.

Warren, M. L. 2000. "Chef Allen's/Aventura." *Sun-Sentinel (Fort Lauderdale, Fla.),* October 6, 54.

Wilson, Mike. 1992. "Lunch: 'I am Never Satisfied with Anything,' the Chef Said. 'And I Never Will Be.' It Must Be Hell to Buy Him a Birthday Present." *Miami (Fla.) Herald,* May 3, 9.

Ziff, Bruce H., and Pratima V. Rao. 1997. *Borrowed Power: Essays on Cultural Appropriation.* New Brunswick, N.J.: Rutgers University Press.

AFTERWORD
Problematizing the Problem
Psyche Williams-Forson

• • •

In 1903, in *The Souls of Black Folk,* W. E. B. Du Bois writes,

Between me and the other world there is ever an unasked question: unasked by some through feelings of delicacy; by others
through the difficulty of rightly framing it. All, nevertheless, flut-
ter round it. They approach me in a half-hesitant sort of way, eye
me curiously or compassionately, and then, instead of saying
directly, How does it feel to be a problem? they say, I know an
excellent colored man in my town; or, I fought at Mechanicsville;
or, Do not these Southern outrages make your blood boil? At
these I smile, or am interested, or reduce the boiling to a simmer,
as the occasion may require. To the real question, How does it
feel to be a problem? I answer seldom a word.

And yet, being a problem is a strange experience—peculiar
even for one who has never been anything else, save perhaps in
babyhood and in Europe. It is in the early days of rollicking boy-
hood that the revelation first bursts upon one, all in a day, as it
were. I remember well when the shadow swept across me. I was
a little thing. . . . In a wee wooden schoolhouse, something put it
into the boys' and girls' heads to buy gorgeous visiting-cards—
ten cents a package—and exchange. The exchange was merry, till
one girl, a tall newcomer, refused my card,—refused it perempto-
rily, with a glance. . . . Alas, with the years all this fine contempt
began to fade; for the words I longed for, and all their dazzling

opportunities, were theirs, not mine. But they should not keep these prizes, I said; some, all, I would wrest from them. Just how I would do it I could never decide: by reading law, by healing the sick, by telling the wonderful tales that swam in my head,—some way. . . .

One ever feels his two-ness; One ever feels his twoness,—an American, a Negro; two souls, two thoughts, two unreconciled strivings; two warring ideals in one dark body, whose dogged strength alone keeps it from being torn asunder.

Though well familiar to most of us, I cite Du Bois at length not only to marvel that we still ask these questions and feel, powerfully, this two-ness but also because we "feel" this two-ness through the everyday acts of food access, production, distribution, preparation, consumption, and even expelling. The issues of food justice painted in these chapters are rendered in the most complicated sets of ways: food trucks and unfunded entrepreneurship; barbecue's historical materiality and cultural symbolism; community participation and the guises of "food justice movements"; community redevelopment; and the moral economy, writ large. For those of us doing food studies and social justice work, these chapters paint a rather familiar picture of racial politics that vests the most consequential and insidious forms of injustice in one of the most quotidian things that appears to pass largely without conversation, unless prompted.

In responding to the early twentieth-century question "How does it feel to be a problem?" asked by scholar and activist W. E. B. Du Bois, Ronald Jackson explains, "Black bodies were inscribed with a set of meanings, which helped to perpetuate the scripter's racial ideology. Through these scripts, race gradually became its own corporeal politics" (2006, 9). As I highlight in *Building Houses out of Chicken Legs: Black Women, Food, and Power,* these "scripts" extended to women and to cultural products like food (2006, 14). Stereotypes and images that sought to denigrate African American men, women, and children using foods such as chicken and watermelon that were—and continue to be— pervasive were perpetrated in large part through popular culture.

As Jackson explains, these narratives that socially assigned Black bodies to an "underclass" had their origins in the institutions of "slavery and the mass media" (2006, 9). Today, this includes social media and its ability to reach vast audiences with haste.

From this standpoint, rather than being seen as resilient and always already resisting trauma, Black bodies are devalued and read as "unruly," constantly in need of taming and controlling, an ideology not far removed from a master/slave mentality. It is these perceptions that fuel beliefs that wholeness and health are not in the interest of Black communities. These misguided viewpoints, propelled in no small part by the surveillance of Black bodies, lead to a constant reading of African American communities as always lacking, no matter how microscopic the differences might be. For instance, it is not that African Americans dislike exercise, but when we are not seen working out in the right places, in the right gear, or in large numbers, then it is assumed we do not care about fitness. When our bodies are saddled with extra fat and/or dis-ease exacerbated by the vicissitudes of life and the myriad systemic inequalities, it is our kitchens that are perceived to be unhealthy. And when we present ourselves as food professionals, we are shorthanded as capable of creating and consuming only what is called "soul food." Thus, we are predisposed to condemnation by virtue of our histories, as if we are a monolithic, one-dimensional community of people, disallowed any complexities.

Thus, the contributors to this volume ask: What interventions into improving or changing food access are taking place, both at the grassroots level and coming from outside the community? Are those interventions considering local food traditions and the complexities of the sociopolitical issues facing these communities? Are outsiders attempting to understand the holistic needs of the community? Is progress being made in improving food access? Improving "healthy" food access? Improving health indicators? Are traditional food-ways remaining intact in the face of these changes? Is there a racialized gaze associated with these relationships? In short, what do we do? How do we "wrest from them. Just how I would do it I could never decide: by reading law, by healing the sick, by telling the wonderful tales that swam in my head,—some way."

The volume does not leave us here with tidy answers—that is for the reader(s) to do. Rather, what I will say is that this is work that Black folk do . . . it is the work we have always done. Now, it seems, we are doing it in the world of food. This does not make it new; it just expands and changes the venue. It is the ongoing, necessary work of liberation: liberatory food work.

And there may not be perfect or neat answers to the dilemmas presented here. What we do know, however, is that on a daily basis, communities are coming together to find solutions that work for them. They are continuously pushing back against forces that restrict their freedoms and limit their access. How this is done will vary at every level and in every locale. This is why anyone taking seriously the work of community organizing will listen to the people and engage the questions posed by the editors, such as: What did the food landscape look like historically in these communities? What are the "traditional" or "culturally appropriate" ways of eating in these communities? How have ideas about traditional foodways changed as the landscape of food access has changed? Are the traditional ways of eating viewed as "healthy" by the community? How are these food consumption patterns viewed by outsiders? How has the food landscape changed in recent decades amid the impact and legacy of urban decline and capitalist ruin? How are these changes tied to broader political economic issues in the community? Were there pivotal events that shifted the food landscape in the area? How have the demographics of the community shifted? What is the role of institutionalized racism in these shifts? If these questions are not a part of your starting point, go back to the drawing board because unless the work is culturally sustainable for those we hope to impact, then our intent is misguided and needs refocusing. As Andrew Newman and Yuson Yung pointedly note, the work and the thinking have to be "across the domains of community, city, self/body, and grocery stores." And it must involve what Rashad Robinson (2018) describes as rebuilding narratives and strategies.

It may be easy to think everyone is an expert when it comes to food work and that the answers are obvious and relatively simple. But that is not the case. We should engage in this work and be careful not to reinscribe the very issues we are critiquing. Here we have to be critical of all perspectives, even those that affect our very sense of self. We should also always recognize that class and socio-economics matter: that any one of us, as humans, might engage in food shaming and regulation; that grocery stores are not a panacea but one avenue to many mouths; and mostly we should remember to deploy multiple strategies because there is no one-size-fits-all.

There is more than enough work to do. The contributors to this volume are helping point the way. It is up to us not only to read and agree and then go on our way but more so to trust that those who are bringing us the messages and who have spoken with the messengers are leading us down the right path. We ignore their wisdom at our peril. If we are to bother with this work at all and are going to hold ourselves up as purveyors of justice, then we need not reinflict the very violence we hope to eradicate.

Bibliography

Du Bois, W. E. B. 1903. *The Souls of Black Folk.* Project Gutenberg. Accessed March 17, 2020. https://www.gutenberg.org.

Jackson, Ronald, II. *Scripting the Black Masculine Body: Identity, Discourse, and Racial Politics in Popular Media.* Albany: State University of New York Press, 2006.

Robinson, Rashad. 2018. "Changing Our Narrative about Narrative: The Infrastructure Required for Building Narrative Power." Othering and Belonging Institute, April 18. https://belonging.berkeley.edu.

Williams-Forson, Psyche. *Building Houses out of Chicken Legs: Black Women, Food, and Power.* Chapel Hill: University of North Carolina Press, 2006.

ACKNOWLEDGMENTS

This edited volume is a product of collective work—not just ours as coeditors but also that of others who have supported this book project from its inception through publication. Though we know we cannot list all names here, we want to acknowledge and thank those who have helped us develop this volume: thank you to each contributor to this volume, for honoring deadlines and writing beautiful chapters; the UC San Diego Division of Social Science for funding the writing workshop and panel we conducted in 2018; Psyche Williams-Forson for feedback on individual papers at the American Anthropological Association conference in 2017 and for writing the Afterword; Lee Cabatingan, Alice Julier, Kimberly Nettles-Barcelón, Brandi Thompson Summers, Mrinalini Tankha, and Saiba Varma for feedback on the concept, framework, and Introduction; our colleagues in our respective academic departments; and audience members who asked thoughtful questions at each of our AAA panels and our panel at UC San Diego.

CONTRIBUTORS

ADAM BLEDSOE is assistant professor of geography, environment, and society at the University of Minnesota.

HANNA GARTH is assistant professor of anthropology at the University of California, San Diego. She is author of *Food in Cuba: The Pursuit of a Decent Meal* and editor of *Food and Identity in the Caribbean.*

BILLY HALL is an AAAS Science and Technology Policy Fellow working as a food policy communications advisor for the United States Agency for International Development.

ANALENA HOPE HASSBERG is assistant professor of ethnic and women's studies at California State Polytechnic University, Pomona.

YUSON JUNG is associate professor of anthropology at Wayne State University. She is author of *Balkan Blues: Consumer Politics after State Socialism* and coeditor of *Ethical Eating in the Postsocialist and Socialist World.*

KIMBERLY KASPER is assistant professor of anthropology and sociology at Rhodes College. She is coeditor of *(In)Visible Women: The Materiality of Gendered Practices.*

TYLER McCREARY is assistant professor of geography at Florida State University. He is author of *Shared Histories: Witsuwit'en-Settler Relations in Smithers, British Columbia, 1913–1973* and coeditor of *Settler City Limits: Indigenous Resurgence and Colonial Violence in the Urban Prairie West.*

ANDREW NEWMAN is associate professor of anthropology at Wayne State University. He is author of *Landscape of Discontent: Urban Sustainability in Immigrant Paris* (Minnesota, 2015) and coeditor of *A People's Atlas of Detroit.*

ASHANTÉ M. REESE is assistant professor in the Department of African and African Diaspora Studies at the University of Texas at Austin. She is author of *Black Food Geographies: Race, Self-Reliance, and Food Access in Washington, D.C.*

GILLIAN RICHARDS-GREAVES is associate professor of anthropology in the Department of Anthropology and Geography at Coastal Carolina University.

MONICA M. WHITE is associate professor of environmental justice at the University of Wisconsin–Madison with a joint appointment in the Nelson Institute for Environmental Studies and the Department of Community and Environmental Sociology. She is author of *Freedom Farmers: Agricultural Resistance and the Black Freedom Movement.*

BRIAN WILLIAMS is assistant professor of geosciences at Mississippi State University.

JUDITH WILLIAMS is a PhD candidate in global and sociocultural studies at Florida International University.

PSYCHE WILLIAMS-FORSON is associate professor and chair of American studies at the University of Maryland, College Park, and affiliate faculty of anthropology, women's studies, African American studies, and the Consortium on Race, Gender, and Ethnicity. She is author of *Taking Food Public: Redefining Foodways in a Changing World* and *Building Houses out of Chicken Legs: Black Women, Food, and Power.*

WILLIE J. WRIGHT is assistant professor of geography and Africana studies at Rutgers University.

INDEX

ACTION. *See* Active Community to Improve Our Nutrition

Active Community to Improve Our Nutrition (ACTION), 115

activism, 6, 21, 139, 208; farming and, 214–16

advertising, 12, 229

Africa, 2, 18, 54, 65–66, 68, 111, 235

African American foodways. *See* Black foodways

African diaspora, 11, 12, 13, 66, 84–86, 87, 116, 243

Africans, 17, 54, 185, 209, 254; colonization and, 84; enslavement and, 85, 235–36; food culture, 55, 60, 68, 74, 185, 187, 191, 196, 259, 269; food production and, 65–66, 192–93, 217

agribusiness, 86, 218, 223, 234

agriculture, 11, 66, 91, 182, 217–19, 244; capitalism and, 238; community supported, 115, 211; cultural knowledge and, 18, 233; enslavement and,

2, 85; racial discrimination and, 21, 231, 232, 242; stigma and, 87; urban, 20–21, 38, 44–45, 118–19, 137–39, 208, 218, 245

agroterrorism, 73, 76

alternative food movement(s), 29, 94–95, 112–13

Amazon (corporation), 153

American Dream, 34, 265

Ames Plantation (Tennessee), 184, 186–87, 193

animal husbandry, 18, 20, 60. *See also* horticulture

anti-Blackness, 3–4, 6, 14, 18, 29, 114, 125, 230; delegitimization of Black food and, 110; education and, 109; entrepreneurs and, 44–45; erasure of Black culture and, 20, 109–10; genocidal conditions and, 98; state violence and, 117

apartheid: economic, 215; food, 2, 95, 100n11; geographic, 134; racial, 215